W9-DBV-959

Editing in the Electronic Era

SHOE

Editing in the Electronic Era

MARTIN L. GIBSON

The Iowa State University Press, AMES, IOWA

Martin L. Gibson is associate professor of journalism, University of Texas, Austin.

©1979 The Iowa State University Press. All rights reserved

Composed and printed by The Iowa State University Press, Ames, Iowa 50010

First edition, 1979
Second printing, 1980

Library of Congress Cataloging in Publication Data

Gibson, Martin L   1934
   Editing in the electronic era.

   Includes index.
   1. Copy-reading.   2. Newspaper layout and typography.   3. Journalism—Data processing.
I.   Title.
PN4784.C75G5   070.4′15   79-9883
ISBN 0-8138-0965-7

Contents

I DID NOT set out to design an instrument of torture with this book. The thought of students struggling into the night with dull homework gives me no pleasure. Consequently, you will encounter a frivolous thought or two among the book's many somber reflections on eternal truths. Moreover, I use the pronouns *I, you* and *we* because I am discussing things of interest to you, and we both may benefit from the discussion. If our luck holds, you and I can go through this work together and have a good time on the trip.

As you get into the book, you will encounter a major structural departure: You will be asked to answer questions. Some of them you can answer in your head. Others will require that you write an answer on a separate piece of paper. I offer these questions—and answers—as a specialized method of reviewing the material we cover. I have tested this approach thoroughly, and I tell you straight out that your benefits will be heightened in direct proportion to the amount of effort you put in.

A book like this has one major shortcoming: the temptation for people to take a shortcut and check the

Introduction

author's answers instead of coming up with their own. That practice will boost an intellectual loafer through the book somewhat faster than the other way, but the loafer will end up carrying a considerably lighter cargo of knowledge.

Do your work this way: (1) Read the explanatory material carefully and absorb it. It contains the wisdom of the ages, so pay attention. (2) Answer the questions. If you are instructed to write something out, write it out. You may want to type it. Or use a pencil. Or use a crayon. That's your business. All I ask is that you write it out—and do so before peeking at the answer. (3) Check your answers against those I have given. Most of the time, you will see what I was driving at and will agree with my answer. You may need to reread the material if I have been foggy. If you understand my answer and still disagree—if you like your own answer better—that may be great. The only requirement here is that you understand the answer. If you concur with it, we can consider that a bonus.

The procedure is simple. The work is moderately pleasant. The task is before you. Go to it.

Editing in the Electronic Era

[1] *Welcome to the electronic newsroom*

YOU ARE ABOUT TO STAND shoulder to shoulder with Benjamin Franklin. If you are a journalist, or are preparing to be one, you have more in common with old Ben than other journalists have had for two centuries. Chances are good that you will enjoy the line of work you are heading into, particularly after you learn what to do. This book is meant to help you learn.

Your kinship with Ben Franklin arises from the profession that took much of his early energy and in return gave him money and time to do all those other things he did so well. Franklin called himself a printer. In reality, he and his contemporaries in the field were editor-printers. They wrote their own material, or edited the work of others, and then set it into type. Progress wiped out that hyphenated job description, and some editor-printers became editors, devoting their time to preparing copy, while others became printers, arranging copy and getting it to the press.

Franklin became a statesman.

Although the electronic era does not bring back the title, it restores the work of the editor-printer. Like Ben, you will edit copy and then set it into type. Frankly, you will be a little slower than Ben at the first half of his job—editing—or at least you will be slower than most good copy editors with pencils. But if Franklin could see the speed you gain with the second half—the printer half—he would get a considerably larger tingle than he got while flying his kite in a thunderstorm. He would be shocked.

As a printer, you will use a video display terminal to carry out your Franklin-like decisions on whether type should be wider or heavier or taller or whatever. You will make the type run around half-column cuts or do other tricks. You will set the type; *you*. Alas, this new authority, this new freedom, is not an unalloyed blessing. With it comes a new responsibility. If you make a mistake—let us say you spell a name *oJhn*—you no longer have a Linotype operator to notice it and automatically correct it. You no longer have a proofreader sitting behind the typesetter to catch and correct any slips of the finger. No; *you* are the

3

proofreader. You goof, and the error will probably appear in print, causing the jeers and taunts of an outraged readership to be heaped on your shoulders.

You and your video display terminal will be a hundred times faster than Benjamin Franklin was at his best. The world will be a better place if you are half as good as he was at his worst.

That thought brings us to a basic principle that governs your work in computerized editing: The video display terminal (VDT) is a lineal descendant of the quill pen. It is a faster way of committing a thought to paper. If you cannot edit on paper, you cannot edit on the tube. The computer people have a word for it: GIGO—garbage in, garbage out. If you learn to edit on paper (and that is still the most common way to learn) you will be able to transfer your editing skills to the VDT quickly.

And where does all this electronic editing take place? Just about everywhere. The list of newspapers converting to computerized editing grows rapidly, including operations as large as the *New York Daily News* and the *New York Times* and as small as—well, you name it and the manufacturers are trying to sell it a terminal.

The wire services are even deeper into electronic editing. Their primary mechanical problem is the rapid transmission of data. Electronic editing, coupled with increasingly fast transmission systems, serves their needs best. News editors at wire service headquarters have unbridled enthusiasm for the tube. The news editor at United Press International, for instance, can call up any story in the system in seconds. It appears on the tube and can be edited, rewritten or merged with another story, with never a drop of paste hitting the desk. After that, the punch of a button sends the story out to the world, or parts of the world, or back to the computer for storage. Or, if the wrong button is punched, to hell and gone. (Not often is the wrong button punched. Most systems require a multiple punch to kill a story. You will hear horror stories about news copy being eaten by the computer, and such things do happen. But their incidence is relatively rare, and it is getting rarer.)

The two major wire services offer an old-fashioned 66-words-per-minute printing system or a new 1,200-word machine. (They do not cost the same.) The 1,200-word device sends messages to news editors, telling them what kinds of stories the wire service computer has just sent to the publication's computer. News editors in Des Moines, for example, can find out from their computer just what is available from the Associated Press computer. News editors can call to their terminals any story that AP has available. If they want hard copy (something on paper) they can punch another button and get a printout of the story, before or after editing.

Magazines have been slower to switch to electronic editing. *Time* and *Newsweek,* which set a great deal of straight matter (body type in a standard size and line length), use a mixture of the old and new. Most writers on these magazines work with typewriter and paper. Stories are checked, edited with pencils and perhaps rewritten. Then they are typed into the electronic editing system (the computer, if you wish to call it that). They can then be re-edited indefinitely, stored for later use, or set into type.

Magazines that produce relatively little straight matter and have less stringent, or at least less frequent, deadlines are slower to move into electronic editing. A big house like McGraw-Hill can ease into these waters, for, with about 40 magazines, McGraw-Hill sets a lot of type. But a single magazine gains little advantage tying up money in electronic equipment; the normal practice is to have the type set by a commercial typesetter, using stories written on paper.

Electronic editing and writing is also of scant value in—let's be ironic—the electronic media. Broadcasters do not gain much speed with the VDT because broadcasters do not set type. Besides, you cannot put a script in your pocket and find a quiet corner for study if the script is on a VDT.

However, we might look a short distance down the road to see what electronic systems can do for broadcasters and for other operations that do not produce much regular type. The terminal can be used as a reference librarian, providing quick access to files and to encyclopedic information. And it can be used to hold stories from correspondents or the wire services, stories that formerly came in (much slower) on regular wires. Dan Rather may never write a word of the evening news on a VDT, but he and other news gatherers can use one to bring in information. The same goes for you in your hometown radio station.

We encounter the same basic situation elsewhere: People are using terminals to go into libraries and bring out information. Not now, but before long, a public relations firm, for example, might lease the right to a university computer or public library computer to gain quick access to information. The company probably would not store its own confidential data in the system, since the world seems full of people who know how to fish out things they are not supposed to fish out. But the company would be able to comb through the whole library full of information from its office miles away. A vast amount of information lies moldering in our libraries. The VDT will help people get it out somewhat less painfully than before.

We also have home screen callup devices, fairly well established in Britain and getting started here. With these, an attachment to your home television set lets you call up all kinds of news. The British Broadcasting Company calls its device CEEFAX (see facts), and a private service terms it ORACLE (Optional Reception of Announcements by Coded Line Electronics). The systems transmit signals across the edges of the picture tube, and decoders put them on the screen, in six colors. Stock market reports, weather, and news summaries made up the early offerings, but those have been expanded.

You can see that these things could have a major impact on news dissemination in any country. Will newspapers become obsolete? I would guess not, for the newspaper format offers many advantages, from portability to divisibility to convenience, not to mention habit. Newspapers can be carried anywhere, with no preparation. They can be divided into sections for families. They can be examined at leisure, and a person can go from page 1 to page 90 in a second without having to scroll through extraneous material on a TV screen. In addition, a properly edited newspaper grades the news carefully and offers the reader many clues as to the relative worth of each story.

Even so, CEEFAX and its cousins are not going to shrivel up. They will grow.

Relax; no matter what wonders are wrought on the tube or in the newsroom, the ultimate core of journalism will be the same. Journalists will continue to procure information, arrange it in some meaningful pattern of words and pictures, and pass it on to people who need it. The copy editor's job will be essentially unchanged—to see that the flow of information is as smooth as possible.

Let's not get ahead of ourselves. Copy editors will be in demand in all systems, and we can talk about editing for news outlets, especially newspapers. Let us look at what VDT systems do and how they affect the people who use them. We will then work our way over to the mechanics, the part that tells you which buttons to press. Figure 1.1 shows the main components of an electronic news system.

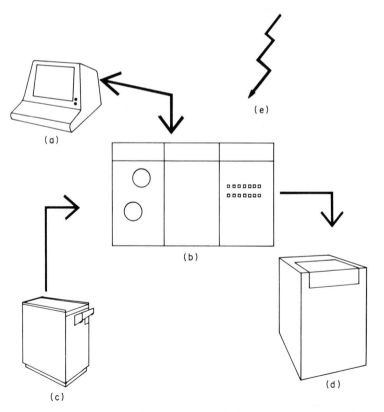

Fig. 1.1. **(a) VDT, (b) computer (central processing unit), (c) OCR machine, (d) phototypesetter, and (e) bolt of lightning representing wire services.**

Electronic editing systems are built around computers. It is not un-common for a newspaper computer to handle ad billings, subscription lists and payrolls as well as news stories. Larger papers are more likely to have a separate computer for the news operation. You can think of the computer as a big file. Before you can get something out, something has to go in. Input is handled in a variety of ways. Here are the four main ways:

1. Direct keyboarding—you type on a VDT hooked up to the com-puter.
2. Scanner copy—reporters type scanner copy and run it through the optical character recognition machine. This machine reads copy elec-tronically and puts it directly into the computer.
3. Computer-to-computer hookups—the wire services send material to your computer at great speed; you hear nothing, but you get notes on what is in the system.
4. Paper tape—human operators called tape punchers read your typewritten copy and from it make a perforated tape that can be used to set type directly or to feed a story into the computer. Because it requires extra work, including a second keyboarding of the story, this system is being supplanted by other methods.

Direct keyboarding with a VDT is the ultimate system in today's technology. It is the system you will someday use as a reporter and editor. With direct keyboarding, you are in immediate contact with your computer. You get the story lined up the way it is supposed to appear in print. Most of this book assumes that you should be trained for work with VDTs.

Scanner copy is another game. *Scanner* is the short term for *optical character recognition (OCR)*. The scanner works with typewritten copy the way your bank's equipment works with checks. The bank equipment has electronic eyes that read those funny little numbers at the bottom of your check. The scanner has the same kind of eyes. They read news copy that reporters have prepared on regular electric typewriters (with letters of slightly different shapes). Instead of bouncing or passing a check, the scanner feeds your story into a computer. In older systems, it punches a paper tape that is then used to feed the story into the system.

Preparation of scanner copy is not terribly difficult, although the degree of difficulty varies with the equipment. I taught myself to write scannable copy in 20 minutes by following the format on a piece of used copy. Later, on another brand of equipment, I blew half a day reading a manual and trying to get a story to run. This soured my outlook on the scanner. Indeed, I once argued unsuccessfully that the student newspaper at my school should bypass the scanner and go directly to VDTs. I was right, of course. And wrong. I was right because scanning is an in-termediate step and is thus technologically obsolescent. I was wrong because scanning lets you get copy into the computer with far less ex-pense than a VDT. A small newspaper might have 20 reporters (each

**Fig. 1.2.   This view of the newsroom at the *Advertiser*
in Huntington, West Virginia, shows VDTs as a dominant feature. Terminals at left and far right are on lazy
susans that can be turned for use by staffers of the *Her-
ald-Dispatch.***

needing only a typewriter) feeding in typewritten copy with a scanner,
and three or four copy editors calling it out of the computer for editing
on VDTs. Equipment for such an operation would be much less expensive
than the purchase of VDTs for all reporters.

No newspaper that I know of has VDTs for every writer. The common minimum is one for two. VDTs have caused newspapers to
reorganize their newsrooms, setting up the desks in a fashion that permits
more than one person ready access to the terminal. Some newspapers
have put swivel bases on terminals to make sharing easier. See Fig. 1.2.
Others set the terminals off to the side so that a reporter might do the
basic preparation at his or her regular desk and then move to the VDT
row, choosing any unoccupied terminal, to input the story. We will no
doubt soon see a time when almost every reporter has a terminal, since
prices are tumbling. We will also see widespread use of portable terminals. With these, a reporter with access to a telephone can unfold a
portable VDT and do from miles away the same things that can be done
in the newsroom.

Our third input system, the wire services, should give you no trouble.
The wires move vast amounts of copy at high speed. You get no evidence
of it except through a small abstract printer, which is something like a
Teletype setup but smaller and quieter and much faster. It identifies and
summarizes the stories and tells you what number each story carries. The

copy editor calls out stories by number, the same as for stories put in by keyboard, scanner or paper tape.

That fourth input system, paper tape, stays with us only because of economics. It is much slower than electronic processing, but it works. Newspapers have been reluctant to throw away things that work. They use paper tape for backup operations or for special kinds of stories—features and other advance copy. Tape is too slow to be used on ordinary news stories at plants with VDTs.

After input comes output. Between the two comes the copy editor—you. If you go to work on an electronic newspaper's copydesk, you will be assigned a VDT. The first thing you will have to do is learn how to get a story onto your screen. Although systems vary, you must have some coded reference to the story. Usually, you give the computer a command such as "get 0216." In that case, the computer will bring to your screen whatever story carries the number 0216. You will then edit the story. When you finish, you write a headline (usually) and put the story back into the computer so the copydesk chief can call it up and look at it. The chief will then send it to the typesetter.

The typesetter is a photocomposition device. It sets type by taking pictures of letters. A typical system has a whirling disk containing little windows in the shape of alphabet characters. When the proper letter whirls into position, a strobe light shines through that little window and makes a picture of the letter on a piece of photosensitive paper on the other side of the disk. A computer tells the strobe when to flash and tells the lens how to move along so the letters come one after the other in proper order, line after line.

When this photo paper is developed, in a high-speed (30-second) machine, these lines of characters make up the story, as edited. This type is then pasted onto a page, and the pasteup looks like the printed page you want. The pasteup is photographed, and the resulting negative is then turned into a printing plate. The entire process is called the *cold type* process.

Effect on editing

Photocomposition has revolutionized the printing industry. I am hoping it does not have the deleterious effect of a previous revolutionary step, the Teletypesetter. The Teletypesetter (TTS) system had much to commend it. It was the salvation of some smaller newspapers, for, when introduced in the mid-1940s, it permitted one person to operate four Linotype typesetting machines at one time. TTS uses a punched paper tape to drive the machines. (Wire services send signals that punch tape, and typists turn local copy into tape.)

I am all in favor of saving money, but not at the expense of editing quality. TTS discouraged quality editing. How? Simple. If an editor removed a word of any substantial length from the first line of a paragraph, say six characters, the second line would have to give up six characters to make the first one come out even. Then line 3 would have to give up a word and get one from line 4, and so on to the end of the paragraph. Since that resetting required the services of another Linotype operator or tape puncher, little was to be gained over the practice of having the operator do the work in the first place. You do not have to be a financial wizard to see that publishers are going to scream when copy editors improve copy so much that every line has to be reset. TTS thus made a major contribution to the decline in the quality of copy editing in this country. The better the editor, the more expensive the work. A publisher would have to have great dedication to improvement of the newspaper before taking the more expensive option. Publishers of that stripe were found primarily on larger newspapers. Smaller newspapers flocked to TTS, and good copy editing went elsewhere.

I have worked on TTS papers and know the subtle pressure that is applied to ignore minor mistakes and low level verbosity. I have worked on newspapers that went the other way and encouraged—no, demanded—that copy be trimmed and polished to perfection. Believe me, the latter kind of newspaper is more enjoyable to work on and to read.

We have some evidence that editing on the VDT is slightly more difficult than on paper. That has been my experience, and a *Miami Herald* study showed that VDT editing requires about a third more time than pencil and paper editing. That study timed editors doing a number of tasks (inserting, transposing, combining, deleting, and so on). Pencil pushers came out ahead on eight of ten tasks.

VDTs have been given other raps. People using one model complained of headaches. The terminals had to be redesigned so that a vent blowing air onto users directed its stream elsewhere. Headaches ceased.

An unanswered question deals with eyestrain. I have talked to copy editors who complain that they get tired of looking at the screen all day, but they do not indicate that they were a great deal more tired than when they stared at paper copy for the same length of time. We have had at least one lawsuit dealing with eyestrain at the terminals (terminal eyestrain?), but that was really a question of who makes the rules—the union or newspaper management. Management won that one without a full trial. No proof of the cause of eyestrain was shown.

Of course, a thought sure to cross your mind as you start this work will concern what your eyes will be like after 20 years of looking at little lights on a green or gray background. We won't know the answer for 20 years, because the current generation of editors is the first to do this kind of work steadily. Airline and hotel people have been using VDTs for years, but they do not concentrate on the screen hour after hour. All I can offer is the thought that somebody had to be the first to eat an oyster.

Despite the extra time required to edit, VDTs have speeded up the overall production of newspapers. The loss of time is quickly made up once the editing is complete. Whereas an old-fashioned editor had to turn the copy over to a Linotype operator for keyboarding (retyping, in effect, only slower), the electronic editor merely punches a button and the copy is converted into type, ready for pasteup, in a matter of seconds. A galley of type, one column two inches wide, could be set in about 20 minutes on old-style equipment, if all went well. Good photocomposition equipment can set the same amount in 10 seconds.

VDT speed has had a good effect on deadlines; they are not as oppressive as they once were. Newspapers changing over from a hot metal operation to cold type normally encounter deadline problems for days or even weeks, but familiarity with the equipment soon reverses the situation. One survey put the average improvement at 30 minutes, meaning the paper had 30 minutes more per edition to spend on careful editing or on getting new stories. One newspaper, the *St. Petersburg Times,* claimed a gain of an hour.

And what has all this meant to the desk, to copy editors? Before the change, people expressed fears that veterans would be unable to switch to this new way of doing things. However, no severe dissatisfaction has surfaced. And even the dissatisfied editors have been able to do the job, though with a little more grumbling than usual. Louis Boccardi, an Associated Press vice-president, said flatly that nobody—*nobody*—who was supposed to work with a VDT at his place was unable to fit right in. AP started out with 16 hours of training on the terminals before letting people work them for real. That amount of time was found to be excessive; writers picked up the skills more quickly than expected. However, wire service people have an advantage over newspaper copy editors because they do not have to worry about coding the story for certain type widths and sizes and so on. Trying to remember that 9-point News Roman type on a 10-point base set 10 picas wide is "Format 131" (unless you want it 12 picas wide instead of 10, in which case you "Change Format to 131 × 12)—trying to remember that will take some doing, but it can be done.

Electronic editing has led to one other problem that may be worse than the frustration of dealing with picky computer instructions—the lack of feedback from veterans, in particular the copydesk chief. The problem arises because the chief cannot determine what the copy editor has done. Copy no longer has pencil marks on it. Whereas edited copy formerly showed clearly what had been done to it (editors used to make mine bleed), material handled on the VDT is always clean. Desk chiefs have no easy way to tell whether clean copy is a reporter's work or the copy editor's. Without knowing, the chief cannot wisely discuss the editor's strengths and weaknesses. This situation retards the young editor's professional growth. And the desk chief has no sound way to make recommendations for pay raises. The chief can see only the negative—if the writing is bad after editing, the chief knows the editor didn't help it; if it is good, the reporter will at least share in the credit.

There's more: The process of handing a story from one person to another is more involved in the electronic newspaper than in the old pencil and paper operation. In the old days, the desk chief would say, "Lemme see that," and the editor would hand over the copy. Now the copy editor has to send the story back to the computer, the chief has to clear his or her own screen by returning the material on it to the computer, and then the chief must call up the story in question. Handing the story back to the copy editor requires substantially the same steps—another trip through the computer. This discourages exchanges, although it certainly does not prohibit them.

The layout process is not noticeably hindered, at least not beyond the problem that a desk chief might have when wanting to take just one more quick peek at a story before deciding what page will carry it. On newspapers in which top editors sit in on the page 1 layout process, the normal way is to get a printout of the stories under discussion. Machines to produce printouts can be found in almost all newsrooms, and they provide paper copy quickly.

What does all this mean to the potential editor, to the young newswriter? Must you learn to edit on the tube be**fore yo**u can get a job? Did you make a mistake when you threw away that comic book with the LEARN ELECTRONICS AT HOME ad on the back? Can you still make a go of it, even if you don't like Ben Franklin?

Fret not. Remember GIGO. Learn to edit. And write. If you can write and edit with a pencil, on a typewriter, or with any other method known to modern science, you will be all right. Two weeks on the tube, coupled with the distilled wisdom and pithy pointers contained in this book, will make you the master of the electronic era, a mechanical marvel—an editor.

You will be ahead if you can get experience on a school newspaper or in labs before you take a job. The number of gentle and kindly persons in a newspaper office is larger than some might suspect, but these people do not like to spend their time teaching newcomers how to run the machinery. A managing editor confronted by two applicants of equal ability and general background has an easy decision if one applicant is familiar with VDTs and the other is not. Fortunately, familiarity comes quickly.

Mechanics of electronic editing

Experience indicates clearly that few people have any great trouble in learning how to manipulate copy on the VDT. Ten minutes at the tube will get most people started, although it will be several days before they are comfortable with typesetting codes. These codes vary from publication to publication and especially among different manufacturers of VDT equipment. But the basic functions, the things that affect your editing, are substantially the same.

Let's look at Fig. 1.3. The VDT keyboard is arranged much like that of a typewriter, except for the extra keys. (If you do not know how to type, you will not be able to edit electronically with much efficiency. For that matter, you will not be able to handle most jobs in journalism.) These extra keys should not intimidate you. Only half a dozen—really, just six—will get constant use. The others are for special functions.

Fig. 1.3. A typical VDT keyboard. Arrows on dark keys control cursor.

Let us start at the beginning. Machines vary in start-up procedures. Some are ready to go with the simple flick of an on-off switch. I have a warm spot for that kind. Others, particularly those designed for multi-purpose use, including bookkeeping, have a more elaborate ritual. The first step is to get the machine ready to go to work. Usually, you select a "file." The process is like opening a file cabinet drawer for sports, news, business, Sunday advances, the family living section, books and so on. Each file contains a number of stories. In a file drawer, folders are usually arranged alphabetically; in the computer, stories are arranged by number. You look at an index of your stories, note the file number on the one you have to edit, and call it to your screen. (One system uses *fe* as the call signal; it stands for *fetch*.)

With the story on your screen, it is time to get acquainted with the big six, the special keys. Four of them, usually bearing arrows, govern the cursor. The *cursor* is a line that shows you where you are working on the copy on your screen. It underlines one character or, on some systems, brightens a whole character or outlines it. Whatever you do on the keyboard will affect that character. The cursor moves one space with each regular keystroke, keeping up with you the way a typewriter does. The arrow keys move the cursor left, right, up and down, without affecting characters. Hold the key down and the cursor will move until you let up.

We will assume you have found where you want to start editing. You now have three choices: You can *change* what you have, simply by writing over the old wording; you can *delete* material; or you can *insert* new material.

Changing copy by striking over it is an unusual experience at first, particularly if you are accustomed to editing out strikeovers in regular copy. VDT copy has no strikeovers. The new letter or word replaces the old. If a reporter has written the words "President James Carter," for example, and you want to make it "Jimmy," you just put the cursor under the "i" (you could start under the "J," since a strikeover of the same letter leaves the copy unchanged) and hit the keys for "immy." Presto! The word is now "Jimmy." (If the new material is longer than the material it replaces you will need to make an adjustment with the insert key; without the adjustment, you would just write over the next word.)

The task of deletion involves the fifth of our six big keys. We will just shorten that last name to "Jim," for illustration. To do so, we simply put the cursor under the second "m" and hit the delete key. This key is normally marked *delete* or *dele* in the middle, with *character* or *char* on the bottom and *word* on the top. If you hit the key when shifted (as in capitalizing a word on the typewriter), you will delete a whole word from your story. If you hit it unshifted, you delete a single character. Your first tap of the unshifted key deletes the "m" and the second tap gets the "y." "Jimmy" is now "Jim." You do not have to worry about blank spots, either, for the copy automatically moves to the left to fill in. (I enjoy watching copy snake up from the following lines to fill in spaces left by deletion, but I am easy to entertain.) If you want to take out a whole word, put the cursor under any part of the word, any letter or punctuation; then you shift and hit the dele key. Away goes the word.

Caution: If you hold the button down, words will keep going away until you let up. Word after word, line after line, will feed up from below and disappear. (Although this has some entertainment value, you will have to retype all the words you cut out when you get carried away.)

Most equipment also has provision for deleting full paragraphs. Usually, you simply tell the computer where the block ends and begins, and then you hit the dele key. Some machines have a separate key to delete a sentence or, shifted, a paragraph. One click, and it's gone.

That leaves inserts, controlled by our sixth major key. If a story about President Jimmy Carter was supposed to say "President and Mrs. Jimmy Carter," we would need some way to insert the two new words. We can't just type them in, since they would write over, and thus eliminate, "Jimmy." We avoid that problem by hitting a key marked *insert* (a universal designation). Now, everything we keyboard will be inserted. Words already on the screen will be pushed to the right, with lines below changing as long as we keep inserting material. When we complete our insertion, we must hit the insert button again to tell the computer we want to stop inserting and go on to something else. (As you might suspect, some equipment has a separate button to stop inserts.)

Minor point: To insert, you place the cursor under the character exactly where you want to start work. In the case above, you would put it under the "J" in "Jimmy." Your new material, "and Mrs.," would thus start after the space following "President." When you finish your insertion, make your last character a space (to the computer, a space between words is just as much a character as a letter).

If you master these six keys—and you can do so quickly—you are on the way. For a while, you will find yourself hitting the space bar instead of the appropriate key when you want to move the cursor. At that point, you become the *curser,* since a stroke on the space bar inserts a space in the place of whatever letter you had lined up. But all you have to do is back up one notch with the arrow and type in the letter you took out.

The operations above will get you through nine-tenths of the work done on a copydesk. You may benefit from knowing one other operation—the moving of paragraphs. Systems vary, but the basic idea is to isolate a block of copy in some manner. On one system, the key marked *define block* does the trick. You put the cursor under the first character in that block and hit the define block key. That tells the computer to lock in on this block. Then you go to the end of the block (which can be a paragraph or two or ten) and hit the define block key again. That pulls tight the net and you have captured this block of type. You have to get rid of it before you can do any more editing. So you move your cursor where you want this block. You hit the insert key and the execute key, and the job is done. No one can tell that the story was not written that way originally. You do not have paste on your hands and the copy is clean—no strikeovers, no hard-to-read scrawls, no coffee stains. Always clean copy. You will like this way of doing things.

I ran in one new key on you in that last paragraph, the *execute* key. This key, which goes by different names in different systems, is usually the last one you punch when you are handling a story. It is a message to the computer, calling for action. In the case above, it told the computer to switch a block of type from one place to another. You will use it most often when you have completed editing your story and are ready to have it set into type. The execute key tells the computer to go to work because you are through editing.

The typical keyboard contains (as you may have noted on the illustration) a number of keys we have not dealt with here. They have special functions, most of which you will use only on occasion. Some are used to set type in boldface or italic. One will let you type everything in capitals. These keys should not frighten you; they do not bite—they do nothing at all until you order them to work. You are the boss, just like Ben Franklin.

[2] *The copy editor at work*

IF YOU HAVE BEEN LED to believe that this book, or a course in copy editing, or both will teach you to turn a literary sow's ear into a silk purse, you have been deluded. Copy editing does not work that way. With any luck, you will learn to make your sow's ear glisten and wave prettily and perhaps win a blue ribbon at the county fair. But what you will then hold in your hand is a porcine prize, not a Pulitzer. You need to understand the difference before you go into this line of work.

About the best you can do with a bad piece of writing is to knock off the rough edges, so a reader can choke it down with as little effort as possible. The proper way to improve wretched material is to rewrite it, but time, the curse of journalism, too often precludes that. Consequently, all you can do is ease the reader's burden as much as possible, making sure everything is understandable on one reading. Few news stories are so good that a reader wants to go back over them for pleasure; the second trip usually means that the material was too fuzzy to grasp—and that you have an irritated reader.

The foregoing admonition does not mean that you are being touted into a life of frustration and general unhappiness. On the contrary, many people find a great deal of pleasure in editing, even when working with bad copy they want to rewrite but cannot. The job almost always provides a chance to be creative, and the news desk is unquestionably the nerve center of the newspaper; there the product is assembled and refined and decisions are made on treatment of the day's news. Furthermore, the copydesk is also the quickest path into the newspaper hierarchy. Being in the hierarchy is no particular thrill in itself, but the money is good.

Newspapers are not the only publications that employ copy editors. Most periodicals have such people, although they may give them additional—or different—duties and a different title. Almost every kind of institution that prepares material for general distribution has employees who handle the editing function, and that includes network television. This function is to examine someone else's work, eliminate all mistakes, and make

sure it is in the form that will be most easily understood by the consumer—
the reader, the listener, the viewer.

Newspaper copy editors are unique in that they handle a far greater
volume of copy under more pressing conditions than other editors. Much of
this book has a newspaper orientation. Two reasons for this approach come
to mind: (1) Most of the book's users will be students, and their first outlet
will be a school newspaper. (2) The transfer value is bigger from newspaper
editing to other kinds than from other kinds back to newspapers. That is, if
you learn the basics of tightening copy, preparing clever headlines and
presenting the work for newspapers, you will find you need change your
work only slightly if you move to another medium.

Copy editors are prized employees on the nation's newspapers. Managing editors shed copious tears in lamenting the demise of good editing and
the lack of replacements. Good editors are simply hard to find.

Also, the move into electronic editing has thrown even more of a
burden, even more responsibility, on the copydesk than we had in pencil and
paper days. So the shortage of good editors is likely to get worse.

Why is that? Three possibilities: (1) Many potential copy editors come
to believe early that life on the rim is an unpleasant mixture of boredom and
hellish pressure, and they are frightened into other pursuits. (2) Many who
spend long hours with television do not have the language skills required for
the job. (3) Publishers believe that fiscal prudence forbids them to lavish
enough money on the copydesk to make it supremely attractive. Copy
editors normally get slightly more money than reporters, but the difference
is not enough to cause a stampede. A shame. Newspapers in general do not
open the treasury to copy editors.

So where do editors come from? Who trains them? How do they
become good at this stuff? What *is* good?

New copy editors often come out of journalism school, usually with a
stopover of a year or more as a reporter. Arthur Laro, former managing
editor of the *Houston Post,* had a rule, bent occasionally, that a person had
to have five years as a reporter before going to work on the copydesk. The
desirability of such a policy is evident—people ought to be able to produce
good copy on their own before they start hacking on someone else's. Also,
the seasoning provides a better comprehension of problems the newspaper
faces, from libel up—or down.

Unfortunately, good copy editors are in such short supply that most
managing editors are unable to stick to a policy like Laro's. They take what
they can get, sometimes including, alas, people fresh out of school.
Although it is probably unfair to thrust a beginner into such work, some
turn out all right. They have laid a foundation in school in an editing course
and, perhaps, with work on the school newspaper. A school newspaper,
especially one whose older staff members or faculty advisers have time to
offer advice, is usually a fine training ground.

We are not overrun with research projects showing the traits that copy
editors possess, so the list you will encounter shortly is based on
speculation—and keen observation, of course. I may be getting onto

dangerous ground by trying to generalize about copy editors, for they are unquestionably individuals. Among my friends on copydesks are a man who annually flies to London for a week of theater-going and who composes headlines ahead of time covering all eventualities for a story he expects to handle; a one-eighth Indian woman whose former husband couldn't drive but who liked to start their Austin-Healey and run through the gears in the garage; several pipe-smokers; a snuff-dipper; a certified bomb-thrower; a Jesus freak; a short, fat man who has written books on education and who has a limited capacity for tequila, and a few normal people like me.

Let us catalog the character traits, the background, the personality flaws likely to be encountered in those who labor on the copydesk. Copy editors should have these things:

1. A long and growing acquaintance with the written word. A person who does not enjoy reading and writing will soon find editing tiresome. A copy editor does not have to know the terminology required for the teaching of an English seminar, but he or she must be able to recognize flawed writing instantly—and improve it.

2. Abundant self-confidence. Editors must feel that every change they make improves the copy and must be ready to correct bad copy from anyone, up to and perhaps including the publisher's son-in-law. An editor unwilling to change copy for fear of erring will thresh around in a sea of indecision forever.

3. A measure of maturity. Maturity is needed to keep that abundant self-confidence from turning into cockiness. If left unchecked, incipient arrogance can cause editors to think there is only one good way—their way—to write something. Maturity causes editors to make changes only to improve copy, not just for the sake of change. An editor who messes with good copy wastes time that could be spent on bad copy—and makes a reporter mad in the bargain.

4. A suspicious streak. Editors who accept everything at face value provide reporters no backup help. Editors should be skeptical—and willing to express skepticism. Editors need not be paranoid but they ought to recognize implausibilities when they come across the desk. The number of opportunities for error in a daily newspaper is manifold: thousands of facts, spellings, dates, quotations, figures. Editors must approach everything as a source of potential error.

5. A dirty mind. You can get by without a dirty mind, but you need to get rid of your naiveté in a hurry. If something in a story or headline can be read two ways, one of them dirty, it will be. My files contain a headline saying, "Sewer system opens; deposits being accepted." That was probably written in total innocence, but it nevertheless enlivened the newspaper editor's week.

6. Breadth of interests and knowledge. The copydesk may be the last home of the generalist. In the first hour of the shift a copy editor might handle stories on an axe murder, an oil embargo and a housing ordinance. Ideally, the editor would know something about all three, including how they compared with past events, what governmental processes were in-

volved, and what English spelling of Arab names the newspaper prefers. No editor knows enough. But good editors store away most of the important information they encounter and constantly search for more. Editors must understand as well as know, must have wisdom as well as knowledge. For example, it is one thing to know that two countries signed a peace treaty in a given capital in a given year, but it is another to grasp the meaning of their recent falling-out.

7. Stability. Some people need the pressure of an approaching deadline to make them function at their best. Some do not. And some find that pressure stifling. This last group needs to avoid the copydesk. Although most of the shift is spent at a moderate pace, things do get taut in the minutes before deadline. (Newspapers have many places in which deadline pressure is a minor factor.)

8. A reduced thirst for glory. The copydesk is not the place for you if you are fond of compliments. No one will cheer you for your magnificent writing. Strangers, upon introduction, will not remark that they are familiar with your by-line. You will occasionally, perhaps even regularly, receive plaudits for good headlines. But this recognition will come from the copy chief or, indirectly, other copy editors ("Hey, who wrote this 3–36 on the ewe turn?"). Unless retirement policies are loosened and you are allowed to continue working in your eighties, you are likely to be able to count on one hand the number of times a reporter will express gratitude for your rescue of a hastily written story. (Perhaps I'm being cynical; reporters no doubt appreciate the desk's help but don't know how to pass the word.) Many newspapers cite their reporters and editors in print in house organs. Others offer their praise with bonus money—always popular among wordsmiths. Even so, you are not often likely to bask in a warm glow of compliments at the end of the day's work.

A dispassionate observer would note that a copy editor's day is marked by wild fluctuations in level of activity. The pace picks up dramatically as edition time nears, rides a great crest as the magic time passes, and then plunges into a trough of relaxation, at which time the next wave starts building. But this picture can be altered. A well-managed desk will spread the work over as long a period as possible, though the deadline's approach will always increase the action. Also, familiarity with the work tends to make the pressure less noticeable; veterans are bothered less by pressure than newcomers, normally. Note the word *normally:* Some people go out of their way to look for pressure. They think they are supposed to be under a strain on the copydesk, and they have conditioned themselves to tense up two or three or seven times a day, every time a new edition nears. Others, including some relative newcomers, find the pressure stimulating but not suffocating. These people will probably outlive their tense companions. I only hope people do not go into (or stay away from) the work with a belief that ulcers are a requirement for employment.

If we downgrade the importance of pressure, we can argue that copydesk work has definite advantages over some other positions on newspapers. For one thing, editors never have to go out into the rain or heat or cold; their comfort is assured if the building has a good roof and adequate heating and cooling. For another, the copy editor does not experience the frustrations of a reporter who, facing a deadline, cannot find a needed source or who has to grapple with people reluctant to part with information. Conversely, the editor does not enjoy the excitement of tracking down and reporting on the activities of the mighty or the simple pleasure of piecing together a story from many and difficult sources—a story of value to readers.

But the copy editor does have a key role in the production of the newspaper. Editors make the final adjustments on copy for the benefit of reader comprehension and top off the work with a headline that, with luck, both delights and informs the reader.

A side benefit, of no financial importance, is that the copydesk is always abreast of what is going on when a big story breaks. A dozen reporters may be working on the story, each seeing only a small part (and all other reporters seeing nothing). The copydesk will have the whole picture throughout. The transfer of information between editors is much greater than that between reporters, for the desk is a self-contained unit. As an editor, you learn about your neighbor's work very quickly.

A copy editor's day

Let's look at a copy editor's schedule. Perhaps we can see better what causes people to flee from the desk or what makes it worthwhile. My main purpose is to show you that goes on there, not to lure you or to run you off. We face a temptation to split this examination four ways: for morning and afternoon newspapers and for the big and the not-so-big. However, though procedures vary widely, the core of their work is the same. We will look at the whole scene first, and we can take up A.M.–P.M. and big-unbig departures as we come to them.

In eight years of desk work on newspapers, ranging in size from a 3,000-circulation weekly to one with more than 2 million circulation daily, I went to work at these hours: 2:30 A.M., 3:30 A.M., 5:30 A.M., 6:00 A.M., 6:30 A.M., 7:00 A.M., 8:30 A.M., 10:00 A.M., 1:00 P.M., 2:00 P.M., 3:00 P.M., 6:00 P.M., 9:00 P.M., 11:00 P.M. and midnight. Somewhere in all that mess you should be able to find a time you like. One can only hope that the time you prefer corresponds with the time your managing editor finds your talents most in demand.

(Speculation: I have nothing to go on except a couple of decades of conversation, but I believe most newspaper people prefer slightly offbeat hours. Although those 5 A.M. and 9 P.M. starts tend to restrict your social life, getting into the race at a different time from the other rats has its advantages. For one thing, you avoid rush hour twice a day. Of more importance, perhaps, is your ability to run errands while most businesses are open. For example, you can take your car in for repair without any time hassle. The 9-to-5 insurance clerk has to get up early and find a place already open or take time off from work.)

Six A.M. is a fairly common time for copydesk personnel to report to work on small-to-medium afternoon papers. These papers do not make a big deal of street sales. They usually get an edition out around lunchtime, and they may make over a handful of pages for the home edition sometime before 2 P.M. Such a schedule gives them time to cover the morning's events and still reach the outer parts of their circulation area with the first edition and then get the second edition into the carrier's hands for local delivery soon after the subscriber's work day ends.

The copy editor on such a paper may also have to handle the wire and do some layout. (A rule of thumb is that the number of tasks handled by a copy editor or reporter grows as the size of the paper decreases. A reporter in Bad Axe, Michigan, may cover the courthouse, city hall and PTA; write the streamer headline; and do a page 1 column. On the other hand, a reporter for the *New York Daily News* may specialize in bad axe murders, or something nearly as esoteric and narrow.)

The difference between morning and evening shifts is less pronounced than between large and small newspapers, but it is clearly observable, nevertheless. Afternoon newspapers have less time to put the product together, generally. They try to handle as much late material as they can, partly in an effort to live up to their near-universal circulation motto: *Today's news today*. Morning newspapers have a delivery advantage in that business activity slackens between 1 A.M. and 5 A.M., possibly excepting sales in some of the older professions, and the dead time can be used to transport newspapers to readers. Afternoon newspapers have no such dead time.

Small-to-medium morning newspapers customarily have a copy deadline somewhere near midnight, perhaps earlier if out-of-town circulation involves much distance. Metropolitan papers run the gamut. Some try to get out an early edition to catch the theater crowd. Most will run a very late edition, closing around 5 A.M., to go after big street sales to people on their way to work.

A typical time for a morning paper copy editor to go to work would be 3 P.M. The well-managed desk will have one or more editors handling advance material throughout the day, perhaps starting as early as 8 A.M. But the bulk of the news will be handled after 3 P.M. or even after 6 P.M. That advance material would include everything from the comics to the bridge column.

The copydesk

We can look now at how a desk is run—how the advance material finds its way into the paper, who decides what goes where, and even who writes what headlines. As usual, we will have to allow for variations because of size. We will look at a day's activity on the copydesk of the *Houston Chronicle,* a P.M. paper with a circulation of about 300,000. It is a large newspaper, although it is dwarfed by a few.

Life on the *Chronicle*'s copydesk begins around 9 P.M. The night news editor is generally the first person to arrive, although someone may be stirring in the sports department and a few late-stayers may be finishing up stories they have covered in the early evening. The news editor's first task, aside from making coffee, is to examine the dummies for the next day's paper. The dummies, prepared by the advertising department, are simply small sheets showing how the ads are arranged on different pages and, thus, how much space is available for news.

The news editor does not have to worry about sports, amusements, business news, or the family living pages. Editors there are allotted space separate from the news and they work independently of the copydesk. Amusement and business copy are funneled through the desk, primarily so the news editor will be better aware of what is going into the paper. This prevents duplication of coverage and can help in the grouping of related materials. (It is quite conceivable, we can say for illustration, that the business editor and news editor would have the same story, one from New York and one from local sources. The New York version might be camouflaged so well that a sleepy news editor would not recognize the local angle and thus neglect to pass it to the business desk. If the business writer's material did not go through the copydesk, both stories could end up in print. This happens.)

The news editor examines the dummies and complains that either (1) there is no way in the world to get all the day's news into that tiny hole; or (2) there is no way in the world the editor and a small overnight staff can fill up that gigantic hole without railroading everything in sight. Thus unburdened, the news editor tries to move a few pages to the composing room and plan out the rest of the paper.

This movement of pages to the composing room is a vital aspect of a vital process called copy flow. Although the news editor is eight hours away from deadline, it is necessary to pace the day's work and not hold everything back until the final moment. The news editor (the copydesk chief in this operation) must send some material to be set into type, so it can be moved to the pasteup tables, so it can be moved to the platemakers, so printing plates can be moved to the pressroom, so the press can be loaded, so subscribers get their papers on time.

Much of the newspaper's production equipment operates at a precise speed; you cannot hurry it. That is, camera operators do not have a high gear to help them turn out printing plates extra fast. The same goes for pasteup people; they can slap that stuff down only so fast. They do not build up extra speed with idle hours. That is, if one page can be pasted up in 15 minutes, two pages take half an hour. If you send one page at 9:00 and one at 9:15, you will have two completed pages at 9:30. If you send nothing at 9:00 and let the pasteup person rest and send two pages at 9:15, you will not have two completed pages until 9:45. Copy flow. It works with pasteup people and platemakers and people who put plates on the press and, Lord help us, even with copy editors. A copy editor can make up a little time by abdicating some duties—putting a headline on a piece of unread copy for instance—but you will find no sentiment for that kind of work here.

The *Chronicle*'s comic page ordinarily has one empty column on it. A column-long story already in hand lets the editor wipe out the page at one stroke. Platemakers and press workers get just as much work out of that page as they do a page that requires 15 minutes and great skill to lay out.

The news editor tries to send pages to the composing room with some regularity as the night progresses. The pasteup people are usually busy with the editorial page and things of that nature for a while, but they start on the news side as quickly as they can.

Any need for moving pages in a hurry must be balanced against the peril of committing too much space too quickly. Even in the quietness of the predawn hours, the wire services move a great amount of good material. (After all, Europe is nearly ready for lunch.) Consequently, the copy chief must save space for important news. Some of this news is unexpected, but much is announced ahead of time by wire service budgets (discussed in Chapter 8).

A little experience will tell a news editor how much space should be saved back through the night. The wise editor will send some optional material to the composing room or, in this day of electronic editing, at least choose it and keep it handy. That material can be popped into the paper if nothing good comes over the wire or it can be omitted without major loss to readers. Electronic editing eases the copy chief's burden a little by requiring a little less care in making space and copy come out even. In the old days, the processing of excess material, called *overset,* was considered basically sinful. Eight columns of overset meant that one typesetter had worked half a day fruitlessly.

Our news editor starts at 9 P.M. Rim help—copy editors—do not come until 10 P.M. or later. Early work involves an examination of the wire and of notes from the day side. The day crew sends some copy down and leaves notes for the night side. The notes give subject matters and identification key (computer number or headline slug), headline designation and length. The night news editor normally will call up the story for examination and then plug it into a page that will be moved early. The headline can be changed if it does not suit the layout plans or the editor's general taste in headlines.

If the ad department has not held up the dummies, if the city side is active and the wire machines are working properly, and if the stars are in proper alignment, copy editors will have plenty to do as soon as they have cleaned last night's sludge from their coffee cups. They may start with a headline change or two and possibly a trim to finish off one of those early-early pages. They may want to re-edit the story, depending on the quality of work done by the first person who had a shot at it. (In theory, copy editors should not have to go over stuff that has been handled by someone else, but in practice it is a rare copy editor who can let a piece of copy go through without just a little improvement.)

The material is returned to the copy chief after the copy editor completes the headline. The chief sends it to the composing room, moving it along in a process that eventually gets a newspaper into a subscriber's hands.

Before we zero in on what copy editors do with a piece of copy—how they edit—Let's reemphasize one point with a question.

Q. *Copy editors normally are unable to turn really horrible copy into monuments of literary beauty. Why is that?*

The answer is, of course, that a thoroughly botched writing job calls for rewriting, and the copydesk is not the place for a full rewrite. The copy editor can knock off rough edges and make copy understandable, so the reader gets maximum return on minimum effort.

Our news editor has already moved a few small pages, as noted, and has given stories to copy editors to handle. None of these pages will be in the front part of the paper, for that section is saved for bigger news. The *Chronicle,* unlike some papers, does not have a basic rule that prescribes what kind of news goes on which pages. (The *New York Times,* for instance, uses the first 8–20 inside pages for foreign news, news of international import; it then goes to national news and finally works its way back to the city news.) Depending on the ad arrangement, the *Chronicle* tries to use page 2 as a local page, especially if the page has no ads. If another open page follows, it is likely to be used as a jump (continued) page, containing several good news stories as well as any stories jumped from page 1. The *Chronicle* will also have an open or nearly open page as its basic world news page. The world page is normally followed by a page containing national news. However, the *Chronicle* is not as meticulous about separating news from different geographic areas as it could be.

Do not get the idea that the *Chronicle* is sloppily put together. You will find a large number of newspapers that appear to be made up by the numbers—using whatever copy is at hand to fill page 2, then page 3, then page 4, and on until they run out of news or pages or time. Although I can forgive a copy chief who draws a loose dummy (a dummy with holes here and there that may have to be filled in with old features or other material that is set ahead of time and saved for emergencies), I have a hard time expressing a fondness for those who do their layouts with a shovel. I am referring to the people who send the composing room an abundance of copy and an assortment of headlines and tell the pasteup people to use whatever fits.

In addition to selecting news and matching it with the available space, the copy chief has to check that proper headlines are written for all stories. In some places, the chief will trust certain well-tested copy editors and ask only for the first couple of words of a headline. These words are written on a layout sheet to show the pasteup people what story and headline go there.

I am not condoning this practice of approving a headline without seeing it; I am just telling you that it happens, and it is more likely to happen in shops with video display terminals than in others. The reason: If a headline is written on paper, it can be passed to the copy chief with a flick of the wrist. On the terminal, it has to go through the computer.

Either way, the copy chief should look at every headline that goes into the news section. He or she should do much more than that. A good copy chief can make a great improvement in the quality of headlines. The first step is to make the rim people (copy editors) aware that sloppy headlines will be kicked back.

I do not believe any writer can satisfactorily tell you how to reject headlines when you become a copy chief. You will have to tailor your actions to your personality and to that of the editor who produced the headline. I do know that you should not rewrite every bad headline yourself. Let the editor have another crack at it. You may want to make a suggestion—a word, an angle. But don't rewrite it and slap the copy editor across the face with it. Do not take the foregoing as an admonition against raising your voice for fear of bruising the psyche of some poor desk worker. If you are handed a wretched headline and your job is to see that wretched headlines do not appear in the paper, reject it. Bruise that psyche if you must. But don't delight in it. A good copy chief is usually surrounded by moderately happy people; the desk is no place for sadists.

We need to complete our peek at the *Chronicle*'s operation. Actually, there is little more to do than fill pages—choose the news, lay out the page, decide story lengths, select headline sizes, assign the copy to rim people, pass judgment on headlines, handle pictures and cutlines, and then do it all over on another page. Editors normally start on page 1 half an hour before the final deadline, and they usually like to have most of the rest of the paper cleared away by then. The copy chief lives in hopes of a good story coming across fairly close to the deadline, a story the opposition newspaper is sure to have missed. However, the chief doesn't want too big a story to break right on deadline, since that would call for a major overhaul of the page. You will find your first postdeadline crisis moderately exciting, but you will probably feel better for the experience. Fortunately, most people suffer through such a crisis or two as copy editors watching a chief bear the big responsibility. If you can keep your sense of humor, you may even have a good time.

How to edit copy

Copy editing books customarily advise you to read every story three times—once for familiarization, once while you edit it, and a third time to check your work. I would not want to disagree with that advice, but I must tell you that it is nonsense as far as most copy editors are concerned. Copy editors do not have time for a triple reading.

However, the advice is good, particularly for people learning how to edit. Seasoned copy editors compress those three readings into one and a half. They skip the familiarization session, preferring to familiarize themselves with the story as they edit it. And their checkup reading is part of the editing pass-through; they may reread a sentence or paragraph that required special pains, but they do not start over and read the whole thing through again.

What should you do? Until you are seasoned, until you have developed the ability to concentrate required of good editors, stick with the triple threat approach. (Veteran copy editors would commit fewer mistakes if they tried it, too.)

As a copy editor, you will operate for the most part on someone else's instructions. The copydesk chief will tell you how long a story should run and what kind of headline it should have. Ideally (and in a college class you have ideal conditions) you should mentally calculate the amount you must trim as you start work on the copy. You may want to scratch the by-line or mark it boldface or do whatever else is necessary, but do not do any heavy editing on this first look. No, just read and try to understand the story. You may take notice of any particularly soft sections, looking ahead to the trim.

If the story has no glaring problems and if you understand it, you may be ready to edit. On this pass, you are concerned with spelling, grammar, punctuation, conciseness of expression, smoothness of writing, general accuracy and comprehensibility. Pay particular attention to the lead, for it is the most important paragraph in the story. Make sure you understand it, and make sure it is supported by the rest of the story. Indeed, you ought to be sure the lead adequately summarizes or sets the stage for the rest of the story.

Although our list of characteristics did not mention it, every copy editor should have a grasp of the mechanics of editing. That is, an editor needs to know how to mark copy for the printer, including the proper symbols to use. Knowledge of the symbols—and knowledge of VDT procedures in electronic editing—will not make you an editor, but lack of that knowledge will keep you from doing your job effectively. Similarly, you need to be familiar with your stylebook. (The stylebook is your guide in capitalization, spelling and such things.) Not one reader in a hundred will know anything about your style, but many will notice if you switch back and forth.

You must learn a new way of reading to be a successful copy editor. Forget what you learned in speed-reading class. Learn to look at every letter in every word and every word in every sentence. Remember that you are the last stop in an electronic newspaper; if you let a misspelled word go by, it comes out misspelled in the newspaper. The reader does not realize, or care, that you really know how to spell the word but just did not see the typo. To the reader, it is a misspelled word.

The requirement that you look at every word has a couple of solid reasons behind it: (1) You learn to weigh sentences and decide when they carry unnecessary words. You decide when one word would do the work of four. (2) You scrutinize each word to see that it is the best for the job of communication you are undertaking. I put that in the positive sense, but the negative aspects are also important; that is, you need to keep wrong words out just as you need to put precisely the right words in.

Fraction of selection

Let me introduce you to the fraction of selection, an idea borrowed from communication theorists. The fraction,

$$\frac{\text{expectation of reward}}{\text{predicted effort}}$$

has applications far beyond communication theory. I consider it a basic philosophical concept: You do things if you expect them to be worth the effort. Keep this in mind in your editing. Remember that the reader has a choice between slogging through your paper for a great deal of news or doing almost nothing in front of the television set for considerably less news. The written word is more difficult to receive; it requires effort. Your goal, of course, is to see that the reader gets a large amount of news (reward) from your newspaper with as little effort as possible.

The fraction gives the copydesk two tasks. (1) The desk must eliminate unnecessary stories and then unnecessary wording within stories so as to provide room for more and better material. (2) The desk must make sure the reader's effort is comfortably low, even if it will never be as slight as the effort required by television.

We might illustrate this with some figures. Say you are watching television. You can lie on your back, balance on your stomach a bottle of beer or a pizza or both (depending on your girth), and open one eye. Let us say this work takes 1 unit of energy. Now let us say 30 minutes of news provides 10 units of information. Don't worry what 10 units of news means; I made that up as an arbitrary figure. If you use the fraction of selection, you get the figure 10—effort divided into reward. Now you set food and drink aside and read the newspaper. We will say, to make up a figure, that it takes you 10 units of energy, since you have to sit up and use both eyes. If this newspaper has a great deal of news, editorials, comics, and other goodies in it, you might get—we will be arbitrary again—90 units of news. The formula now says you have a score of only 9 (10 into 90) for the newspaper. Television is easier even though the newspaper used here offers nine times as much information.

The copydesk's job, to repeat, is to lower the amount of effort or raise the amount of information. If the desk can make the paper easier to read, perhaps the bottom of our fraction can be cut to 9, or even 8. Alternatively, the desk can put more information into the newspaper. One hundred units divided by 10 units of work makes the paper equal to television.

What usually happens is that your effort to make stories easier to read causes you to shorten them, which opens more space for news. Consequently, you improve both parts of this fraction of selection.

Remember that these figures were picked arbitrarily. I do not mean to suggest that it is 10 times as hard to read a newspaper as to watch television. It may be 5 times. Or 20. And a newspaper may have only 6 times as much news. Or 50. The point is that newspaper copy editors must make their product easier to read and of more benefit to readers. They do that by careful editing.

Ten timely tips

We will turn now to some thoughts on what a copy editor might do with a pencil.

Although I have made an effort to avoid retreating into generalities, some of the suggestions in this chapter tend to be less specific than they could be. A few are almost the equivalent of this command: "Catch all errors." Such a command has much to be said for it, but the beginning copy editor may want to latch onto something a bit narrower. Fair enough. We will look at 10 habits you might cultivate, as a copy editor, to do your work better.

1. Mumble.	6. Do the work only once.
2. Verify or duck.	7. Be alert for repetition.
3. Ask the old-timers.	8. Avoid procrastination.
4. Compress.	9. Add it up.
5. Chop fearlessly.	10. Recheck.

These deserve a closer look, particularly since you cannot understand them without some explanation. A few words of explanation follow.

Mumble. If you try this and start getting dirty looks from fellow denizens of the rim, switch to the silent mumble. I am suggesting that you repeat to yourself every name you run across in copy—names of persons, names of organizations, names of places. Say them, and fix them in your mind. Why bother? Well, as a copy editor for the *Chicago Tribune* I once slept through a story in which we gave a man's name and address and then in all subsequent references called the chap by the name of his street. Had I mumbled his name at first, had I locked onto it and truly understood what I was being paid to edit, I would have caught it.

While we are at it, I ought to warn you against sonic writing—the use of a word with the same general sound as the correct word it replaces. For example, this sentence, "Smith was found innocent of all the charges that Jones levied against him," is 92 5/7 percent pure. One wrong word. "Leveled," not "levied." That one got by the desk of a major newspaper several times. You have to concentrate. Reporters do not put little red flags beside words they misuse. Such words just sneak in there amongst all the perfectly good words, and they will flit right past you if you doze.

Another way to phrase this advice, obviously, is to say, "Pay attention." Speed-reading is forbidden. Slow down. Read the copy carefully. Understand it. Expect errors from reporters under pressure. Catch all errors.

Verify or duck. Every time a reporter writes a statement of fact, the copy editor confronts three possibilities: (1) The statement is presumably correct. (2) The statement is questionable, and we have handy ways to check it out. (3) The statement is questionable, but we have no convenient way to prove it right or wrong. You do not have time to look up every spelling, every address, every date. Some things you know, and some you take on faith. If a story says Frank Knox, a former newspaper reporter, was secretary of the navy for Franklin Roosevelt, you may pause for an instant and reflect on Knox's ability to rise faster and higher than the average reporter, but you will not dash to the encyclopedia to verify the information. (You might if your story was an advance to be used a couple of weeks later.) If the story says Knox ran for vice-president with Alf Landon, you would realize the information must be wrong, because it means he ran against Roosevelt, the man we are saying made him secretary of the navy. You check it out. (Don't change it; check it.) Hey! The story was right. FDR must have seen the goodheartedness of a reporter shining through. But at least you checked.

Let's say now that our story states that Knox was a strong backer of the Spanish-American War as a Hearst newspaper publisher. Could be. But if so, Knox was either a child publisher nearly 40 years before he became secretary of the navy, or he was well past the age of Social Security eligibility when he got the navy job. You think the reporter meant World War I or maybe meant that Knox wrote editorials then and became a publisher later. Either way, you cannot readily verify the statement. So you duck it—you simply delete it. You might alter it to say only that before he became secretary he was a Hearst publisher and a writer of strong editorials, but you would duck out of saying which war he supported or when he was a publisher or when he supported a war. Readers get a little less information than they might otherwise—but none of it is wrong.

Another case: If in one place the story calls Knox secretary of the navy and in another says that as secretary of the army he was very close to Roosevelt, you look it up or duck use of the title, saying only that he was close to FDR as a cabinet member.

Remember that you cannot duck major parts of a story. If a fact is critical, you have to take time to verify it, even if you delay the story's publication. Try not to do this regularly.

Ask the old-timers. In a sense, asking the old hands is another kind of verification. Large numbers of facts are readily available nowhere but in the memories of copydesk veterans. Or maybe a veteran could quickly recall a fact you would have trouble looking up or could remember enough of it to steer you to the right source. If you are handling a weather story, for instance, and you think it needs to be fleshed out, a veteran editor might suggest that you look up the storm that hit Galveston in nineteen-oh-something. You could depend on Galveston being the proper location, but you should not take the old-timer's word (or anyone else's) on the date or number of dead or any other precise measurement. Still, you would have saved a little research time with your inquiry.

This practice has another aspect. You have to feel your way along in questioning other people, whether seasoned desk help or other beginners. Generally, people do not mind being asked sensible questions unless they are terribly busy. But you should not bother co-workers with minor stuff that you ought to know. Much depends on the way you ask your questions. An occasional question about the stylebook will bring a ready answer from someone glad to demonstrate knowledge. But you use up your credit in a hurry if you do not learn the stylebook on your own and if you continue to rely on others to make your decisions.

A final thought: Never hesitate to ask a question because you think you may be considered ignorant. Copy editors, especially beginners, often leave questionable material untouched, thinking that the writer must know the facts. Writers do not have to be ignoramuses to misstate a fact. The great ones do it. But copy editors who pass material they should question are ignoramuses of the first order. If they pass enough of it, they soon become former copy editors.

Compress. Go through every story with the intention of replacing four words with one, or six with two, or anything else involving that kind of arithmetic. If you see one thought spread thinly over two sentences, take the best parts of each for a new sentence. Cut out words that add little to your communication. An example:

> The scientist said the boom was either locked in position or so close the difference is unimportant.

You can tighten that to say:

> The scientist said the boom was firmly in position.

Although you need the full context to evaluate the editing properly, I assure you the writer was trying to say the boom was satisfactorily placed. The word "locked" would freeze many writers and editors; they would not be able to construct the sentence without it. Do not let yourself be frozen. Note also that this was not a rewrite. We merely made some substitutions:

> The scientist said the boom was ~~either locked~~ *firmly*
>
> in position~~, or so close the difference is unimportant.~~

We substituted "firmly" for "either locked" and deleted the part about an unimportant difference. If it is unimportant, we don't need it, do we?

Chop fearlessly. Beginning editors often hesitate to perform major surgery on a piece of copy. They look at the story, see the hard work that went into it, and read and enjoy the information it contains. If they like it, they figure everyone else should. Well, new copy editors must become accustomed to going home at day's end with more knowledge than some of their readers. Life is a bowl of compromises. You can run less than 100 inches of type plus headlines and art on a six-column newspaper page. The desk must decide whether your readers get all 100 inches in two stories or 10. You must be ruthless occasionally. You get paid to decide whether your readers can get by without the information you are deleting. Chances are that most will never know what they missed. Chances are that you do not know what you missed in the newspaper you read earlier today. You try to give your readers as much information as possible, but you do not have space to give them everything, and they do not have time to read all a day's news. In a sense, readers are paying you to go through the day's news report and choose the stories they want and need.

Do the work only once. A story that must be cut in half should not be edited meticulously before you make a major trim. Do not spend time compressing two paragraphs into one, only to kill it later. Kill the two grafs first, and spend your time in careful editing of something else.

Be alert for repetition. You would be astonished at the number of times people say something in one paragraph and then repeat it, in different words, in the next paragraph.

Many writers merely change words around from one paragraph to the next and offer the same thought.

Good copy editors recognize that flaw in writing, because they read the material carefully and grasp what the writer said. Then the idea is familiar when it comes back in other clothes.

The editor who is paying attention will see that the same thoughts and information have been offered once before. Even though the repetitive idea may be approached from another angle, it is still old hat and not worth using a second time.

Perhaps the worst sin is to make a statement in the lead and come back later with a quotation saying the same thing almost word for word. This transgression occurs most often when the quote provides a snappy summary of the action. The writer may use a paraphrase or partial quote in the lead, calling the source "an official," or something like that, name the source in the second graf, and then use the full quote in the next graf. Looks bad every time.

Repetition of a quote, even when paraphrased, is almost always bad. Few things make you look worse. You must be particularly careful when the quotation does a great job of summarizing what you want to say; the temptation to put part of it in the lead and then come back with the full quote later is hard to resist. Seldom looks good.

I suppose this paragraph will insult half or more of you, but I fear that a few will have missed the little trick in those preceding six paragraphs—every other one is a duplication. My apologies to the alert. To the others: You were not reading copy on this, so you have committed no crime. But you could have been paying closer attention, and you must pay closer attention when you start taking money for editing.

Avoid procrastination. Do not trust your memory to bring you back to a place that you have mentally marked for reexamination. Do not say to yourself, "Hey, I will look that up when I finish editing this story." Do not put it off; do it. If you plan to come back to something, at least put a mark by it on the copy. If you are an electronic editor, make a note on a piece of paper. Better to write notes than to see an error in the paper and say, "Oh, yeah; I intended to check that."

Also, write down any tricky phrasing you think of instead of trusting your memory. That is, you are reading copy and you see a sentence that could be stated more clearly. You think of a better way to say it, but you decide to insert it after you complete the story. At that time you turn back to the inserting place and suddenly draw a blank. The clever phrasing you had so firmly in hand has flown out of your head, possibly never to return. You can only groan in frustration.

Add it up. Einstein never worked in a newsroom, and most newsroom inmates have reciprocated by staying out of his territory. A pity, both ways. Einstein survived adequately without getting ink on his hands, but newspaper people—particularly those on the copydesk—could stand a better acquaintance with math. You do not have to be in Einstein's league. You learned the basics long ago; now you need to develop the habit of using your math when you come across figures in a story. You remember the tale about the enterprising necktie salesman? He summarized his business philosophy: "I buy the tie for a dollar and I sell it for two dollars, and I'm happy with my 1 percent profit."

His business is better than his math. The trouble is that a great number of copy editors might let those figures pass. Many who would boggle at such an egregious error will never question clearly questionable material on their own. The *New York Times* ran a story noting that 900 cases of lead poisoning had been found in 27,000 children tested—0.033 percent of the total. The copy editor should have known a little more about percentages. The reporter probably took the correct first step, dividing 27,000 into 900. That tells you that one is 0.0333 of the other, or three one-hundredths. You know that three one-hundredths is 3 percent. But our reporter and copy editor didn't pick it up. Readers did.

You need to know how to figure percentages and how to add. Next, to repeat, keep an eye out for all kinds of figures. Check them out. Add them up. If they do not add up, and believe me, they will often be wrong, the copy goes back to the reporter. (If you are in a hurry, see timely tip number 2 in this list.)

Recheck. Copy editors do not have time to memorize the stories they read, but they should make every effort to skim back over a story after they complete work on it, mainly because the lack of time will have caused them to work too fast. Copy editors can think faster than they can write. Consequently, they may form perfect sentences in their minds but move along to something in the next sentence before their fingers can commit the words to paper. The same disease strikes VDT operators; they remember thinking a perfect sentence but they are unable to type it as fast as it goes through their minds. If they go back over the story, they may encounter these rough spots and be able to smooth them out. Otherwise, the reader catches the bumps.

Should you memorize the ten timely tips? No real need to. However, you need to make them part of your method of operation. You can become a successful copy editor without mumbling or even without moving your lips at all as you read. But you do help yourself if you lock onto names and other facts at first reading and stay with them. You may develop ten other habits I have not thought of that are of greater benefit than these. Fine; copy editors need all the help they can get.

Editing runs into work, but it can be fun, too. Your fun increases as you learn to do the job better.

Reference works

The dictionary in a newspaper office is traditionally located within a few steps of the copydesk. Affluent papers may have another one elsewhere in the newsroom for the primary use of reporters. The dictionary is an essential tool, of course, and its importance grows in an electronic editing system because no proofreader sits behind the copy editor. If the copy editor, with

Webster's help, cannot handle a word, it comes out wrong in the newspaper. A poor speller can survive in the newsroom as long as he or she recognizes the weakness and looks up doubtful words.

However, *Webster's* has plenty of company on the journalist's bookshelf. The good copydesk should be well supplied with reference works, some of them indispensable. If the desk's world almanac is a year old and not beginning to look dog-eared, the crew should be tested for sleeping sickness. A world almanac answers questions on everything from the population of Pinellas County, Florida, to the amount of deposits in the nation's leading bank, from the name of the president of Iowa State University to the difference between the flags of Italy and the Ivory Coast. Many companies put out world almanacs. You will find at least one new one every year, though most come out or are revised every other year.

You will find state almanacs in some places; they range in size from overgrown pamphlets to books as large as a typical world almanac. And they are nearly as useful to a copydesk as the broader scope effort.

A copydesk would have a difficult time, too, without an atlas—that book of maps and other geographic data. The *New York Daily News* takes another step and uses a collection of large maps mounted on wall hinges. Reporters and copy editors can quickly turn to whatever map they want, from a borough to a nation.

Telephone books and city directories for all cities and towns in the area covered by the newspaper are also required. The *Cross Reference Directory* (Criss Cross), which lists telephone numbers by address, can be exceedingly helpful for reporters.

The average newspaper publisher probably has most of the titles cited so far. These less essential but valuable references are also needed: *Bartlett's Familiar Quotations,* the *Bible, Book of the States, Congressional Directory, Facts on File, Film Daily Year Book of Motion Pictures, Statesman's Yearbook, Statistical Abstract of the United States, U.S. Postal Guide,* and *Who's Who.*

That barely gets us into the list of resources available. William L. Rivers did an annotation of reference books, called *Finding Facts,* which contains more than 400 citations. Of course, only a big library would normally carry that many references, just as a library or major newspaper would be the most likely place to find one other valuable reference tool: the *New York Times Index* and microfilm file. The index tells you the date and page number for most stories the *Times* has carried, and the microfilm lets you look at it. The index is too cumbersome and the process too laborious for a copy editor to use in checking a minor fact, but reporters should take advantage of it.

Time out for a secret: Although librarians are human and subject to the frailties of the species, they are almost invariably among the most helpful people you encounter. Cultivate them. Love them. Count on them. Usually, all they want is a trace of civility and moderately specific inquiries. (They do not want a question like this: "What do you have on the Russian tsars?" Be specific: "How many times was Peter the Great married?")

Just as you do not depend on other editors to answer every question you have about a piece of copy, you do not depend on a librarian to tell you where to look for information. Practically anything you want to know is written somewhere, and you make yourself much more valuable if you know where to look it up. You do not acquire that knowledge from a cursory examination of this book. You acquire it by constantly resorting to reference books when you have questions and by looking through them in idle moments. Reference books are a tool; your job is to learn the best use of that tool.

I am not by nature inclined to crawl out on limbs, but it is time for a peek at what lies ahead in reference works. Most of the discussion about hotshot technology in this book is based on ideas that have been brought to fruition at the time of writing. I have tried to avoid the error of those seers who, three decades ago, predicted that newspapers would shortly be extinct and the news would be delivered into each home with a printout right at the breakfast table. That prediction, involving facsimile transmission, has yet to come to pass and may have been superseded by systems involving the television screen. I want to deal with technological innovations in references.

It seems unlikely that the full implementation of electronic editing can clean off the copydesk totally, but I fully expect it to eliminate—someday— the need for most reference works that now clutter up the place. The electronic editor will be able to pause in the middle of a story, switch to a blank screen, ask for the dictionary, and no doubt get all definitions and spellings for any word. The editor will then switch back to the story and continue, knowing that another misuse of a word has been avoided.

You can readily see that at least in theory it is but a step from an electronic dictionary to an electronic encyclopedia, and then to an electronic library. Computers do not now have the storage capacity to handle your library's billions of pieces of information, but you are shortsighted if you think that problem will not be overcome in your lifetime. With a link to an electronic library, you could call up, say, H. Allen Smith's autobiography, *To Hell in a Handbasket,* and read it over a week's lunch breaks. Of course, *To Hell in a Handbasket* will not have top priority when we start computerizing our information system. The almanac will be ahead; so will the dictionary and the tables in an atlas.

Do you want to know what comes first, though? The morgue (the clipping files from your newspaper). Computerization of newspaper clipping files is already upon us. The *Boston Globe, Toronto Globe & Mail,* and *Los Angeles Times* are leaders in this work, and they are well into it. The Boston paper had 9 million clippings in its files when it went electronic and stopped clipping in 1977. Eventually, the 9 million clips will be stored in microfiche or in the computer, clearing a great amount of space for other work. (The microfiche system is kin to microfilming; it uses a small piece of film, mounted with others on a card, that fits into a reading device. Each piece of film, less than an inch square, covers a newspaper page or several pages of other documents. Microfilm uses the same principle, with the film in a roll.)

You are perhaps by now aware that the public is not totally convinced that people in the news media are all saints. Our readers and viewers and listeners too often distrust us. Part of their distrust springs from their repeated observations of our errors. We will not be able to eliminate the distrust, any more than we can eliminate all error, as long as we have regular broadcasts and daily newspapers. But we can cut down on one by cutting down on the other—we take aim at our errors and hope that a by-product will be increased trust. And the way we go after our errors includes more double checking with the references, with our morgue, with the sources, to get nearer the impossible goal—an error-free piece of communication.

[3] *Editing symbols*

NOW WE TAKE UP this book's least exciting but most basic topic, editing symbols.

We might liken editing symbols to the symbols musicians use. Apprentice songwriters may be able to draw magnificent signs for sharps and flats and treble clefs and such things, but that knowledge in itself will not make them good musicians. Songwriters use musical symbols as a handy way to tell people what to sing or what notes to play on instruments. Similarly, copy editors (and writers) use editing symbols as a shorthand way to pass information to the person setting copy into type.

Although the bulk of editing for most periodicals will soon be handled on video display terminals, enough editing will be done with pencil and paper to make it worth our while to study the editing symbols. When every home has a computer in the rumpus room and terminals are as common as handkerchiefs, we can forget the symbols. In the meantime, we may find it easy to learn them with this program.

For the sake of convenience, all normal editing symbols are shown in Fig. 3.1. These are the customary symbols, universally understood. You will find minor variations in other books. Ignore them—stick with these; they are infinitely wiser. You may find yourself in someone else's employ someday, and in that case you will use the symbols the boss suggests.

These symbols are an agreement between the typesetter and the writer-editor. If the composing room knows that a given mark always has the same meaning, we are all in good shape.

One of the first symbols you use is the one calling for a paragraph indentation. This symbol $\llcorner$ is used on every paragraph, even those already indented. Why? So the typesetter can see quickly that you want a paragraph to begin at that spot. Do it about like this:

```
⌐This is an example.
```

Sometimes it is necessary to tell the printer that you would like to start a paragraph at a point other than at the beginning of a typed line. That is, you want to break a paragraph into two paragraphs. If so, you may use the same symbol used at the beginning, $\llcorner$. Or, better, you

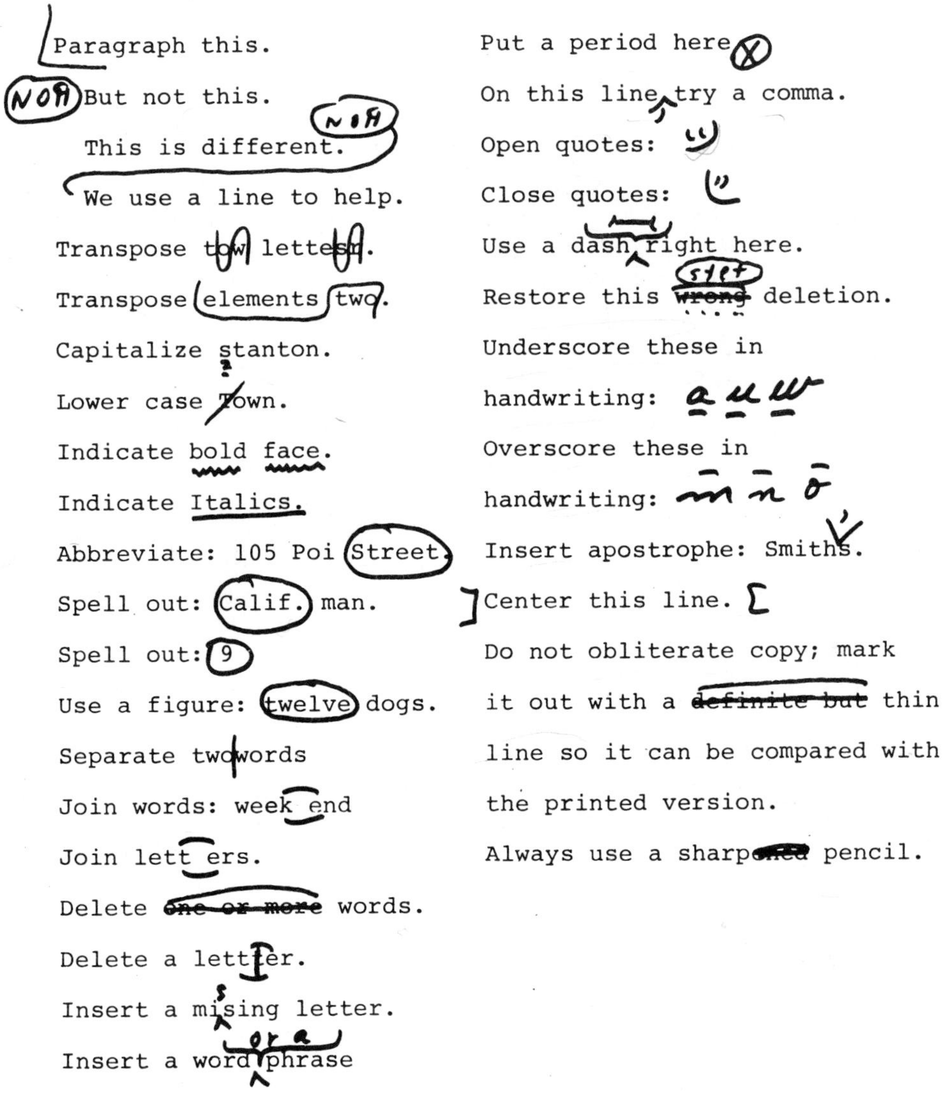

Paragraph this.

NON But not this.

    This is different. *NON*

We use a line to help.

Transpose tow lettesr.

Transpose elements two.

Capitalize stanton.

Lower case Town.

Indicate bold face.

Indicate Italics.

Abbreviate: 105 Poi Street.

Spell out: Calif. man.

Spell out: 9

Use a figure: twelve dogs.

Separate twowords

Join words: week end

Join lett ers.

Delete one or more words.

Delete a lettter.

Insert a missing letter.

Insert a word phrase

Put a period here⊗

On this line try a comma.

Open quotes:

Close quotes:

Use a dash right here.

Restore this wrong deletion.

Underscore these in

handwriting: *a u w*

Overscore these in

handwriting: *m n o*

Insert apostrophe: Smiths.

Center this line.

Do not obliterate copy; mark

it out with a definite but thin

line so it can be compared with

the printed version.

Always use a sharpened pencil.

Fig. 3.1. Editing symbols.

may use another symbol, ℔ , which is a proofreader's mark that has crept into the editing side of things. It is widely accepted. Its advantage, used within a paragraph, is its uniqueness; it will not be mistaken for something else. The L-shaped symbol might appear at first to be just a vertical mark for some other insertion in the copy. Consequently, the ℔ is preferred when you are turning one paragraph into two.

On occasion, a copy editor will need to turn two paragraphs into one. That is accomplished with the same symbol plus the word "no" (makes sense), like this:

```
    Video display terminals are here to stay, as a

look at any newspaper office will show. (no #)

    They are driving the pencil cartel crazy.
```

Notice that the instructions were circled. The circle is to tell the typesetter not to set these instructions into type. Typesetters would not set the *#* symbol, of course, but they might start on the "no" before realizing that the word was an instruction. The typesetter would then have to reset the line.

A major point on this minor point: Put the mark at the end of the upper sentence, not at the beginning of the lower one. Why? It is a convenience for the typesetter. When reaching what appears to be the end of a paragraph, the typesetter will hit the equivalent of the carriage return on a typewriter, moving to the beginning of the next paragraph. Then the typesetter, finding your *no #* mark there, will probably say something unkind, because at that point the upper line must be reset, with the next sentence at the end of it. However, if you are thoughtful enough to indicate *no #* at the end of the upper line, the typesetter will not return to the beginning of a paragraph but will hunt for the rest of the paragraph and will think nice thoughts about you.

Finally, experience indicates that many newcomers tend to throw in an extra *no #* anytime they cut out part of a line. That is needless effort. If there is no period, the end of the line will obviously not be the end of a paragraph. Save yourself a little effort.

And with that we can move on to other, less exhausting symbols.

Sometimes a reporter types a capital letter by mistake. The editor must uncap it. Uncapping is done with a slash, from top right to bottom left. Like this. Here is a sentence, with unnecessary capitals, that has been edited:

```
People sometimes /capitalize /Words they /shouldn't.

We /journalists would /Never do /Such a /Thing.
```

We're rolling. Maybe we should stop. How do we stop? We use a period. And the best mark for a period is this: ⊗ . You will meet people who say the x need not be circled. Shun them. The x gets a circle for a reason: A circled x is never mistaken for a plain *x*. If you can draw an x that has no chance of being taken for an *x*, you will cause no problems by leaving your x uncircled. If you are in doubt, circle it.

You should know that copy editors sometimes use one other mark to indicate a period: a circled dot, like this: ⊙ . The mark is circled so it will be more easily spotted. This mark is properly a refugee from the proofreading department, but it is so common that most editors accept it or at least recognize it.

Let's look at another paragraph and some of the other symbols. First, the unmarked copy:

```
when people talk about Cold Type, they are not

referring To the welldigger's weekly from the fargo,
```

```
N.D, area   They are referring to Type set with Pho-

tocomposition Equipment.
```

Here's how this paragraph should be marked:

```
 when people talk about ¢old Type, they are not

referring to the welldigger's weekly from the fargo,

N.D, area  They are referring to Type set with Pho-

tocomposition Equipment
```

We had a minor problem: The comma after "N.D," was exactly where we wanted to put a period. Note the solution. We just indicated the period on the comma and then added a comma. If there had not been enough room to do it that way, we would have scratched out "N.D," and written it in properly above the line. Remember, we are not playing a game in which a circle must be round and every mark must be made with machine precision. No, we are communicating our ideas to a typesetter. And the quicker the typesetter gets the desired message, the better off we are.

If you are overly sensitive, you may complain that you were not told about commas before we tackled that last job. A good point; we should remedy the shortcoming. We'll take up the comma now.

With the comma comes an all-purpose mark, the caret. If the caret is in the normal position, with the point at the top, the comma goes under it, $\wedge$. If the caret is upside down, $\vee$, punctuation goes above, as for an apostrophe:

```
We'll be home early, mom.
```

There's more. The caret is also used on the colon and semicolon: $\wedge$ $\wedge$. Note that the marks are large and clear. Get into the habit of making bold marks on copy; timid ones are likely to be overlooked by hasty typesetters.

Now, we'll mark up a paragraph with the caret for commas and the upside-down caret for apostrophes. We will put in all the other required marks while we are at it.

```
 Electronic Editing, relatively new in the U.S.A.

is rapidly increasing in importance.  It Is quick,

¢lean, Quiet and Efficient  Although it requires

Relatively greater concentration by the editor, elec-

tronic Editing offers many many advantages.  By Dec.  No !

31, 1999, the American newspapers will have aban-
```

doned paper. Lets hope they wont have abandoned

news too

[Electronic Editing, relatively new in the U.S.A.,
is rapidly increasing in importance. It is quick,
clean, quiet and efficient. Although it requires
relatively greater concentration by the editor electronic Editing offers many ~~many~~ advantages. By Dec.
31, 1999, the American newspapers will have abandoned paper. Lets hope they wont have abandoned

news too

Did you note the paragraph mark? How about the period at the end? The copy editor is responsible for catching those things. And, as said, electronic editing places a premium on careful, thorough examination of the copy.

We are not through with the caret. We need it to show where we want to insert a hyphen. Like the apostrophe, the hyphen (-) gets an upside-down caret. Ah, but here's a twist: The hyphen is indicated in copy editing with *two* marks, one atop the other like an equal sign (=). Strange, you say. Well, not too strange; we use two marks because the dash uses a single mark. We will handle the dash later. Right now, let's pop an apostrophe and a hyphen into this sentence:

We cant cross the Vermont Canada border.

The caret also comes into play when we insert words or letters, with one major distinction: If we insert a word, which will have spaces on each side, we throw in sort of a bracket arrangement. If we insert only a letter, we use only the caret or perhaps the caret and a vertical line. Witness:

See how we insert (our) extra words and leters?

Once more, using a song title:

The (old) gray mare (she) ain't wat she usd to be.

Here is how that sentence would appear with the vertical line mentioned earlier:

The (old) gray mare (she) ain't wat she usd to be.

No big deal. If you have to use the vertical line to indicate clearly where the letter goes, use it. Otherwise, the caret will carry you.

We will finish up our time in caret land with a dash. The dash is not a hyphen, despite the steadfast belief of many journalism students. The hyphen is an overworked little mark as it is, and we ought not to impose a greater load on it by making it do the dash's work. Besides, the dash is a big, lively—perhaps even dramatic—mark, and we ought to at least give it the proper symbol.

On a typewriter, the dash is made with consecutive hyphens, with no space between them and the words on either side. In copy, the dash is made with this mark, ⟩——⟨ . It is a long mark with tiny reversed parentheses on the ends. Here is how it looks when edited into copy:

```
    Journalists are among the world's happiest
    ⟩——⟨
people⋏especially if they have outside income.
```

Although this chapter deals with the marks and not grammar in general, I must unburden myself with a few words about this lively and dramatic punctuation mark—the dash. You will encounter dashes sprinkled about in this text. And this amount is proper. Anything more than a sprinkling will be noticeable, and you have trouble if your punctuation becomes noticeable. The young journalist should learn to use the dash for flavor, for it is a good punctuation mark. But it cannot do everything, and it is so strong that its repeated use wearies the reader.

Let us look at some things the dash can do. (1) The dash is used to emphasize words or phrases or even clauses. It sets them apart, like a souped-up pair of parenthesis marks.

> She had blue eyes—clear as a bell—and auburn hair.
> The Buckeyes—playing without their star—were underdogs.

(2) The dash quickly takes a sentence off on a tangent. It provides a twist in thought, as in the note about rich journalists above. Also, look at these:

> "That didn't hurt," he said—picking up his teeth.
> Pillsbury got a taste of something sweet today—in court.

(3) The dash does duty as a muscular colon.

> That's his strength—the crosscourt kill shot.
> He has one weakness—lack of stamina.

A diligent search will turn up numerous other uses for this mark. You should learn to use it, but you should also restrain yourself and not wear it out. It deserves use—not abuse.

So far, our emphasis has been on introducing new material into our copy. Now we need to take a look at how to delete what we do not want.

You will find disagreement on the best way to eliminate a paragraph. Some people would ask that you mark through every line. Others would agree, with the added requirement that you draw a diagonal from the last used word to the next one. Others would scratch through all lines and add arrows. Still others would draw a rectangle around the material to be deleted, adding arrows if that suited them. See examples below.

~~This is a short paragraph that will be used to illustrate a technique of deleting a block of material.~~

In this material, we'll have three paragraphs. ~~The second one will be eliminated, and we'll get a line from the last used word to the next.~~ It should look pretty.

This is still another. ~~In this paragraph, we delete the material with marks through every line.~~ The arrows go to the next usable graf.

~~Finally, we reach the rectangle stage. This is as good a marking as any, as long as it is understandable to the people setting type.~~

Of course, the problem vanishes when you go into electronic editing. Your copy there is always neat.

Back to pencil work. Sentences get a treatment different from that we just gave to paragraphs. Normally, a sentence is simply scratched out, deleted, with one line through it. On most kinds of publication, you will also draw a line from the end of the sentence before your deleted sentence to the beginning of the one after your deleted sentence, like this:

Copy editors should not delete material so vigorously that it cannot be read under the graphite if, for some reason, reconstruction is needed. ~~On the other hand, the editor must mark through the sentence firmly enough to guarantee that the typesetter will not set it.~~ Moderation and common sense serve as the basis of a good policy.

Before we dig further into this particular trove, it might behoove us to mention a sin often committed by journalistic apprentices, the yo-yo sin: taking typesetters down to a lower line and then jerking them back up to the original. In some union shops, this kind of copy will be kicked back. Here is an example of such a forbidden editing practice:

```
Trenton, with 105 slayings, listed for the year

on the bureau's records, 'was second in the state
```

Don't do that. The printers go crazy. Don't even do this:

```
Trenton, with 105 slayings listed for the year

on the bureau's records (was second in the state)
```

Instead, write it in, like this:

```
            was second in the state
Trenton  with 105 slayings listed for the year

on the bureau's records, was second in the state.
```

"What nonsense!" you may be saying. "Any fool could figure out what the marks mean." That may be true, but, as you recall, the editor's job is to send the printer copy that does not have to be figured out. The typesetter must be able to read it without pause.

Look at this editing:

```
We heard his troubled cries for water, water.
```

Ah, but that's only half the job. To help the typesetter, we draw a little bridge over the deleted matter.

```
We heard his troubled cries for water, water.
```

With this mark, we tell the typesetter not to try to read what is under the bridge; we make a bridge for the typesetter's eye.

Sometimes you use two bridges. When? When you want to eliminate the space between characters. The single bridge, as used above, tells the typesetter to leave the appropriate space after the word. Two bridges, under and over the deleted matter, call for a joining of the characters. Material written this way

```
week end        sin gle         sinngle        tom boy
```

would be edited this way

week‿end   sin‿gle   sin⁀gle   tom‿boy

and would be printed this way: weekend, single, single, tomboy.

Note the second "single." It contained an extra character. We deleted that character with a vertical line, | . Then we asked the typesetter to close up the space. Typesetters with half a brain would figure out that they were supposed to close up "sin" and "gle," even if you made only one bridge over the word. Mark both bridges anyway. Take no chances.

Similarly, you should not take chances by placing the lower bridge where you do not need it. You probably will not get burned, but you could. That is to say, no typesetter in good health and of reasonable sobriety is going to believe that you want no space between "The" and "president" (Thepresident) when you make the following wrong mark:

The ~~U.S.~~ president lives in the White House.

You have no guarantee that, somewhere out there, you will never run into a typesetter who is temporarily not in good health or of reasonable sobriety, or both. Besides, your mark made the typesetter pause and reread the material to see if there was more to it than was apparent. Good copy editors do not cause typesetters to boggle often.

Remember: One bridge *over* a deletion means that a space will be left after the word. *One over* and *one under* means that the words will be set solid, with no space between (set together: settogether, likethis).

We move on. So far, we have deleted characters within words only. Now we tackle a character on the end of a word, either end. Again, we have a simple operation: Just scratch it out. If you feel moved to throw a bridge over the scratch, no one will complain. The main thing is that the typesetter must understand you. Example:

We̸ have too̸ many characters.

No one could misunderstand us on that mark, with the bridge or without it.

Having crossed that bridge, we come to the task of deleting punctuation marks. Be advised that you will run into people who will suggest that you use this mark ⚲   to take out punctuation. Humor them. If that is the mark most often used at your new place of employment, use it, like this:

People often put⦰ commas where they⦰ do not

belong.

However, you need to know that the mark is properly used only in proofreading. (Proofreading is what you do after the material has been set into type.) Again, the main thing is to do what is most readily understood.

Usually, therefore, the proper editing mark for deletion of punctuation is the same as for a letter on the end of a word—the scratch.

```
He scratched out / the comma.
```

Most of our recent work has been toward joining elements. Now we need to see about moving them apart a little. Copy editors have to backstop reporters on this sort of thing, so you will need to know the marks. (You need to know them even if you never edit anything but your own stuff.) To separate characters (actually, words are more commonly run together than isolated characters), we use a plain vertical line: For instance:

```
Separate two|words.
```

Now we turn to transposition. We have two basic items to transpose: words and characters. The same mark works for both. (Transposition of paragraphs is usually done by cutting and pasting; by rewriting; or, on the tube, by punching the proper keys.) In pencil editing, here is how we transpose words and characters:

```
These |words/ two| somehow g|t|o| in bac/w|k/ard.
```

You may be wondering whether square marks or curved ones are proper. Yes; either is fine. Furthermore, you can draw the first horizontal part either under or above the words.

```
It |not |matters| how straight |line |the|, how up
|down (or) the loops.  As (as / long) a typesetter |read \can/
it, we'll praise |yells/with| and whoops.
```

Quotation marks come next. And here's the thing about quotation marks and copy editing: Typewriters do not have opening and closing quote marks; they are all straight up and down. In type, opening marks slant to the right and closers slant to the left. See: ''Ooo.'' (Digression: The period and the comma always go inside the quotation marks.) Therefore, the copy editor is obliged to show direction on all quotation marks. (The VDT has separate keys for openers and closers.) This means you have to mark them *all*. Even if they are clearly at the beginning or end of a sentence, mark them all. To mark them, simply use an arc that opens to the left when you have opening quotation marks and use an arc opening to the right for closing marks. Open to left, ⌣ , begin quotes. Open to right, ⌣ , close quotes. Example:

```
⌣"I am sorry you don't believe it,⌣" he said.
```

Some people put a caret in the line to show the typesetter where to start. This mark is usually unnecessary.

We progress naturally from an arc to a full circle, the next copy editing symbol. Actually, the circle is more often an ellipse; but we will call it a circle, since we are more interested in grammar than geometry. The mark means the same, no matter what you call it. If drawn around a full word, like this,

```
. . . in Chico, (California) the . . .
```

it tells the typesetter to abbreviate the word: "Calif." If drawn around an already abbreviated word, like this,

```
. . . to the people on Lakemoore (St.) every day . . .
```

it means we spell out the word: "Street."

The same principle is used on numbers. If you circle a figure,

```
I have (9) dogs.
```

it will be spelled out: "nine." If you circle a spelled number,

```
I have (eleven) dogs.
```

it will be turned into a figure: "11."

Here's a sneaky one:

```
He worked for the state's ABC before moving to

N.Mex.
```

You can't circle "ABC" because the typesetter won't know whether you mean Alcoholic Beverages Commission, Audit Bureau of Circulations or Anti Balloon Congress. You, the copy editor, must see that it is spelled out, and that means you have to write it out yourself. You could probably get away with circling "FBI" or "CIA," but you are wiser not to take a chance. On the second abbreviation in our sentence, "N.Mex.," you have to make it clear. Do you want both spelled out, "Mex." abbreviated to "M.," or what? Take the time to write out what you want when you confront some weird typing. In the case at hand, we would have to write out "New Mexico," since names of states standing alone are not abbreviated.

Occasionally an editor mistakenly deletes something and has to put it back. The thing to do then is to examine the material carefully and see if the typesetter can read it through the markings. If not, the editor must write it back in, carefully. But if the original version can still be deciphered, do this:

```
Do not make these exceedingly picky deletions.
                    (stet)
Do not make these exceedingly picky deletions.
```

Draw some dots under the deleted material and write the word "stet" above. If you had only one or maybe two short words to put back in, it would probably be just as easy to write them in as they were. If you have several words, stet will save you a little time. Should you want a full paragraph restored and it is readable, write a stet at the side and bracket the graf.

Boldface and bold caps come into play now and then. Many publications use bold cap read-ins to begin occasional paragraphs. Markings for read-ins vary from publication to publication. Usually, a wavy line under the word will produce boldface. If you want a mass of bold material (inadvisable, since it is hard to read), you might bracket the graf and mark "bfc" at the side. But for just a few words, you do it like this:

(bfc)
The full truth will stun you.

And if you want only boldface, not bold caps, do this:

(bf)
The full truth will stun you.

Try a bfc read-in first; then do a single word (born).

(bfc)
The only blue items were borrowed.
(bf)
I was born to edit.

Normally, bfc read-ins are two–three words. But in this case four were required because three would have left us dangling: **THE ONLY BLUE** items. But bold cap read-ins should never run more than a line (indeed, a full line is too much).

Some publications ask that you circle the words you want in bold caps and make a marginal notation:

(bfc) ——— (The only blue items)were borrowed.

If that is what the editor wants, go along. Either method will do nicely.

If you have the symbols down pat, take a bow; you are better than average. If you are still unsure about some of them, stay on the job. These symbols have to become second nature to you.

[4] *A good start*

WE HAVE NOTED that copy editors do more rewriting with VDTs than they did with pencil and paper. Although editors should not get into the habit of rewriting all copy, they can do a full-scale revision on VDTs with little trouble. If a story is thoroughly inadequate, the editor should kick it back for revision by the city desk and the offending reporter. But if one paragraph of rewrite will expiate all sins, the editor may be justified in doing the job, especially if time presses. With that thought in mind, we are going back to the basics of newswriting.

News has a number of characteristic elements. Among them are consequence, immediacy, prominence, oddity and proximity. You may be able to list more. But the five just cited bear most directly on a majority of stories. Let us examine the five.

Consequence is by definition important. A fierce typhoon that does nothing but agitate the fishes in the Pacific deserves scant news play. But a storm of much less intensity will get at least some mention in the press if it delays the wheat harvest a week or so. A brief storm that kills someone and causes heavy damage in a single town will receive better display. Try another example: If high schools in Peoria permit the use of an extra pompon girl at football and basketball games this year, the consequences will not be widespread, although presumably the quality of cheerleading will be improved, with all the benefits to society such a change implies. The story will receive little notice. But if the president signs a bill setting a national auto speed limit of 45 miles per hour, the story will be of major value because of the consequences.

Prominence comes into play in most stories. If a journalism professor gets hurt playing handball, few people will take note. But if a state's lieutenant governor takes a header in a game and needs a few stitches to get himself together, we have a more interesting story.

Proximity gets to us all. More than 100 Americans die in car wrecks every day. Unless the circumstances are unusual or the number of deaths is abnormally high, most of those accidents go unreported outside the immediate area. But a fatal wreck that occurs locally will be covered. Why? It is close to home, and it is more likely to have an effect on readers.

Readers may know the victims or may have passed the wreck site recently.

Immediacy is of some importance. News grows old quickly. Indeed,
sometimes news of great importance is downgraded because it has lost its
timeliness. The clock is the curse of journalism, but it is what separates news
from history.

Oddity rounds out the list. A garter snake with two heads is of precious
little consequence to the world, but it is an unusual thing—so it gets some
news play. If a state official padlocks a business establishment that has not
paid its sales taxes, the closing is news because it is unusual. But if such
events occur day after day, they soon lose their oddity and their news value
diminishes.

Although these elements come into play in discussions of all kinds of
news, this chapter is concerned primarily with straight news. Features
belong in another category. Straight news, sometimes called *hard news*, has
a strong sense of immediacy, and it informs more than it entertains. Such
news is usually written with a summary at the beginning and its facts
arranged in order of decreasing importance.

We run into our question and answer format in this chapter. Here's a
challenge to answer the questions as you come to them.

Q. *Decide which item below is the best example of straight news.*

    a. A bus driver makes expensive jewelry as a hobby, working with
gold and precious stones.
    b. Three students signed up as VISTA volunteers today.
    c. Two 75-year-old men signed up for law school aptitude tests.
    d. The local university administration building was evacuated
because of a bomb scare.

Story *d* has consequence, oddity, proximity, immediacy and prominence.

Q. *Which of the following is the better hard news story?*

    a. The city planning commission recommended disapproval of a
development along a local lake today.
    b. It may soon be possible for a poor family to slowly buy a roomy
apartment.

Story *a* has news in it. The other has a feature approach. Although story
b is heavily laden with consequence, it will never have the immediacy of
story *a*. One of the problems facing journalists surfaces here: How do
you peddle a news story that is only a situation report, no matter how
important the story may be? Answers are not plentiful.

The lead

Without question, the most important paragraph in a news story,
probably in any kind of story, is the first. We call it the lead. (Most leads

are only one paragraph long, but they can run longer.) The lead sets the tone for the entire story; it grabs the reader; it gives the reader the essence of the story.

A diligent scholar could quickly turn up a dozen names for different kinds of leads. Most of these names are used only in classroom discussions of leads; reporters do not spend their idle moments chatting about such things. We will deal with summary, question, background, quotation, picture, contrast and offbeat leads.

No other lead approaches the summary lead in importance. It does the bulk of the work in news stories for newspapers, magazines and broadcast media. A summary lead normally answers half or more of the key questions—who, what, when, where, why and how. And it does so briefly. Rarely will a lead answer all six questions (known as the five *W*s and *H*). The need for brevity requires that some be held out of the first paragraph and used later. *Who, what, when* and *where* get the most play in leads. That leaves two other elements in a secondary role: *why* and *how.*

Most news stories are written in a form known as *inverted pyramid,* although few writers give this kind of architecture much thought as they put a story together. Like the kinds of leads cited earlier, this term is used primarily for discussion. The analogy is nevertheless valid. The term means that the big end of the pyramid—the broadest information—is placed at the story's beginning. The story then tapers to smaller and smaller details until it disappears.

> **Q.** *The following lead leaves one or more key questions unanswered. Which ones?*

> HARRISBURG, Pa.—Gov. Milton
> J. Shapp signed a bill making June
> 11–16 Mental Health Week in Penn-
> sylvania.

We left out *when, where, why* and *how.* Although not mentioned specifically, *where* the event took place was implied. Governors normally sign bills at the office, and any change is likely to be mentioned. Also, the dateline (Harrisburg, Pa.) makes a strong indication of location. One *where* is covered—where the event has effect. The *how* (with a ball-point pen, a flourish, or both) is unnecessary unless it was unusual. But we ought to tell *when* in the lead (today), and we ought to tell *why* soon afterward.

We could have put a *why* in the lead, but that might have crowded it:

> HARRISBURG, Pa.—Declaring
> that mental illness must be eradicated in
> his state, Gov. Milton J. Shapp signed
> today a bill making June 11–16 Mental
> Health Week in Pennsylvania.

This lead is usable, although it borders on being too long (28 words). Let us look at its parts:

> Declaring . . . Shapp . . . signed . . . today . . . a bill
>   (*why*)   (*who*)   (*what*)   (*when*)   (more *what*)

One point occasionally causes confusion: the case of the *what/what*. Some people believe the following lead, which has no person in it, is not a *who* lead; they would call it a *what* lead.

> A chest full of pirate gold was
> found here today.

There is no *who*, to be sure. But if we break this one down as we did the Pennsylvania job, we get:

> A chest . . . was found . . . here . . . today.
> (*what*)   (*what*)   (*where*)   (*when*)

Thus we have the *what/what*. Forget that. Call the subject of the sentence a *who*, no matter whether it is a chest of gold or the guy who draws Dick Tracy.

Chances are you do not remember all the kinds of leads; that's no major problem. But you ought to be able to write examples of the seven different kinds of leads. Let's see what we have:

A *picture* lead paints a word picture for the reader. You might describe a woodland scene after a snowstorm. You might describe a shaggy-haired rock band's pelvic contortions. You might even describe the beauty of a rainstorm sweeping across the desert. Your goal is to get readers to see a picture in their minds.

The *question* lead is fairly common. It does a satisfactory job on some features, and it can be used on a hard news story occasionally. With this lead, you speak directly to the reader, a practice usually avoided. You might begin this way:

> Ever wonder what it's like to ride a
> bicycle 100 miles in a day?

Some readers will take the bait immediately: They have wondered. Others will be harder to sell. If they answer "no," you have lost readers. A better use of the question lead is:

> Will school taxes go up?
> That question will be answered
> tonight by the county school board.

Quotation leads can be helpful for a change of pace. The greatest danger in their use is that the speaker may come up with one really spiffy quote but never refer to it in the speech or interview. That is, the quote, though readable and interesting, may not have much to do with the meat of the story. The writer must show strength of character and choose something less exciting but more germane for the lead. A quotation used in a lead should summarize the major point of the story. For instance:

> "I shall return," Gen. Douglas
> MacArthur said today as he evacuated
> Corregidor.
>
> "That's one small step for a man,
> one giant leap for mankind."

On occasion, it is necessary to get things in perspective before ringing in new information. In such a case, we find the *background* lead helpful:

> In 1520, Vasco da Gama's men released a few goats on an island off the coast of California. In the four centuries since then, the herd has grown to number 10,000. The resultant heavy grazing has almost defoliated the island, and now the government wants the goats removed.
> Bill McWilliams plans to do the job.

A summary lead would look like this:

> The federal government called on a professional trapper today to remove some of the 10,000 goats that are defoliating an island off the California coast.

Not bad, but the backgrounder lets us start at a more leisurely pace and is thus considerably more effective. Presumably, this story will be three-fourths feature, growing out of a news situation. We can let our readers ease into it rather than being thrust into it headlong. Indeed, this change of pace is another reason for using the background approach—we try to keep the reader from tiring of a steady diet of summary leads.

A *contrast* lead is probably more of a change in writing style than a new kind of lead. The contrast emphasizes differences in two things or situations. For instance, these three:

> Greg Luzinski is a nice guy—but he hates pitchers.

> A four-cent washer almost aborted a million-dollar rocket launching today.

> The world's sweetest woman turned sour today.

Finally, we get to the *offbeat* category. This term is helpful because it includes all the kinds of leads that do not fit in other categories. Some people would prefer to use another term, perhaps *freak* or *catchall*. Offbeat leads would be leads such as:

> Granny, what a bear track! Brother, what a basketball game!

> I think that I shall never see a poem lovely as a tree. . . . Joyce Kilmer might change his mind if he saw what a heavily fruited old mulberry is doing to the courthouse sidewalks.

> Skunk was the cry and panic was
> the game at the Caliche County Con-
> solidated Church Revival last night.

The leads examined here do not exhaust the field. Other kinds of leads will come up. New names will be offered and admired. If you prefer other terms, use them, but now you know that we can stray outside the confinements of the summary lead. However, be aware that the summary lead is still the best for most news stories, even though it does not cover all the key questions.

Let us look now at just what the summary lead does cover. We must have some sort of pragmatic balance between vagueness and wordiness. We must be specific, and yet we cannot be redundantly detailed. That is, the reporter must summarize the main point of the story at first, but the lead need not be crammed so full that the reader chokes on it. As a general rule, you should examine every word of the lead and decide whether the facts requiring that word cannot profitably be delayed awhile.

At this point, English majors may leap to their feet to protest. Their objection will be that literate people should be able to understand a sentence, any sentence, if it is constructed in accordance with rules of grammar and good sense. True, but not all readers have reached the level of literacy of our English majors. And even those with a wall full of diplomas find their reading comprehension enhanced when we write in simple, direct sentences, usually limiting ourselves to one idea per sentence. We need not go back to our "Run, Spot, run" days, but we need to feed the reader one basic thought at a time for maximum understanding.

Let us grab a skeleton and flesh it out to illustrate the point:

BARE BONES: The state may be losing sales tax money.

SOME FLESH: A state Senate committee thinks the state is missing out on $2 million daily in sales taxes.

FULL-BODIED: The state gets $8 million every day in sales tax revenue but loses $2 million that businesses fail to collect, a state Senate report indicated Wednesday.

The bare bones offering can almost be called a teaser lead—it only cites the subject. You will use such a lead occasionally, probably on a feature.

Our second lead contains most of the necessary elements for a good lead. It does not tell *how,* but that information can easily come in a second paragraph. Its shortcoming, perhaps, lies in its use of present tense—the committee "thinks." We get a little stronger sense of urgency and immediacy if we tie our committee's view to a specific action.

The full-bodied offering ties that view to a report that did its indicating Wednesday. This third lead also puts the amount of money in perspective—$2 million lost out of $10 million—and it shows that the loss occurs because businesses fail to collect the tax. This lead runs 26 words, which is a trifle longer than the wire service goal of 22 but still within good readability range. And it has many facts.

Do we need more facts? Take a look:

> A report on the state sales tax released Wednesday by the Republican-dominated Financial Affairs Committee of the state Senate disclosed that the state is collecting $8 million daily in sales taxes but is losing $2 million more that businesses fail to collect.

You have seen sentences like that in reputable publications. Some of the problem comes from the writer's failure to let the reader make inferences. For instance, our full-bodied lead said the state is losing sales tax revenue, "a report indicates." The reader can surely infer that the report is about the state sales tax. You need not start off by saying someone has issued a report. No; start off by telling what the report says. Indeed, the main fault of our second lead, the one with "some flesh," is that its first words name the source rather than state the fact.

Let's reverse our process and try to strip away the unnecessary wording. Although it is conceivable that other facts could alter our opinion, in a typical story we would start by moving the name of the committee out of the lead. This does not mean we never use the name; it means only that we save the information for a later paragraph. Unless the story is about partisan politics, about Republicans trying to hang someone with this sales tax report, we need not say in the lead that the committee is Republican dominated. If the story *is* about a hanging, then we have our lead on the wrong subject.

Q. *Check back over what we have considered so far and think about how you would trim this lead:*

A report ~~on the~~ state sales tax released Wednesday by the ~~Republican-dominated~~ Financial ~~Affairs~~

~~Committee of the state Senate disclosed that~~ the

State is collecting $8 million daily in sales taxes

but is los~~ing~~ $2 million ~~more~~ that businesses fail

to collect⌃ a state Senate report disclosed Wednesday.

A report on the state sales tax released Wednes-

day by the Republican-dominated Financial Affairs

~~Committee of the state Senate disclosed that~~ the

(takes in)

State ~~is collecting~~ $8 million daily in sales taxes

but ~~is~~ los~~ing~~ $2 million ~~more~~ that businesses fail

to collect,¡ *a state Senate report indicated Wednesday.*

Q. *How about the following? Can you hold it to 25 words? (Twenty would be better.)*

Five ~~young~~ men, all close to 6-6 in height ~~and~~

~~all wearing ski masks and carrying pistols, took~~

~~over Abe Malone's delicatessen last night~~, cleaned

Abe Malone's delicatessen last night

~~out the cash register~~ and robbed∧ ~~the 14 customers~~,

getting $3,000 ~~in loot before flee~~ing.

Possibilities abound, but you might do it something like this:

(tall young men held up a)

Five ~~young men, all close to 6-6~~ in height and

~~all wearing ski masks and~~ carrying pistols, took

~~over Abe Malone's~~ delicatessen last night, ~~cleaned~~

(and took)

($3,000 from the store and)

~~out the cash register and~~ robbed ~~the~~ 14 customers.

~~getting $3,000 in loot before fleeing.~~

The revision contains 19 words. It could be shorter. We could have left out mention of height with no major loss, depending in part on what develops later in the story. The similarity to a basketball team will surely strike some readers, and that angle would liven the story. Reporters want to be alert to take advantage of anything that sets a story apart from others, but they also should be leery of forcing such comparisons.

What else is interesting about the revision? We did not name the deli. Sometimes the name helps. If Abe Malone's deli is known far and wide, we do the reader a service by naming it. But if the spot is relatively unknown, naming can wait until the second or third paragraph while we focus on more important things. A fire at Tiffany's produces a name in the lead, but a fire in a five-and-dime, though more serious, would be handled differently.

Another point: We dropped mention of masks and weapons. The assumption here is that anyone in this line of work is going to be armed. We said they held the place up. That should be sufficient for the lead; let the reader make an inference that the holdup men were armed. Later we will say thay had pistols, as opposed to shotguns, and we will mention that they wore ski masks. But that is not essential to the lead. Nor do we need to say here that they cleaned out the cash register, since the cash register is the normal place to keep money. If the crooks knew Abe had his big bills rolled up in his garter, we might find that worth mentioning. But a simple trip to the cash register produces nothing special for the lead.

One other thing: We did not say where Abe's joint is. If we were in Indianapolis, we might refer in the lead to "an Indianapolis delicatessen." Or we could say "a delicatessen here." One or the other of those would be proper and required.

Q. *Consider the next one a local story, to be run in a newspaper in the town where the event occurred.*

Gov. Ralph Henson Tuesday said that he doubts that Martin Elred will serve another full four year term as director of the state highway department, even if he is reelected by a majority of the state highway board in next month's voting.

Gov. Ralph Henson Tuesday said that he doubts that Martin Elred will serve another full four year term as director of the state highway department, even if he is reelected by a majority of the state highway board in next month's voting.

We can review that point by point. First, we had to take "doubts" out of quotes. Unless our governor has a monarch complex and uses second person in his speech ("The governor doubts . . ."), our quote is inaccurate. If accurate, the governor must have said, "I doubts . . ." That is unlikely; governors normally talk better. The only good solution, therefore, is to get the word out of quotes. We might take a hard look at the entire quote. It doesn't sing, does it? If we kill the quote marks, we can take out "four year," which is just an expansion of "full." Unless we want to make "director of the state highway department" into a title preceding the name (Highway Department Director Martin Elred), we need do nothing more until we get to the last clause.

The last clause cries for help. Phrases like "even if he is re-elected" usually get brighter with removal of the "he is." Next, we ask how one gets reelected. The answer in almost all cases is by a majority, so we can scratch that. And what is the process called? A vote. So we do not need to tell our readers Elred will be elected in voting. You might also get away with delaying for one paragraph the name of the group that will elect him. However, you would have to make sure you were not close to a normal election, which could make readers think the directorship was up for popular vote.

Your work on leads has not made you an expert, no doubt, but at least you have a start. Remember to pay attention to every word of the lead. Say enough to give the reader the idea, then stop.

First day–second day

News reporters are beset by many minor problems, one of them being that news events do not always occur well in advance of the deadline. Indeed, some news events have the effrontery to occur after a deadline, thus missing an edition or even a whole day. (If you are an optimist, you may argue that the event has merely occurred far in advance of the next day's deadline; do not try to sell this idea to a city editor.)

This situation is worst when the event occurs after the deadline but before the reader gets the newspaper. Afternoon newspapers, in particular, have to grapple with this problem. They may have a 1 P.M. deadline but not get papers to subscribers before 5 or 6 P.M. Thus an event that occurs at 2 P.M. will not get to the reader until 5 P.M. the next day, 27 hours after it happens. (If the town has a morning paper as well as an afternoon paper, the event is said to have occurred "on the opposition's time.")

That brings us to a different kind of lead—two, actually. Or maybe they are different kinds of stories. We will call them a folo (follow) lead or story and a second day lead or story. For purposes of discussion, we will define them this way: A *folo* story is based on an event already reported; the folo has some new information, perhaps including a major new development. A *second day* story is based on an event already reported, but it has little or no new information. However, the emphasis of the story has been changed.

These terms are used almost interchangeably in most news shops. Ideally, every story about a previously covered event would be larded with new information, but new information is not always easy to come by.

Do you need examples? Try these.

FIRST DAY, HARD NEWS: Three children died early today when flames raced through their West Side apartment.

FOLO: A short circuit in the wiring of an electric heater was blamed today for a fire that killed three children early yesterday.

FOLO: City Manager Dan Danielson launched a full-scale fire prevention program today in an effort to head off repetition of yesterday's triple-fatality fire.

FOLO: Apartment owner Martin Elred was cited for felony negligence today in the fire that killed three children in one of his apartments yesterday.

You certainly might find more than just these three angles for a folo story. You will want to learn what the fire means to insurance rates, for one thing. And you want to go after perspective with statistics—how many fatal fires have we had this year, what are the causes, who are the victims, and how much does it all cost?

Occasionally, however, even the most diligent reporter cannot scratch up something worth turning into a folo story. Sometimes, nothing new has happened. And at those times you see leads like this pure, unadulterated second day example:

FIRST DAY: Five tall gunmen held up Abe's Delicatessen last night and got away with $3,000.

SECOND DAY: Lincoln police were combing the west side today in their search for five tall gunmen who got $3,000 in a holdup at Abe's Delicatessen last night.

This second day lead shifts the emphasis. We assume that all our readers know about the holdup. Our first story no doubt mentioned that the police were hunting on the west side. Our second day story focuses on that angle, because the police are still hunting there.

Our police story may appear a bit lame to you; it should. Blame overwork. This kind of weak second day approach shows up in newspapers—and in the broadcast media—every day. The police always search for crooks. Our lead is safe, though it is unmatched for dullness.

You get a related situation on many other kinds of stories. Take the stock market. A 3 P.M. broadcast, or a late afternoon newspaper lead, might say: "The stock market closed at 986.14 on the Dow Jones index today, up two points in a day of active trading." Nothing new will happen between the market's closing and a publication or broadcast the next morning. But news reporters do not like to repeat leads. So the next day's newspapers or early morning broadcast may say: "The stock market stood at 986.14 today as investors prepared for another round of trading."

This lead is misleading if it conveys a picture of investors scurrying about to prepare for another round of trading. The writer will argue that the market did indeed stand there today, starting at midnight and continuing until the bulls and bears showed some activity, and investors prepared for the round of trading simply by getting out of bed and dressing. (No wonder newspaper people make good lawyers.) Although we can't nail our writer with a charge of total inaccuracy, at least we can suggest laziness in writing this pure second day stuff. The good reporter will seek something livelier.

Let me cover one more point. You may be perplexed by the time element in our holdup at Abe's. How can it be a first day story if it happened last night, a day away? Simple, the first day lead is our first report of an event. If opposition newspapers and the broadcasters have not already taken the shine off this news event, we use a first day lead. If the news event has been thoroughly reported, we try the folo approach.

And if we hit a dry hole there, we fall back on a second day offering.

You need to recognize different kinds of leads and know when and how to change them. As a copy editor, you will rewrite leads with some regularity, perhaps one every other day. The usual procedure is to kick the story back to the reporter if much rewriting is required.

> **Q.** *Look at this next lead. Decide whether it is first day or folo or second day. Then rewrite it in one sentence in a different style; that is, if it is first day, make it a folo lead or second day. Don't try to put all this information into one sentence; you are given an extra amount so you can find something you like for the new lead. Use only facts given here.*

> ST. LOUIS—Outstate Missourians overcame heavy urban support today to vote down the legalization of pari-mutuel betting. However, both urban and rural voters approved a $150 million water pollution control bond issue. The gambling defeat puts off for at least two years George Milne's plan to bring horse racing to Missouri. Milne said he will try for another election as soon as legally possible.

It is first day. Try something like this for second day:

> George Milne, whose effort to bring horse racing to Missouri was voted down today, plans to try again.

I want to bring in still another kind of lead here. It is a first cousin of the folo and second day leads. We will call it a *first day, soft news* lead. Such leads are often derided for backing into the story; they do not just haul off and summarize the facts. However, more and more afternoon newspapers are using this kind of lead on occasion, simply because they have to compete strongly with broadcast media, and the broadcasters invariably get most news to the public first, no matter how thin their reports are.

Look at a soft lead, first day version:

> Maybe Missourians just don't want horse racing in their state.
> They seemed to indicate that today by voting down another proposal to legalize pari-mutuel betting.

The first paragraph in that two-graf lead was running interference—sort of a blocker—for the second graf, which was carrying the ball. Look at another:

> INDIANAPOLIS—Will Overhead can recite the turtle-and-hare story by heart. He likes it, especially the ending.

> He flashed through the pack at the Indianapolis 500 yesterday, passing all those hares with broken equipment, and won auto racing's most prestigious event.

We have mentioned four kinds of time leads: hard news, first day; soft news, first day; second day; folo.

Now we will apply that knowledge to some other leads. In these next examples we first decide what kind of lead we have. If it is not first day, hard news, we will rewrite it, tightly, into that kind of lead. If it is already a first day, hard news lead, we will turn it into a second day lead, using only the material available. Get a piece of paper and go after this vigorously to get full benefit.

> State University journalism professors think the administration has been too generous in the matter of money for equipment.
>
> One professor, Martin Elred, said the department gets funds too fast and "has been compelled, by the sheer availability of money, to spend unwisely." Elred testified at a trustees' meeting yesterday. He said the administration lacks direction and does not keep close tabs on how the money is spent.

This lead is soft news, first day. A hard news approach would go something like this:

> The State University journalism department has had so much money showered upon it that it has "been compelled" to spend some of it unwisely, a professor told the school's trustees yesterday.

The next lead is first day, hard news. We will revise it as a second day lead, according to instructions. (You will probably not be able to tell the difference between this and a soft news lead. There isn't much.)

> Will Overhead flashed through the pack on the final turn and straightaway yesterday to capture auto racing's most prestigious event, the Indianapolis 500.
>
> Overhead, driving a quadraphonic Coyote, nipped heavy-footed but trouble-plagued Jim Tom Blair by the width of this newspaper page. The victory was worth $250,000 immediately and perhaps a million more over the next year.
>
> Blair, disconsolate despite $68,000 in

> lap prize money, said overconfidence cost him the race. "I had it won on the last lap," he said, "but I backed off going into the traffic. Overhead didn't, and caught me. I have nobody to blame but myself."

Here's a second day approach:

> Jim Tom Blair thought he had the Indianapolis 500 locked up yesterday, and he eased up when he got into heavy traffic near the end. The move cost him the race and a large part of a million dollars.

Or we might have done something like this:

> Jim Tom Blair doesn't blame anyone for his one-foot loss at the Indianapolis 500 yesterday—anyone but himself and overconfidence.

That kind of lead might easily be called a first day, soft news lead; I would not quarrel with you over that or the second day category. Your terminology would probably not get you into any trouble in most of the nation's newsrooms. The terminology is not what is important here. What is important is your ability to recognize when a reporter is backing into a story and when the story is met head-on and also that you learn, as both reporter and editor, to take different approaches to stories on occasion.

> Montana doctors got their wish yesterday.
> The state legislature, meeting in special session, set a limit of $4,000 on the amount a doctor must pay for malpractice insurance. The vote was expected to cause doctors to call off their strike at most major hospitals.

Looks like soft news, first day to me. The hard news lead would be straightforward. If you scratch out the first sentence of the lead above, you have most of a satisfactory hard news lead. Try another.

> Montana doctors called off their strike at major hospitals this morning.
> Their move came eight hours after passage of a new medical malpractice law. The legislature voted to limit liability to $4,000 per doctor.

This is a folo story. It reports a major new development in a continuing story. You could call it a first day, hard news story and not be wrong. As for the revision, we would have to return to the first day report in the preceding example.

> Abe Malone may have been held up by a basketball team.
> Five tall young gunmen robbed Malone and 14 customers last night at Abe's Delicatessen. They took about $3,000 and the customers' jewelry. Then they fled north from the 2501 Guadalupe location in a green Studebaker. Police and the highway patrol are searching for the Studebaker.

This is a soft news, first day lead. It has a throwaway line at the beginning. This line, though clever, contains some danger. It immediately turns the story into something moderately light. The reporter has to back up the lead, including the light feeling, with a couple of snappy quotes and another observation or two about the young felons' height. The single reference in the second paragraph ("five tall young gunmen") cannot carry the load imposed by this lead. (If Abe says he was afraid they were going to slamdunk him or were going to bump into his light fixtures, or if the police point out that they will have little trouble in eliminating suspects, you may be able to use this basketball angle. But, again, only one reference will not do; we would have to force our joke, and we should not do such things here.)

For a hard news lead, start with the second paragraph.

> Cattlemen were reflecting today on the possibility that their animals will be worth perhaps twice as much in six months as they are now. Their hopes were raised yesterday with the announcement that meat imports will be curtailed shortly. The announcement came from the White House.

This lead is a second day. The first day, hard news lead says, "Meat imports will be curtailed shortly." You may want to add, "the White House announced today." You can get away without naming the source until the second graf, since the announcer has the authority to do what is being announced. (Did you lead with "The White House announced today that . . ."? That's all right for now, but you need to read the section on attribution in Chapter 6 soon.)

> Montana doctors are looking forward today to a sharp drop in the cost of their malpractice insurance.
> Their relief came from the state legislature yesterday in the form of a bill limiting insurance prices to $4,000 for any doctor. The governor signed the bill into law within hours of its passage.

The above is second day. (Please don't argue; this is pure blue sky stuff.) It differs from the first lead on the Montana doctors, a clear case of soft news. This one treats the event as something in the past and looks ahead to its effect. It can't be a folo story because it has no major new information. Regardless of the category you assign it to, the first day, hard news lead comes out something like this: "The Montana legislature passed a bill limiting medical malpractice rates to $4,000 per doctor yesterday."

> Helena doctors, questioned about the state's new medical malpractice law today, were unanimously enthusiastic about it.

This is a folo lead based on a totally new development. In one sense, it is a first day, hard news story about a continuing situation. Ideally, we would have had this story in the same edition as the story announcing passage of the bill. But we couldn't get to the doctors in time, I would guess. So we will run this story today, another story in a month or two or six, saying what the law has meant to medicine in our state.

We have spent some time on leads. A good lead will grab the reader, set the tone for the entire story, and win us the general approbation of our peers.

Links

The battle is not over when you finish the lead. You still have to move on to the body of the story. A careful writer will build a smooth bridge from lead to body; in fact, a careful writer will provide clear connections between *all* paragraphs so that the writing flows. Too often, writers have all the facts in their heads and fail to realize they have not put enough of them on paper—they have omitted a bridge from lead to body. Copy editors get paid to spot the shortcoming and correct it.

Sometimes the bridge will cover one of the five *W*s not used in the lead. For example:

LEAD: The school board postponed Monday a decision on whether to pay $14,500 an acre for a 42-acre tract as the site for a new Thurgood Marshall High School.

BRIDGE: Board members complained they were given insufficient time to consider the proposal.

The *why* element is the basis for the bridge in this paragraph.

Sometimes the bridge paragraph or sentence will handle the attribution. However, it is poor form to make a flat statement in one paragraph and then indicate in the next that the first paragraph was only somebody's opinion. Here is an example of the poor form cited:

> America will be worse off with the
> metric system.
>   That's the opinion of Jody
> Taylor. . . .

The danger is that the flat statement will seem like an editorial, and editorials belong elsewhere.

> **Q.** *Using the following lead, select a bridge of attribution to go with the story:* "State University announced today a plan to recruit 1,000 members of minority groups as students over the next three years."
>
>> *a.* The announcement came immediately after a luncheon given by the university president.
>> *b.* The announcement, made by President Martin Elred, said the recruitment would double the minority figure at the 27,000-student school.
>> *c.* The announcement was made in response to a federal requirement that the university enroll more minority members.

The attribution *b* to a high official lends authenticity to the announcement. Answer *c* would have made a good bridge, but it explains the *why,* and our task was to pick a bridge of attribution.

Another function of the bridge can be to provide perspective—to place an event in context. For example:

LEAD: A tornado struck the West Texas hamlet of Lenorah yesterday, destroying a cotton gin and three of the town's 11 houses.

MORE LEAD: There were no deaths or injuries.

BRIDGE: The twister was one of four sighted across the South Plains in a day of wild weather.

ANOTHER BRIDGE: None of the other tornadoes caused any damage, but the storm system brought hail that ruined hundreds of acres of cotton.

Had the Lenorah tornado done more damage and perhaps caused loss of life, we would have dealt with it at greater length before crossing our bridges to the rest of the storm story. Indeed, we might have dealt with nothing else in that story, putting the rest of the storm system in a separate article.

Look again at how connections are made between thoughts. Note that our first bridge starts with a reference to something from the lead, "The twister . . ." That takes us from the lead to new information. We would have the same effect if we said, "Twisters were also seen . . ." The word *also* would connect our two grafs.

Look at our second bridge. It mentions *other tornadoes,* which makes a connection to the preceding paragraph and adds still more information. It says that no damage is there but some damage is elsewhere. Thus, *damage,* or the lack of it, becomes the connecting thought.

The tie-back

Now we take up one other form of linking paragraph, the tie-back. The tie-back is an essential bit of information in every folo story. It lets new readers, who missed the story yesterday, catch up quickly. And it reminds yesterday's readers just what went on. You should try to rehash the *whole* story, and you must at least give the new reader enough information to put the story in perspective. An example:

LEAD:

Thomas D. Finch, manager of the Guadalupe Street Cobblery, will go before City Judge John Watkins today to answer charges of operating his store in violation of the city's new Sunday closing law.

TIE-BACK:

Finch was arrested Sunday, the first day the law was in effect. He had defied the city council to "tell me how to run my business" and had advertised that he would be open.

Which part is the tie-back? One sentence? The whole paragraph? Here the entire paragraph is used to bring us up to date.

Sometimes a sentence—maybe even a clause—will handle the tie-back work. Sometimes you need a full paragraph. Your job is to decide, to make sure that people seeing the story for the first time will have a reasonable idea of what is going on. At the same time, you balance that with a concern that you not make yesterday's readers feel they are neck deep in old news. Balance. It takes effort.

[5] *Trimming the fat*

NEWSWRITERS have not always used the summary lead and inverted pyramid approach. Until a century or so ago, stories were commonly told chronologically, building to a climax. A battle story might begin with a description of a military camp at sunrise, a little frost and tension in the air, smoke over the breakfast fires—that sort of stuff. It would go on to describe the skirmishing, throw in a little gore to keep us awake, and then conclude by informing us that we lost the war and that tomorrow we have to start speaking Celtic (or French or Spanish, depending on the enemy).

But things changed in the 1860s.

In the 1860s, during the Civil War, correspondents at first stayed with that chronological style and tried to send their material over telegraph lines. The trouble was, telegraph lines were often cut or broken in neighborhoods where they were having battles. Thus many newspapers received wonderful descriptions of military camps at dawn and of tension and the early bloodletting, but the wires sometimes went down before the story got around to naming the victor. This was a drawback. Therefore, astute editors asked their correspondents to fudge a little and start by telling who won. Then northern editors could read the lead and see whether they should rejoice over a victory or start learning to eat grits.

The overall effect has been salutary. It has made news stories much easier to understand quickly.

It has also had an effect on the newspaper copydesk. Copy editors know that the normal way to trim a story now is to cut it from the end. That's where the campfire smoke and predawn tension are now found.

But you will never be a respectable copy editor if you trim from the bottom indiscriminately. Good newswriters put the least important material at the end in most cases, true; but good copy editors do not assume infallibility on the part of good newswriters, and certainly not on the part of lesser lights. Good editors go over the whole story thoroughly, backstopping the reporter to make sure that none of the later material is better than something up front. (This practice of putting the best information first and letting the story trail off is called, you will remember, the inverted pyramid approach.)

On an old-style news desk, the big trim is made with a ruler or other straightedge. You plop the ruler on the copy where you want to end the story and rip off what you don't want. Into the trash can it goes. (Seasoned editors do not crumple the trimmed part severely; they may have to fetch it back to recover a fact or two.)

In electronic editing, major deletions are normally done one paragraph at a time. Some early editing systems deleted only a character with each keystroke. You had to hold down the delete character *(del char)* key until the material was deleted as desired—amazingly cumbersome. Programmers had trouble telling the computer what a sentence or a paragraph was. (It's not as simple as it might seem: If you use a period to define the end of a sentence, you end one every time you have an abbreviation.) Current programs permit you to delete a sentence or paragraph at a time—and larger blocks with just a few keystrokes. Even so, a copy editor can tear off half a story with a ruler about as fast as the electronic editor can delete something graf by graf. (The relative slowness is made up in dozens of other ways by the electronic editor.)

We mentioned the trash can a moment ago: What happens when an electronic editor realizes that an error was made in making a trim? Say an editor is working with a six-paragraph story and mistakenly zaps the last two paragraphs—how can the copy be fished out of the electronic wastebasket? Is it possible?

It can be done. The process depends on the editing system (the computer program) in use at the publication. Some systems retain the original version of the story, even though it has been handled. In that setup, several versions of the story might be in the computer if the story had been called out for editing more than once. This arrangement is the best of all for the copy editor, for he or she can always get the original version. Its drawback is that it requires more computer storage room. If this system of duplication is used at the publication where our editor just made the wrong trim, the editor corrects the mistake in one of three ways:

1. The editor calls up the unedited version again and starts over, this time leaving the required paragraphs in the story. Unfortunately, our editor must also reedit the first part of the story. If that part was edited only lightly the first time, this may be the quickest method of restoring the material.

2. The editor calls up the unedited version, makes notes on what should be included, sends that version back to the computer, recalls the edited version, and keyboards (retypes) the material back into the story. Slow. Imperfect. But workable.

3. The editor puts the edited version back into the computer, so the computer has two versions. Now the editor links the two. Let's say the original is story number 0742, the number the computer uses for it. We will say further that the version our editor nipped too strongly got the number 0884 when sent back into the computer. (More likely, it would be 0742:b, indicating the second version of 0742.) Our editor tells the computer to link the two stories. On one system, the command would be: *0884 chain 0742.* Pretty easy. (The editor doing this with paper would simply paste one story to the bottom of the other; here, the same thing is done electronically.) The chaining, or linking, gives our editor the version already handled, plus the original, unedited version pasted to its tail electronically. The resulting ten-

paragraph story has four edited paragraphs, the same four paragraphs unedited and the two paragraphs that were mistakenly deleted. Our editor skips over the top four (which are already edited), kills the next four (which duplicate the four above), edits the two paragraphs that were zapped, writes a headline, and goes home.

Other tricks abound. Equipment manufacturers by and large have seen an advantage in having a split screen, in which two stories, or two versions of one story, can be displayed side by side. If your publication has such equipment, you do not need to fling stories back into the computer to do some of the work noted above.

Unfortunately, the most common approach to computer programming leaves you with only one version of a story; you kill a paragraph and it is gone forever. You have no way to go into your electronic wastebasket for what you have lost. Editors who make bad kills in such circumstances have only two choices (or three if you count early retirement):

1. They say all the prayers that come to mind and then ask if there is any hard copy (paper) on the story. If the newspaper gets hard copy as a wire service backup, if it uses scanner copy, or if it gets printouts from its own reporters, the prayer is answered affirmatively. The editor then takes hard copy and keyboards information from it onto the story being edited.

2. If the newspaper does not get hard copy (and some are abandoning it), the editor has to telephone the wire service and have the story retransmitted. (This is not as big a deal as it might seem. The same thing happened in the old days; wire editors might lose stories, or more commonly, teleprinters would break ribbons or run out of paper or go haywire, causing a publication to miss something important. Then a wire service would retransmit a story when it found slack time on the wire, inasmuch as a story re-sent to one publication appeared simultaneously on the printer of everyone else on the line. With speeds 20 times as fast as before, a retransmission does not tie the wires up as long as formerly.)

As an electronic editor, you will have little trouble in learning how to manipulate the parts of a story as described. Nor will you have trouble picking up other editing techniques.

What to trim

One problem remains: How do you know what to edit? What goes? What stays? First you always take out general wordiness and repetition. No one has to tell you to do that. You have been urged by this book and other sources of inspiration to cut the fat out of copy. Second, you make trims as directed by the copydesk chief, news editor, or other decision maker. These directions will come in two categories: (1) You will be given a length, usually in column inches, and told to trim the story to fit that length. This means the person in charge has decided to put the story in a specific place on a specific page, fitting it in amongst the ads. You cannot put a 20-inch story in a 15-

inch hole; there is no such thing as spillover. (2) Alternatively, you are given a story and told only to cut it back a bit—meaning a third or perhaps as much as half. The copy chief will probably put this story on a loose page, one with space left after your story is spotted. The presumption is that your story is good and should get as much space as it needs, after editing. After the desk chief sees just how long it runs with the fat out, he will know how long any other stories on the page must be. These other stories will be trimmed to a specific length.

Next question: How do we measure? People making up brochures and doing other bits of close copyfitting commonly use a character-count chart. Such a chart lets you determine precisely how much space you will need for a given typeface. (Typefaces, like people, vary greatly; some are fat, some thin.) Newspapers do not need to be quite so precise because their size gives them room for adjustments. (A digression: Most newspapers keep a supply of fillers on hand to pop into those holes inevitably left by measurement error. The trend is toward using advertising-type fillers—a promotion blurb for your staff cartoonist, for example, or perhaps a suggestion that you give blood or support the heart fund. Some newspapers, bless them, still throw in little items gleaned from the world's trivia warehouses. My favorite filler, found long ago in the *Houston Chronicle,* said simply, "Fish have no eyelids." Took up a quarter-inch.) Newspapers measure not in words or characters but in column inches. A column inch is a block of copy one inch deep by one normal column wide (whatever the newspaper's normal column is).

In electronic editing, the computer tells you how long your story will be. You do not need to count, although you must tell the computer how wide your columns are and what size type you are using. Obviously, wide columns mean your story will take up less depth on the page, but more width, than narrow columns. If the figure the computer offers you is not what you want, you trim some or add some until it is.

It is impossible to say how many column inches a given piece of copy will produce "in a newspaper." Why? Because newspapers vary widely in their choice of column widths. At last measurement, for example, the *New York Times* had a column nearly 14 picas wide, the *Washington Post* had one of 13, and the *Los Angeles Times* one of 12. Those were all on a six-column format. Newspapers on an eight-column format commonly use 10 or 10½ picas. (Twelve picas are two inches.)

Depending on column width and type size and face, newspapers usually get an inch of body type out of about 3 lines of typewritten copy. This copy was once customarily typed on lines of 60 characters, but the figure varies now. If you use a 50-character line, or 79, or something between that gives an inch of type from 3 or 4 lines of type (as opposed to a fraction like 2½ or 3¼), you simplify the math considerably. You will learn quickly how much copy produces a given amount of type at the place you work.

Let's deal now with the questions you might have and the procedures you would follow when given a long story and told to trim it sharply.

Ideally—and ideals are often compromised by the clock—you would have time to go through the entire story at a moderate pace and absorb its meaning, without editing. Then you would go back through, eliminating excess wordage here and there but generally concentrating on taking out the biggest chunks you could properly remove—paragraphs, probably. Finally, you would hit the copy still another lick, trimming words, phrases, clauses and sentences. Above all, you would concentrate on meaning, so the reader could understand the information being imparted.

That's the way you ought to learn to edit copy. Try to learn it that way; you can always telescope two or three of the steps together when time makes you compromise.

A veteran will make most of the clause-sentence-phrase-word deletions on the first pass-through. If the story is 30 inches long and must be trimmed to 15, the veteran will probably edit the first 20 inches fairly carefully and then make an effort to lop off most or all of the final 10. If an extra soft paragraph or two appears in the top of the story, it goes out, of course. Also, the editor must read that final 10 inches carefully to make sure it contains nothing vital that has not been dealt with earlier. The veteran will make the final 5-inch trim a paragraph at a time if possible and by sentences and words otherwise.

When you get past trimming by sentences, you are not going to lose much length. It takes many individual words and clauses to add up to a paragraph. This is not for a moment to say that you should not trim words and clauses and phrases. Indeed, ability to trim on that level is of utmost importance in any assessment of a copy editor's work. But this sort of skill usually comes under the heading of "polishing" the copy.

Common mistakes in trimming

Trimming ordinarily requires a judgment on the part of the editor. He or she must weigh the reader's needs and desires against space limitations. Quite commonly a copy editor will tell the copydesk chief that good information must be trimmed from a story if the story is cut to the designated size. Desk chiefs normally do not have time to read all of every story, and they occasionally err by basing a judgment on the top part of a story. Copy editors read all of every story they get, so they will sometimes find within a story some information suggesting the story deserves more space (or less) than the desk chief thought. (I have never met a copydesk chief unwilling to listen to an editor make a pitch for more space. True, most of them give up space reluctantly, but they listen.)

The editor must beware of a pair of major pitfalls that await the heavy trimmer. Both mistakes are aided by a failure to reread the edited story attentively. The first error is the *unfulfilled promise*. In this case, an early paragraph indicates that explanation or elaboration is forthcoming—but those later paragraphs have been cut out by the space-conscious editor. An example: A story mentions in its second paragraph that a book had caused "quite a national stir." The story never returns to the book and leaves us wondering how it created a stir. Was it scandalous? Was it magnificent? Was it . . . ?

The second common error we will call the *headless snake*. Here the reader suddenly stumbles on a quotation or a paraphrased statement from someone identified only by last name. What has happened, frequently, is that the editor deleted a previous paragraph or sentence with the person's first name and identification in it and then did not notice when the name came around later in the story. (Yes, it is rank carelessness, but it happens.) It happens most often when the first reference is separated from the second by a great amount of copy and when the story contains several other names and quotations.

The problem is not limited to identification. Careless editors can leave in about any kind of headless second reference you care to mention. One story in print not long ago had a reference to "the other storm" midway through the story. The editor apparently cut out the mention of the second storm in the early part of the story, preferring to deal only with the big storm that was the main subject. Later—and this is speculation—the editor realized a little more space was available than expected and let the story run longer. The reference to "the other storm" did not register with the editor, who, unfortunately, forgot the first mention of it had been cut. And then the editor forgot to read over the finished work. Thus the error glided on by into print. Readers were no doubt kind enough to bring it to the editor's attention.

The copy editor guards against these errors with simple vigilance. Concentration helps. The editor who pays attention should be able to avoid these mistakes; be particularly careful when taking out a paragraph with someone's identification and full name and be alert to promises of information.

And then there is a general category of editing error called *striking the color*. To commit this sin, the copy editor develops the habit of shortening stories by eliminating all colorful description automatically. If it's colorful, out it goes. Now, I have made an earnest effort to encourage brevity and to press for the excision of unnecessary detail. Moreover, I freely admit that unnecessary material most often shows up in flowery writing. Nevertheless, the copy editor must not routinely strike the color. A paragraph of description, of color, of background may make a major contribution to the reader's understanding of an event or a situation.

Editing time

We have spent a bit of effort on wholesale deletions in copy, so now we try the retail work. Your assignment is to delete superfluous wording—clause, phrase or word at a time—from these sentences. Some of the sentences are inventions for this book: They have extra words pushed into previously acceptable sentences. Most of them, however, were published as you see them.

Q. *How would you edit this first one for a Kansas publication?*

Topeka ~~was the leading city in~~ the state ~~of~~ *led*

~~Kansas~~ in ~~the number of~~ traffic deaths ~~recorded~~ in

~~the year of~~ 1978, the State Highway Department said

today, in an announcement.

That made-up sentence contains some quality verbiage; you don't see that many errors in the average sentence. Here is one way to edit it, along with reasons:

Topeka ~~was~~ *led* ~~the leading city in~~ the state ~~of Kansas~~ in ~~the number of~~ traffic deaths ~~recorded~~ *in* ~~the year of~~ 1978, the State Highway Department ~~said~~ *reported* today~~, in an announcement.~~

Our reasons? (1) We toughen the sentence by switching to an active voice for our verb: "led." The verb "was" lacks punch. (2) Almost everyone knows Topeka is a city, so we have no good reason for saying it is. (3) Kansas is certainly a state, so we need not double up there, either. If this is for a Kansas publication, we can simply refer to the area as "the state"; readers would expect us to name the state if some other were involved. (4) We delete "the number of," because a number is implied whenever you do any counting. That is, if you lead in traffic deaths, or jelly beans, or whatever, you are automatically going to lead in the number of them, so drop those words. (5) We delete "recorded" because that is the only kind of deaths anyone can lead in. Nobody leads in "unrecorded" deaths. (6) We need not point out for our readers that 1978 is clearly a year. Similarly, we would not point out that January is a month. (7) We should delay mention of "in an announcement" for a paragraph or two, since "reported" covers the field satisfactorily. (Ideally, a later paragraph would tell how this information came out—something like this: "The department's annual statistical report indicated that . . . ")

Get all that? Let's go over it again. Yes, the same sentence. This is sort of like batting practice—you get a chance to hit a fat pitch. Here it comes. Edit it out of the park.

Topeka ~~was the leading city in~~ *led* the state ~~of Kansas~~ in ~~the number of~~ traffic deaths ~~recorded~~ *reported* in ~~the year of~~ 1978, the State Highway Department ~~said~~ today~~,~~ ~~in an announcement~~.

Q. *Try another.*

~~Union~~ *Union* Negotiations ~~dealing with the labor aspects~~ were completed~~, with the unions involved in the case~~ last month.

Labor Negotiations ~~dealing with the labor aspects~~ were completed~~, with the unions involved in the case~~ last month.

Let's look. Do not assume that you can solve all your editing problems by switching adjectives around freely. But if you see that moving one word sums up the situation, you may be able to tighten a sentence considerably. That happened here: "Labor negotiations" is much tighter than the other way of saying it. We took out "in the case" because we obviously are not going to negotiate with unions involved in some other case. Then we take out "involved," because there is no profit in negotiating with unions not involved. Finally, we take out "with the unions," since labor negotiations almost by definition involve unions.

Q. *This next offering is for real, and it is the wordiest of the lot. Could you trim it to 25 words?*

The policeman ~~entered the building, stopping to~~
call^{ed} for assistance before ~~attempting to~~ making an arrest~~, the~~
~~subject.~~ Aⁿ ~~female~~ officer, ~~in the area when the~~
~~call went out~~, arrived within seconds and ~~together~~
the two ~~tried~~ attempted arrest ~~to apprehend~~ the suspect.

and another officer who had been nearby went into

The policeman ~~entered~~ the building, ~~stopping to~~
~~call for assistance before attempting to arrest the~~
~~subject. A female officer, in the area when the~~
~~call went out, arrived within seconds and together~~
~~the two~~ and tried to ~~apprehend~~ arrest the suspect.

Don't fret if you did not do it exactly that way; the paragraph should have had a full rewrite. Sometimes, editors have to do the rewriting.

Here are the reasons we revised this one so drastically. (1) Depending on the circumstances, we normally do not need to go into great detail on how the police work was accomplished. If the officer's decision to stop and call for help was critical to the story, we would have to report it. Since it isn't, we can leave that information out without any loss to readers. (2) We should not use the word "subject," which looks fine on the police report but does not appear in ordinary conversation often. (3) We might as well drop our isms and treat female cops the same as male cops: call her another officer. (4) You surely see the redundancy in "together the two," and you surely did not overlook "apprehend" in a spot that would look nice with "arrest" or "catch" in it.

Q. *Here is another.*

Commercial forests could ~~be made to~~ yield more
by ~~implementing programs such~~ with proper ~~as~~ fertilization, ~~re-~~
~~placement of slower growing inferior trees with~~
faster growing tree ~~types~~, genetic improvement, thinning

of ~~weeds and~~ competing growth ~~trees~~, and ~~reducing losses~~ greater protection

from fire, insects and diseases ~~through better for-~~

~~est protection,~~ Spurr said.

Commercial forests could be made to yield more

with better ~~by implementing programs such as~~ fertilization, ~~re-~~

the use of ~~placement of slower growing inferior trees with~~

faster growing trees ~~types~~, genetic improvement, thinning

of ~~weeds and~~ competing growth ~~trees~~, and ~~reducing losses~~ better protection

from fire, insects and diseases, ~~through better for-~~

~~est protection,~~ ·Spurr said.

Q. *Now we will try a troika, a three-sentence item. Your task is to make one tight sentence of it.*

Eleven acre along the Missouri, near L+C apartments, ~~The~~ garden plots can be rented ~~for a~~ one-year

at $15 per year ~~period,~~ starting March 1. ~~The rent will cost $15~~

~~per year. The gardens will~~ be on an 11-acre plot of

~~University-owned land along~~ the Missouri River, near

~~L&C Apartments.~~

(which) The garden plots can be rented for a ~~one~~-year ($15)

~~period,~~ starting March 1. ~~The rent will cost $15~~

~~per year. The gardens~~ will be on ~~an~~ 11/acre ~~plot~~ of

University~~-owned~~ land along the Missouri, ~~River,~~ near

L&C Apartments.

That leaves us with a 28-word sentence. Most readers will be able to handle such a sentence. However, we might improve things slightly by breaking it into two sentences—let's try.

The garden plots can be rented for a ~~one~~-year ($15)

~~period,~~ starting March 1. The ~~rent will cost $15~~

~~per year. The gardens~~ will be on ~~an~~ 11/acre ~~plot~~ of

University ~~owned~~ land along the Missouri, ~~River,~~ near

L&C Apartments.

Much can be said, and should be, about limiting yourself to one idea per sentence. In our first try above, we stuffed two ideas into our sentence. We ran no great risk of being difficult to understand, for it was a fairly short sentence. Now we need note only that our choice is between a 28-worder and a couple of shorties of 13 and 15. The short ones will be easier on your readers.

Q. *Now we tackle a pair from the sports page. The first story tells about a track meet between women from two universities. Turn these two sentences into two or three tighter, more understandable offerings.*

The Lakey Field affair ~~will be a~~ tuneup ~~for~~
will help rank
~~both squads, but for~~ the LSU women ~~it will also help~~
in   *Despite*
establish the hierarchy ~~within~~ certain events, ~~as the~~
a shortage of
women attempt ~~to demonstrate~~ their abilities. ~~The~~
s
~~team has not been able to~~ work out, ~~as much as~~ Coach
said the team is strong
Jim Daniels ~~would have liked, but the women still~~

~~possess the capability to put on a strong showing,~~

~~he said.~~

The Lakey Field ~~affair will be a~~ tuneup ~~for~~
will help rank   *in some*
~~both squads, but for~~ the LSU women ~~it will also help~~
Despite
establish the hierarchy ~~within~~ certain events, ~~as the~~
a shortage of
women ~~attempt to demonstrate~~ their abilities. ~~The~~
~~team has not been able to~~ work out, ~~as much as~~ Coach
said the team is strong
Jim Daniels ~~would have liked, but the women still~~

~~possess the capability to put on a strong showing,~~

~~he said.~~

third
The Tigers finished ~~as the No. 3 team~~ in the
at
nation ~~after~~ the NCAA Championships last summer.

third
The Tigers finished ~~as the No. 3 team~~ in the
at
nation ~~after~~ the NCAA Championships last summer.

Or maybe either of these:

The Tigers finished ~~as the No. 3 team~~ *third* in the
nation ~~after the NCAA Championships~~ last summer.

The Tigers finished ~~as the~~ No. 3 ~~team~~ in the
nation ~~after~~ *at* the NCAA championships last summer.

Q. *Try another:*

~~Knowledgeable~~ political sources predicted that
as the large towns began sending in results, the
~~vote for the~~ Socialist candidates would hold steady
~~and possibly~~ *or* even climb ~~slightly~~. They said the
Democrats' share of the ~~day's~~ votes would ~~in all
likelihood~~ show an increase at the expense of the
Communists ~~who have lost some strength of late~~.

~~Knowledgeable~~ political sources predicted that
as the large towns began sending in results, the
~~vote for the~~ Socialist ~~candidates~~ *(vote)* would hold steady
~~and possibly~~ *or* even climb ~~slightly~~. They said the
Democrats' share of the ~~day's~~ votes would ~~in all
likelihood~~ *probably go up* ~~show an increase~~ at the expense of the
Communists ~~who have lost some strength of late~~.

A few thoughts on the editing: First, "knowledgeable" raises a
question: Do we ever use sources that are not knowledgeable? No, so we
need not say our sources are knowledgeable. The same logic might cause
us to delete "political," but euphony compels us to leave it in. Next,
"the vote for the Socialist candidates" is not wrong. However, the only
people who get votes are by definition candidates (except for a few write-
ins), so there is some overlap here. We can say "the vote for the
Socialists," making the word plural, or, better yet, say "the Socialist
vote." In the next part, "possibly" and "even" are poor roommates,
particularly since they are part of a prediction; one must go. Also,
"slightly" is implied in the sense of the sentence; if the toll is going to
hold or "possibly" climb, one would assume that the climb would be
slight.

In the second sentence, we have an abundance of trash. The "share of the day's votes'' is wordy; ''day's'' is unnecessary. And what about that ''would in all likelihood show an increase''? Tell readers it will ''probably go up,'' or ''rise,'' or ''should rise.'' Finally, one could easily infer that the Communists have lost strength, since this paragraph tells about others' gains. We need a little more of the context to be sure, but, once sure, we could delete our last clause if we were cramped for space.

Now we change gears. The next sentences contain minor but common flaws that have been corrected by deletion or replacement with phrases or single words. You will be familiar with the wordiness on some of these sentences, but some will probably have escaped you. Then you will say, ''Of course. Why haven't I seen that?'' You need not be embarrassed. Even professional copy editors are not perfect. However, the pros pick up most shortcomings as a matter of routine because they recognize them. With any luck, you will learn to recognize these old standbys—and nip them.

Wright said he never expected to make money while ~~he was serving~~ in Congress.

Westmoreland was almost certain to be upset by any |response ~~of a~~ hostile| ~~nature.~~

Franklin helped erect a church for the ~~use of the~~ congregation.

He said the surplus would eliminate ~~all of~~ the *his* campaign debts ~~he had piled up.~~

Laredo ~~was~~ ranked first on the HEW's list.

or

Laredo was ~~ranked~~ first on the HEW's list.

Baxter has ~~now~~ scored ~~a total of~~ 111 points in three games.

They ~~contacted such organizations~~ *sought the support of* as fraternities, ~~and~~ sororities *and* ~~as well as~~ other campus groups ~~for support.~~

Discussion centered on ~~the topic of~~ survival in
the wilderness.

or one of the next two:

(They) ed
⌊Discussion ~~centered on the topic of~~ survival in
the wilderness.

(They) ed
⌊Discussion ~~centered on the topic of survival in
the~~ wilderness/~~survival~~⊗

The Franklin Award could have gone to either ~~of
the two~~ youth$.

(often)
She visited ~~with~~ FDR at Campobello, ~~a great number of times.~~

Middleton ended ~~his talk to the assembled audi-
ence~~ with a joke.

~~The~~ archeologists turned up an oblong ~~shaped~~
tool.

We have met a large number of our enemies from the Land of Verbosity. We will have to keep up our guard, for we did not confront all the
world's verbiage, all its writing flaws. Moreover, the copy editor is sometimes called on to take out good material, perfectly proper wording that
simply will not fit into the given space.

We need to try a couple of United Press International stories. They are
not bad stories. They were no doubt run just about as you see them in many
publications. However, our news editor has decreed that we trim them.
Look them over and decide where you would take out at least 15 of these
short lines. They are short because this was the Teletypesetter monitor
copy—the version in which lines of type sent by the wire service match line
for line those appearing in the newspaper. A line of typed copy usually will
make about two lines in a paper, depending on width of columns.

BULAWAYO, Rhodesia (UPI)--
Three Roman Catholic
missionaries gunned down by a
terrorist eight days ago were
buried today and their deaths
were called "a sacrifice of
reconciliation."

The three--the Rt. Rev.
Adolf Gregor Schmitt, former
bishop of Bulawayo, Rev.
Possenti Weggarten, director of
the Regina Mundi Mission and
Sister Maria Francis van den
Berg--were all from Germany
and had spent several years
working in black tribal areas.

Following a 1 1/2 hour mass of
the resurrection in English and
Sindebele, a local African
language, in the grounds of a
convent near St. Mary's Cathe-
dral, the three caskets were
taken to Bulawayo's main
street cemetery and buried
in the Catholic section.

As the coffins were lowered
into the graves, nuns of the
order of the Missionary Sisters
of the Precious Blood filed past
and threw in symbolic handfuls
of dirt and gravel.

More than 1,200 persons--
predominantly black Africans
--attended the mass celebrated
by the Roman Catholic Bishop
of Bulawayo, Rt. Rev. Henry
Karlen, a Swiss. Hymns were
sung to the accompaniment of
six marimbas (wooden xylo-
phones) and maracas.

Giving the funeral sermon,
the Bishop of Gwelo, Rt. Rev.
Alois Haenex said the death of
the three missionaries was a
sacrifice which he hoped would
bring the country together the
same way as the mourners
were brought together.

"It was a sacrifice of
reconciliation," he said. "As we
are united here, let the whole
country be united."

He noted that missionaries in
this country almost had no
choice but to be involved in the
escalating guerrilla war.

"The missionary cannot remain aloof as much as he
tried," the bishop said. "He is
inevitably thrown in one way or
the other." The only way to
understand the slayings was
"through faith," he added.
----
upi 12-13 09:59acs

Here is how one might edit this piece, with comments on the reasons.

[BULAWAYO, Rhodesia (UPI)--

Three Roman Catholic

missionaries gunned down by a

terrorist eight days ago were

buried today and their deaths

were called "a sacrifice of

reconciliation."

[The three--the Rt. Rev.

Adolf Gregor Schmitt, former

We do not need to do a great deal to the first two paragraphs. You may want to say "killed" instead of the well-worn "gunned down," but that is hardly major surgery. We can improve the end of the second paragraph by using one verb to replace two; instead of saying "spent years working," we say "worked for years." That they "spent" the years would be obvious.

bishop of Bulawayo, Rev.

Possenti Weggarten, director of

the Regina Mundi Mission, and

Sister Maria Francis van den

Berg--were all from Germany.

(They) (worked)

~~and~~ had ~~spent several years~~

~~working~~ in black ~~tribal~~ areas *for several years*

¶ *The three were buried after*

~~Following~~ a 1 1/2 hour mass ~~of~~

~~the resurrection~~ in English and

~~Sindebele,~~ a local ~~African~~ *dialect* ¶

~~language, in the grounds of a~~

~~convent near St. Mary's Cathe-~~

~~dral, the three caskets were~~

~~taken to Bulawayo's main~~

~~street cemetery and buried~~

~~in the Catholic section.~~

~~As the coffins were lowered~~

~~into the graves,~~ nuns of the

~~order of the~~ Missionary Sisters

of the Precious Blood filed past

the graves

and threw in symbolic handfuls

of dirt and gravel.

More than 1,200 persons--

most of them

~~predominantly~~ black Africans

--attended the mass, ~~celebrated~~

~~by the Roman Catholic Bishop~~

~~of Bulawayo, Rt. Rev. Henry~~

~~Karlen, a Swiss.~~ Hymns were

sung to the accompaniment of

~~six marimbas~~ (wooden xylo-

phones) and maracas.

The third paragraph has 42 words piled into a single sentence. It gives us more detail than we really need. We might go along with it if there were no ambiguity about that cemetery. Is it the main cemetery. A street cemetery? A cemetery on main street? If we guess "a cemetery on Bulawayo's main street," we run a risk of error. Rule: If it is doubtful, extra hard to check, and relatively unimportant, duck it. Edit around it.

It does no harm to say they were buried in the Catholic section, but our readers will not suffer without the information. The same goes for the name of the local dialect and the full name of the mass.

The paragraph about nuns throwing dirt into the graves is poignant, but I would mark it as a soft paragraph that could be cut if necessary. You do not need to mention coffins being lowered into graves, since that is normal.

We can save space here by deleting a reference to the bishop. If some grander church figure came from Rome to handle the funeral, we would want to point that out, but this was a local clergyman, and this is his only appearance in our story; we will delete it.

Giving the funeral sermon,
the Bishop of Gwelo, Rt. Rev.
Alois Haenex, said the death ~~of~~
~~the three missionaries was a~~
were a
Sacrifice ~~which~~ he hoped would
bring the country together ~~the~~ *as it*
had
~~same way as~~ the mourners ⊗
~~were brought together.~~

"It was a sacrifice of
reconciliation," he said. "As we
are united here, let the whole
country be united."
He ~~noted that~~ *said* missionaries ~~in~~ *have*
~~this country~~ almost ~~had~~ no *in Rhodesia's*
choice but to be involved ~~in the~~
escalating guerrilla war.
(30)
~~"The missionary cannot re-~~
main aloof as much as he
tried," the bishop waid. "He is
inevitably thrown in one way or
another." The only way to
understand the slayings was
~~"through faith," he added.~~

~~upi 12-13 09:59acs~~

We noted in the lead and again in the second graf that we have three bodies. Consequently, we save four words by referring to the deaths, plural.

The final two paragraphs contain some pretty good material, but they seem to be almost part of another story. They actually belong in a story about missionaries entering the struggle for rights in Rhodesia; they are too good to be tagged on as an afterthought. I would either put them near the top, which would require a recasting of the story, or cut back on them. Presumably, this angle will be dealt with at length in other stories and has been handled in past stories.

Now we turn to the sports page. Our story here gets the classic kind of trim—big piece from the bottom, another graf or two here and there, some sentences, and maybe some word editing.

SEATTLE (UPI)--Guard Calvin Murphy scored 18 points to become Houston's all-time leading scorer Sunday night, passing former Rocket Elvin Hayes, as the Rockets broke a 29-game home court winning streak for Seattle, 96-92.

To Sonics Coach Bill Russell, the game was just another loss. But to the fans, who were kept waiting until 35 seconds before the buzzer to find out who won, the game was visibly a disappointment.

"I honestly wasn't concerned with the winning streak," said Russell. "I've never paid much attention to our winning streak."

Not since Phoenix defeated Seattle last Feb. 8, had the Sonics lost at home. Thirteen of those games had been won at home thus far this season. Only Philadelphia, with 36 wins in 1966-67, had gone longer without a home loss.

"It's a cliche, but we just take one game at a time," Russell said. "We played pretty well, but some nights that isn't quite enough. They took advantage of every mistake we made."

Houston Coach Tom Nissalke pointed to the rebounding as the key to victory. The Rockets, playing their third road game in three nights, outrebounded Seattle, 52-43, including Moses Malone's 20 rebounds.

"We made Seattle play our tempo and it's something not many teams have been able to do in Seattle," said Nissalke, who preceded Russell as coach of the Sonics.

The teams battled evenly through the third period, entering the final quarter tied at 72-72.

Midway through the fourth quarter, Rudy Tomjanovich had a driving hook shot to give Houston an 86-85 advantage. The Rockets quickly extended that to 90-85, but Leonard Gray hit two free throws and Fred Brown an outside jumper to tie the game at 90.

With 35 seconds remaining, Mike Newlin hit a 20-foot jumper for what proved to be the winning basket. Malone added two free throws and Newlin a breakaway lay-up to close out Houston's scoring. Willie Norwood laid in a rebound at the buzzer for Seattle.

Six Rockets scored in double figures, led by Rudy Tomjanovich with 22, while Bruce Seales had 22 points to lead Seattle.

----

upi 12-13 06:42acs

This story is fairly interesting. It has action, quotes, a little color—most of the things you need. You could run it as is, but the touch-up improves it. Depending on how much the copydesk chief wants it trimmed, here is one way to handle the story:

SEATTLE (UPI) --Guard Calvin Murphy scored 18 points to become Houston's all-time leading scorer Sunday night, passing former Rocket Elvin Hayes, as the Rockets broke a

This story gets off to a bad start with a long, crowded lead. It might have been better to say that Murphy became the leading scorer here and wait a while to mention whom he passed; then we could have told how many points both scored. Wire service reporters on the West Coast carry a special burden; they are three hours behind everyone east of Indiana (give or take a little), and two hours behind another large part of the country. Thus a reporter

29-game home court winning
streak for Seattle, 96-92.

To Sonics Coach Bill Russell,
the game was just another loss.
But to the fans, ~~who were kept
waiting until 35 seconds before
the buzzer to find out who won,~~
the game was visibly a
disappointment.

"I honestly wasn't concerned
with the winning streak," said
Russell. ~~"I've never paid much
attention to our winning streak."~~
Not since *(a Feb. 8 defeat by)* Phoenix ~~defeated
Seattle last Feb. 8,~~ had the
Sonics lost at home. ~~Thirteen of
those games had been~~ *They had* won ~~at~~ *(13)* *(games)*
home ~~thus far~~ this season. ~~Only~~
Philadelphia, *(set the record)* with 36 wins in
1966-67, ~~had gone longer without
a home loss.~~

"It's a cliche, but we just
take one game at a time,"
Russell said. "We played pretty
well, but some nights that isn't
quite enough. They took advantage of every mistake we
made."

Houston Coach Tom Nissalke
called ~~pointed to the~~ rebounding ~~as~~ the
key to victory. The Rockets,
~~playing their third road game in~~

covering a game in Seattle starts a story at
10:00 P.M. for an editor in New York whose
clock says it is 1:00 A.M. That excuse won't
hold on this overnight story, however; this one
was sent at 6:42 A.M.

If you have a large number of Houston (or
Seattle) fans in your readership, you may want
to keep this information; otherwise, it can go.
If you keep it, you may want to tighten it to:
". . . to the fans, who saw their team lose in
the last 35 seconds, the game . . ."

We trim the quote by half because it borders
on redundancy: He was not concerned and he
paid little attention. Same idea.

The paragraph requires some tightening.

Here is a soft paragraph; mentally mark it
to go if we need the space. Russell is right in
calling his answer a cliché, and we do not need
to spread clichés.

This tidbit of information makes a minor
contribution. The clause would be in order if
the story were about how the Rockets showed
weariness. Or if the story were about the
Rockets showing superior stamina, it would
indicate they were doing something extraordinary. But the story does not tell of any effect

~~three nights,~~ outrebounded
Seattle, 52-43, ~~including~~ with Moses
Malone ~~% 20~~ getting rebounds.

"We made Seattle play our tempo and it's something not many teams have been able to do in Seattle," said Nissalke ~~who preceded Russell as coach of the Sonics.~~

The teams battled evenly through the third period, entering the final quarter tied at 72-72.

Midway through the fourth quarter, Rudy Tomjanovich had a driving hook shot to give Houston an 86-85 advantage. The Rockets quickly extended that to 90-85, but Leonard Gray hit two free throws and Fred Brown an outside jumper to tie the game at 90.

With 35 seconds remaining, Mike Newlin hit a 20-foot jumper for what proved to be the winning basket. Malone added two free throws and Newlin a breakaway lay-up to close out Houston's scoring. Willie Norwood laid in a rebound at the buzzer for Seattle.

Six Rockets scored in double

from playing three games in three nights; out it goes.

This paragraph explains things well, and we would probably keep it for that reason. It could go in a pinch. The last clause is interesting but extraneous unless some of the Sonics' victories came with Nissalke as coach.

The play by play starts here, providing us a convenient cutoff spot—we could end the story here without loss. However, it is customary to name the high scorers, so we fish those out of the last paragraph while wishing again that we had just a little more information on Calvin Murphy's performance.

figures, led by Rudy Tomjan-

ovich with 22, ~~while~~ Bruce

Seales had 22 ~~points~~ to lead

Seattle.

--------   (30)

~~upi 12=13 06:42aes~~

We will do one more.

HOLTON, Kans. (UPI)--A smouldering divan caught fire Sunday, destroying a turn-of-the-century hotel and killing five elderly residents.

State Fire Marshal Floyd Dibbern said investigators blame careless smoking for the fire at City Hotel.

Dibbern said the fire began early Sunday in a divan in Albert Jardine's room. He said Jardine, 54, left the door to his room ajar when he went to tell the manager that smoke was coming from the divan.

"When he left the door open, it let air in," Dibbern said. "A woman reported it sounded like a small explosion. What she heard was a back draft. When oxygen got to it, it really took off."

Witnesses said Jardine went back into the building to save his cat. Dibbern said, because of the location of Jardine's body, he thinks Jardine actually returned to awaken other residents.

"It went up just like that," Holton Fire Chief Warren Baum said. "When we got to the scene, the fire was poking through the roof."

Officials identified the vic-

tims as Jardine, Mike Hodges, 75, Marguerite Pauline Hayes, 83, Everett Williams, 63, and Adolph Posten, 70.

Baum said 24 persons were registered in the two-story brick structure. Many of them walked out of their first-floor rooms but several residents on the second floor jumped to safety or slid down ropes anchored inside their rooms.

"There was no fire escape on the building," Dibbern said. "What they had were dead-end corridors."

The fire marshal said his office has no record indicating City Hotel was ever inspected by the state.

"We've already been inspecting these hotels and we're finding them like this all over the state," Dibbern said. "They're either going to have to bring them up to the code-- put fire escapes on them and have alarms on them--or they're not going to operate."

Dibbern said a fire in August that killed five young men in a Baker University fraternity house has spurred his department's investigations of such multistoried residences.

Two residents were injured when

they jumped from second story windows. Another escaped by an old-fashioned chain fire escape.

Chester Frear, 23, an ambulance attendant who suffered back injuries, sprains and contusions when he slipped on ice created by water from fire hoses, also was hospitalized.

----

upi 12-13 10:49acs

As before, here are some suggestions and some thoughts on how you might want to edit it. Your requirement for length would have to be considered.

HOLTON, Kans. (UPI)--A *fire attributed to careless smoking* ~~smouldering divan caught fire~~ ~~Sunday,~~ destroy*ed* a turn-of-the-century hotel *(Sun)* and kill*ed* five elderly residents.

State Fire Marshal Floyd Dibbern said ~~investigators~~ *the* ~~blame careless smoking for the~~ 'fire at City Hotel.

~~Dibbern said the fire~~ began early Sunday in a divan in *the room of one of the victims's* Albert, ~~Jardine's room. He said~~ Jardine, 54, ~~left the door to his room ajar when he went to tell the manager that smoke was coming from the divan.~~

~~"When he left the door open, it let air in," Dibbern said. "A woman reported it sounded like a small explosion. What she heard was a back draft. When oxygen got to it, it really took off."~~

Witnesses said Jardine *got out of* ~~went~~ ~~back into~~ the building *but went back* to save

You can go two ways on this lead: The writer first mentioned the smouldering divan that burst into flames. We can settle for that, or we can take the approach shown and start right in on the fire. Both approaches mention the divan.

As edited, the second graf now notes that Jardine was a victim. That information came at the end of the fifth graf in the original.

The third and fourth paragraphs, though colorful and quite good at explaining the situation, were the reason I changed the lead. They make us spend a great deal of time on chronology and pyromechanics.

Let's say he got out before we say he went back in. The change of wording to tell about

his cat. Dibbern said, ~~because~~
~~of the location of Jardine's~~
~~body,~~ he thinks Jardine actually returned to awaken other
residents, *judging from where*
his body was found ⊕ *#.*

~~*#"It went up just like that,"*~~
~~Holton Fire Chief Warren~~
~~Baum said.~~ "When we got to
the scene, the fire ~~was~~ poking
~~through the roof."~~

 # The building burned quickly ⊕
~~Officials identified the vic-~~
[*The victims were*]
~~tims as~~ Jardine, Mike Hodges,
75, Marguerite Pauline Hayes,
83, Everett Williams, 63, and
Adolph Posten, 70.

 # Holton Fire Chief Warren
[Baum said 24 persons were
registered in the two-story
brick structure. Many ~~of them~~
walked out, ~~of their first-floor~~
~~rooms~~ but several residents on
the second floor jumped ~~to~~
safety
~~safety~~ or slid down ropes ⊗
~~anchored inside their rooms.~~

 # Five of the jumpers and *an ambulance attendant*
[~~"~~There was no fire escape on   *who slipped on ice*
                                    were hospitalized ⊗
the building," Dibbern said.
~~"What they had were dead-end~~
~~corridors."~~

[The fire marshal said his
                an
office has ~~no record indicating~~
                        ion
~~City Hotel was ever~~ inspec~~ted~~
program under way and
~~by the state.~~

~~*"*We've already been inspecting~~

Jardine's body was made only because it
seemed clearer.

We need the idea that the building burned
quickly, and we could use the chief's colorful
quote if we had a lot of space. His first
sentence is a cliché, and the second is meaningless if we do not know how long the department took to respond. But you could leave the
paragraph in with no harm.

Reporters and editors habitually try to protect themselves with the words used here,
pointing out that someone else did the identifying. My only quarrel is that I suspect readers
will blame the newspaper just as harshly with
the original wording as with the edited version
if one of the names is wrong. If we do err, we
will run the correct name promptly, no matter
what our original wording.

We can tighten this paragraph and bring in
a tight version of the final two paragraphs.
The injuries find a natural resting place immediately after the paragraph on how people
got out.

A tough decision. Should you report a
negative decision—the department has "no
record" of inspection—or should you just
duck out? I ducked out, since the next
paragraph implies that the hotel had shortcomings.

~~these hotels and we're~~

is   *hotels* "*like*

finding ~~them like~~ this all over

the state." ~~Dibbern said.~~

"They're either going to have

to bring them up to the code--

put fire escapes on them and

have alarms on them--or *he said*

they're not going to operate,"

(30)

~~Dibbern said a fire in August~~

~~that killed five young men in a~~

~~Baker University fraternity~~

~~house has spurred his depart-~~

~~ment's investigations of such~~

~~multistoried residences.~~

> You could leave this background material in if you have room and think readers want it. It's soft.

~~Two residents were injured when~~

~~they jumped from second story~~

~~windows. Another escaped by an~~

~~old-fashioned chain fire~~

~~escape.~~

> We have said this, in as much length as non-Kansas readers will want, in a single previous paragraph.

~~Chester Frear, 23, an ambu-~~

~~lance attendant who suffered~~

~~back injuries, sprains and~~

~~contusions when he slipped on~~

~~ice created by water from fire~~

~~hoses, also was hospitalized.~~

~~upi 12-13 10:49acs~~

That's how it's done, sometimes. The *New York Times* would not give this story a big ride for its Manhattan readership. But in Manhattan, Kansas, the *Mercury* will run the story in its entirety or, more likely, send a news team to cover it.

One other point: The thoughtful editor, on reading this story, will ask, "Can that happen *here*?" If all goes well and your newspaper is alert, the city desk will set out to answer the question. Your newspaper will have accomplished something. But that's another story.

[6] *The king's English*

ONE OF THE GREAT TRAGEDIES of modern America lies in the vast literary ignorance of its youth, particularly with reference to H. Allen Smith. If you were born less than 25 years ago, chances are good that you have never even *heard* of H. Allen Smith. A pity. Smith was a newspaperman who went bad and became an author of humorous books. In *Low Man on a Totem Pole,* he told how he prepared for the writing racket. As a lad of 5, in McLeansboro, Illinois, he was idling away an afternoon in the loft of a barn when he lost his footing and slipped. He landed headfirst in a bucket of empty beer bottles. He survived that, but soon thereafter he tumbled into an old cistern, again landing pointed end down. He was discovered there some hours later, quietly eating dirt. These two experiences, Smith contended, adequately prepared him for a life as a newsman, being the equivalent of four years in journalism school.

Smith was prone to exaggerate. But there was a trace of truth in what he said. Smith did not go to college. In fact, he maintained for years that his formal education ended in the eighth grade. As he told it, he and a friend were in the school rest room and Smith indiscreetly explained just what he proposed to do to the school principal if the principal messed with him. Smith's indiscretion lay in his failure to notice that one of the rest room stalls was occupied—alas, by the principal.

It's a fine story, and Smith was put out when a biographer turned up information 50 years later to indicate that Smith at least had enrolled in high school, though he didn't last his freshman year.

Now we turn to the point of this whole digression: H. Allen Smith, a high school dropout, supported himself for half a century with his writing. He did not learn to write by watching television. He learned by reading—and writing. That is also the way you will learn.

If you are reading this book, chances appear good that you are interested in journalism. If you are interested in journalism, you do indeed need to learn to use the basic building blocks of the profession—words. You need to learn respect for words and the way they are strung together. I do not want to sound preachy; let me say only that you need to read more than you are reading now, in all probability, and you need to pay attention to what writers are doing.

If you already have an interest in words, in syntax, in grammar, you are off on the right foot. If you had an incompetent English teacher or if you goofed off when you should have been learning punctuation, you can overcome your handicap, but not without work. Fortunately, many people have been through this wilderness ahead of you and have blazed some moderately good trails. You can choose from a number of writers. Most of them are entertaining, particularly to people who like writing, and most of them make sense.

You ought to be exposed to H. W. Fowler's *Modern English Usage* at some point in your writing life. Fowler wrote (he's dead now, as is Smith) with a subtle, sophisticated humor. His dictionary tends to be long-winded on some points, telling you more than you really want to know about certain nuances of words. Still, the work is generally enjoyable, and you can sit down and read it for pleasure or you can use it to enlighten yourself on a single word.

You should also become familiar with Theodore M. Bernstein and Roy H. Copperud. Bernstein, a *New York Times* editor, uses his newspaper for examples in *Watch Your Language* and a couple of similar efforts. The title of one, *Miss Thistlebottom's Hobgoblins,* will give you a clue to the kind of work Bernstein does. Among other things, Bernstein nips at the pedants in the crowd, the Miss Thistlebottoms who believe that our language is frozen for eternity and there is only one right way to use a word. (Wait! Do not get the idea that Bernstein is one of those like, you know, what's-happenin'-baby? fellows. He has a tinge of pedanticism himself, but he believes that an infinitive can be split without doing irreparable harm to the republic. Read him.)

Copperud also found the dictionary approach handy. He used it first in *Words on Paper* and then in *A Dictionary of Usage and Style.* Copperud has a pragmatic approach; he is considerably less academic than other writers (though he is himself a professor). You are likely to be able to use his material immediately, rather than store it against the day you will need to know something special about a word.

The newest superstar in the field is Edwin Newman, the television news reporter. Newsman Newman put out a pair of quite popular books on plain speaking—and writing. He runs to pedanticism at times, but his work is delightful for its examples of tortured prose, of long-winded, obtuse ways of conveying small pieces of information.

These people are fun to read, and their books can be of some help to aspiring writers. (So can *The Elements of Style* by W. S. Strunk, Jr., and E. B. White.) But these fountains of knowledge are not for sips; you have to go to them and drink deep. You have to soak up knowledge of grammar and word use. Don't despair, though; it can be done.

That brings us to the dictionary. You have as wide a choice in dictionaries as in anything else you can name—from the multivolume *Oxford English Dictionary* to a vest-pocket midget. The big Webster (that inches-thick monster that has its own stand or desk) is common at newspapers. The latest title is *Webster's Third New International Dictionary,* or *Webster III.* This dictionary has been widely criticized for its permissiveness; it lists as acceptable a number of uses that many grammarians had not come around to accepting at time of publication. The *New York Daily News* rejected *Webster III* and went out and bought a supply of *Webster II*. These were stored and used to replace other *Webster II*s as they wore out.

The Associated Press and the United Press International opted for *Webster's New World Dictionary* when they brought out their joint stylebook in 1977. This book, the second college edition, covers most of the words a writer is likely to worry about, and it costs less than a tenth of the big *Webster*'s price.

Webster's New World made its appearance in 1953. It has had new copyrights—revisions of one size or another—more than a dozen times; the second edition is the first wholesale revision. (Noah Webster died in 1843. Today's dictionaries have no solid connection to him other than that they have something to do with words. People like the name; traditions die hard.)

Do you know how dictionaries are put together? If you do, you realize that dictionaries do not establish the language; they only report what it is. To repeat: They only follow; they do not set the pace. They are just a measure of the way most literate people use the language. They are necessarily behind the times, since it takes years to bring out a dictionary. Thousands of words may bloom and fade in that time.

Anyone can publish a dictionary, but normally the work requires a large staff—extra large. The staff must read everything written in the language, note how words are used, pick out new words, and then somehow decide when to stop and put it all into their book, which of course will be outdated before it gets off the press. Some dictionary makers rely further on special boards to judge "correct" usage. Still, all they are saying is that at the time editorial work was completed on the dictionary, a majority of readers had certain meanings for certain words.

Consequently, you are on thin ice if you get dogmatic about what is right and what is wrong with a word. Take the word *presently,* for instance. Until the past decade, the word was largely confined to a meaning of "soon" or "in a short while, " as in "Presently, she came upon a troll sitting under the bridge." Now, however, a more common meaning is "in the present" or "now," as in, "Presently, she is a waitress." I would never stoop to that, but it is more common than the old way. I do not get exercised about this loss of the meaning of *presently.*

Hopefully is another story. The battle for the preservation of *hopefully* is lost. Even Theodore Bernstein threw up his hands in 1977 and embraced the degenerate use of the word. He apologized, but he made it clear he would stand and sweep against the tide no longer.

Let us look at it from the beginning. We old folks who carry pocket watches and have cuffs in our pants used *hopefully* this way: "The tear-stained ragamuffin sat by the candy store, looking hopefully into the faces of departing customers." That's a fine way to use the word. As an adverb, *hopefully* tells us how he looked into faces—hoping someone would sweeten his life.

However, nowadays the most common usage is this: "Hopefully, someone will give the little rascal a piece of candy." This means someone else is doing the hoping. It means someone hopes he gets candy, or we hope it, or it is hoped, or one hopes. Granted, *one hopes* is unacceptably awkward. Nevertheless, the loss of a good adverb can only be lamented. The language is cheapened; we all suffer. Perhaps the people will see their error and return to a better day. But don't count on it.

My general view is that newswriters should take a conservative approach to the language. They should shun fad terms and not be found leading the parade for linguistic reform. I do not call for a returne to ye olde English. No; I mean that you should let the fad words become established, become familiar to the bulk of your readers, before you use them in a normal context. If a fad burns itself out before you get around to using it, your loss is not severe. Remember these?

Let it all hang out.	Telling it like it is.
Doing his thing.	Sorry about that.
Get your head on straight.	In this time frame.

All were household phrases at one time, but they have lost popularity or even disappeared now.

The writer's goal is to communicate with the largest possible number of readers. You hope to get across to every reader a piece of information that you or your reporter gathered and turned into words. You have an idea (a series of abstractions or pictures in your head) and you reduce it to words on paper. These words are bounced off a printed page to the eyes of readers, who, you hope, convert them into ideas and abstractions and pictures in their heads. Your goal is to make the pictures in their heads resemble the pictures in your head. If you agree on certain things—the meanings of most words, for instance—this process will work.

Grammar plays a role here. Grammar is worthwhile and dictionary usage of words is worthwhile, because they help in the communication process. Grammar is a kind of agreement among literate people that helps them communicate. We say, "The three little pigs were going to town," instead of, "The three little pigs *was* going to town," only because literate people have an agreement that plural nouns take plural verbs. Would people understand us the other way? Yes. Would they throw rocks at us for being so ungrammatical? Probably not. But if a newspaper (or a broadcaster) continually makes such departures from the norm (mistakes), the audience will soon wonder just how bright its communicators are. Moreover, mistakes have a cumulative effect. Readers who see a grammatical mistake in a newspaper will remember it far longer than they will remember the thousands of correct usages. If they see another mistake tomorrow and still another a day later, they are apt to think the paper is falling apart.

Lest you think I am suggesting that grammatical perfection be written into the Constitution as one of the eligibility requirements for citizenship, let me mention the Luckenbach story. One of the big song hits of 1977 was about going to Luckenbach, Texas, and getting back to the basics of love. It was a country song, sung by Waylon Jennings. One line noted that "out in Luckenbach, Texas, ain't nobody feeling no pain." Friends, you have just been exposed to a triple negative. Your own Miss Thistlebottom told you, correctly, that you should not never use double negatives. Miss Thiss would no doubt blow a fuse at Waylon's indiscretion with the language. We editors would immediately revise that line to say "nobody is feeling any pain."

The point of this story is that Waylon Jennings earned, from this song alone, just about as much as the faculty of the average journalism department makes in a year. (That's the whole faculty, not each teacher.) If it weren't for the inner warmth and satisfaction that come from my realization that I have a better grasp of grammar than Waylon and Willie Nelson put together, I would probably see something inequitable in this situation.

To return to our original theme, that grammar is an agreement that helps people communicate, let me give you another illustration, with no side trips. If you say, "Born in McLeansboro, Illinois, he became one of the nation's premier humorists," your readers (some of them, anyway) will ask just what was so special about McLeansboro that a nativity there could cause a person to be funny. Born in Michigan, you probably get curious about such things. However, if you say, "Brought up in West Texas, he thought eggs were supposed to be flavored with salt, pepper, and sand," we may be able to sustain the logic.

You will find the "Born in" construction used frequently in newswriting today. It is called a non sequitur, and it is hard to eradicate because of its convenience. ("Born in . . ." is mechanically smoother than "Smith, who was born in McLeansboro in 1906, . . .") The non sequitur's permanence does not make it logically correct. I know you will shun it as evil henceforward, striking it as both an editor and a writer.

Recurring problems

Now we shift gears and deal with sentences that could use some grammatical patching. We will look at only three areas: punctuation, syntax and word choice. I do not mean to slight spelling and style errors. Spelling is of increasing importance in the electronic era, since the copy editor has been turned into a proofreader, too. Alas, I am unable to offer any shortcuts to spelling prowess; you have to read, you have to learn to question spellings, and you have to learn to look up words you question. You can get a measure of help at the bookstore, where you will find books that try to change your spelling habits. However, even the guys who write that ad copy for book covers will not promise to turn you into a Webster overnight. You can learn by concentrating on what you are doing wrong and remembering not to do that anymore. No matter what crutches you use or how much help you get, you will have to work at it; you have no choice if you intend to work in journalism.

The stylebook is another matter. After years of labor, the Associated

Press and United Press International brought forth a joint stylebook late in 1977. They are not precisely the same (AP's is 50 pages longer), but they agree on most points and their word has been adopted in most of the nation's newsrooms. Newspapers usually have some variations from wire service style to allow for local conditions. The advantage of using wire service style is that you do not have to devote your brainpower to decisions on capitalizing and abbreviating. The disadvantage is that you are letting someone else make your decisions for you. If you become a publisher, you can use my advice: Go along with the wires on most things, but establish your own style when you disagree with AP-UPI.

The main purpose of a style manual is to produce some degree of consistency in the publication. You look strange if you spell *employee* with a double *e* on one page and a single *e* on the next, or if one person lives on Main Street and another lives on Main St.

PUNCTUATION

Let's look at those problems now, starting with punctuation. Punctuation problems start and almost end with the comma. That little mark causes more trouble than the rest put together. Oh, many people fret over the semicolon, but a good writer can work for days without really having to use a semicolon. Everybody uses commas.

The plan of attack in the material below is to have you decide how you would edit the material. Previously, we have had some explanatory material to precede the questions; we will switch things around now, inasmuch as you should have been exposed to the explanatory material in earlier schooling.

When the scales fell from his eyes, Saul said he became a Christian.

Check the chronology on that. The sentence says Saul was standing around with a faceful of scales. The scales fell from his eyes and Saul blurted, "I've become a Christian." More likely he said, "Wooie, that light is bright." Our sentence says the scales fell and Saul thereupon spoke. It says he made the statement right after the fall. But what happens if we use a different punctuation? The scales continue to obey the laws of gravity, but other things change:

When the scales fell from his eyes, Saul said, he became a Christian.

The extra comma makes a great difference. Now we are no longer restricting Saul's time of speaking. He is still talking, maybe years later, but we have made our attribution parenthetical. We could remove the "Saul said" and still grasp the sentence easily: When the scales fell, Saul became a Christian." The moral is that you should attend to your grammar lessons religiously.

Turning on his VDT he prepared for a day's work.

The rule book says you must set off a beginning participial phrase that modifies the subject. Since "he" is the subject of that sentence, we need a comma after "VDT." The participial phrase modifies "he."

> Drinking steadily he soon drained the bottle.

You should have no trouble seeing the kinship of this sentence and the one you finished a minute ago. I put it here for another reason: to take a quick look at a dangling participle. Put a comma after "steadily" and then contrast that sentence with this:

> Drinking steadily, the bottle was soon emptied.

That "drinking" part has to modify the subject; the subject is "bottle." So this won't work. The subject has to be someone who drinks. Although a bottle can have an important role in this endeavor, it cannot drink; the sentence needs some editing.

> Waiting for the game to start, many birds entertained the stadium crowd. Darting and diving around the stadium, I enjoyed their tricks tremendously. Often swooping near the players, their antics delighted the spectators.

Did the triple-header get to you? Probably not. We can look at the mistakes one by one. The first sentence says flat out that the birds were waiting for the game to start. It should say, "Waiting for the game to start, the crowd was entertained by many birds." Our second sentence is the ridiculous one, for in it our writer reveals that he has uncommon talents. The third sentence is the kind that produces errors most often. It errs by saying the antics were swooping. Antics do not swoop, not ever. Watch your participles.

Sorry, I lost my head. Waiting, darting, diving and swooping, I flew off and left our discussion of commas before we were through. Let us grapple with some restrictive clauses and other appositives:

> The VDT, which is hooked to the computer, has speeded up composition. The scanner, which is slower, is also on line to the computer. The scanner that I like best is the one you bought.

All those sentences are perfect in punctuation. The first two have material in apposition. Such material, set off by commas, is nonrestrictive; it merely adds something to our discussion of the VDT and scanner. The third sentence has a restrictive clause; it limits our discussion of scanners to a specific scanner, "the one you bought." If you write, "After getting the award, Jones introduced his wife Mary," you are telling us about a bigamist. Without the comma, we have restrictive terminology—he introduced his wife named Mary, not his wife named Betty. Use the comma: "He introduced his wife, Mary." He introduced his wife; her name is Mary. The "Mary" is in apposition; use a comma before "Mary."

We also have introductory clauses:

When VDTs entered the newsroom many old-timers sighed.

You need a comma after "newsroom." The rule book tells you to separate introductory clauses and phrases from the main clause. I should leave the discussion right here, in all probability, because confusion is lurking in the exceptions to this rule. Grammarians commonly tell you to omit the comma if the introductory material is very short: "When he retired he felt better." I will not quarrel with that, but I will warn you to be careful and think twice before dropping the comma. If in doubt, use it.

Commas give us trouble in other ways, too. Some writers, seem to throw them in at, random. I suspect these writers grow fearful when they see a sentence with no internal punctuation despite the use of an inordinately large number of words and clauses and such things that grammarians like. Commas are omitted, one might guess, by writers who read sentences in their minds and insert pauses without bothering to commit that pause to paper. Such writers see the pause in their minds and expect others to see it the same way. Copy editors get paid to make sure the necessary punctuation appears on the paper, not just in a reporter's head.

Our final comma problem is the splice. You see it often. Or, as some would say:

Our problem is the splice, you see it often.

We have here two separate sentences. If we consider them to be independent clauses, we have to connect them with some kind of conjunction (probably "and") or slightly more muscular punctuation, such as a semicolon. The comma simply cannot splice two independent units like that. It really can't; it never could.

I do not know of any major problems with other punctuation marks. Oh, I feel as if I am being set upon by P. T. Barnum every time I see an exclamation point. We have too many! They make me nervous! Also, I long for the use of a period on occasion, usually about 25 words deep into a long-winded sentence. But for the most part we solve our problems when we master the comma.

SYNTAX

Syntax, our next subject, is simply the arrangement of words as elements in a sentence. We will probably stretch our definition a bit in this section, because some of the discussion will concern pronouns and adverbs and even the number of ideas that can profitably be crammed into a sentence.

We can start our syntactic outing with this sentence:

The women's swimming team also
got into the act, beating Indianapolis,

> 74–26, behind the triple victory of
> Sharon Smith, who captured the 500-
> yard freestyle, the 1,000-yard freestyle
> and the 200-yard butterfly.

This sentence tries to do too much. It ought to be broken into two parts. Follow the general rule of one basic idea per sentence. We should end this one after "Smith." Put a "She" on the front of the next clause and you will help readability. You may have made several other improvements, perhaps putting "led by Sharon Smith" after the fourth word to produce this:

> The women's swimming team, led
> by Sharon Smith, beat Indianapolis,
> 74–26. Smith captured . . .

To repeat: The plan is to hold your sentences to one basic idea. Try another:

> The chairmanship battle--the latest in a series
> that has flared this semester in such departments as
> history and English--that will be resolved Thursday
> in a meeting in the Union auditorium may also be the
> last appearance of Prof. Martin Elred, the 68-year-
> old founder of the journalism department, who is
> likely to step down soon as chairman and perhaps re-
> tire from the University, no matter who is named to
> replace him.

This example should be cut into at least two sentences, probably three. You might do it this way:

> The chairmanship battle--the latest in a series
> that has flared this semester in such departments as
> history and English--~~that~~ will be resolved Thursday
> in a meeting in the Union auditorium, *the meeting may* ~~may~~ also be the
> last appearance of Prof. Martin Elred, the 68-year-
> old founder of the journalism department, *He* ~~who~~ is
> likely to step down soon as chairman and perhaps re-
> tire from the University, no matter who is named to
> replace him.

Another problem of syntax has to do with parallelism. In the next sentence, we try to parallel two modifiers and a verb, but they refuse to team up. See if you can help.

> The advantages are that the rates are easy to understand, easy to implement and require no tax revenue.

Break it down: The rates are:

> easy to understand
> easy to implement
> require no tax revenue

They cannot "be" require no tax revenue. We have to make our material parallel. These ways will do it:

> The rates are easy to understand, are easy to implement and require no tax revenue [three verbs: are, are, require].

> The rates are easy to understand and to implement and require no tax revenue [compound verb: easy to understand and to implement, and they require no revenue].

Similarly,

> To demonstrate his strength, he stands on his hands and does cartwheels, in the process knocking over the umbrella stand, bridge lamps and putting his elbows through the windows.

What did he knock over? He knocked over the umbrella stand, he knocked over some bridge lamps, and he knocked over a piece of furniture called a "putting his elbows through the windows." No, he knocked over the stand "and" the lamps, and then he put his elbows through an unspecified number of windows.

Here, try another:

> The revised lead is shorter, more compact and includes a mention of New York as a runner-up to Los Angeles as the games site.

To be grammatically sound, you simply replace the comma after "shorter" with an "and."

We move now to one that I call the sportswriter's syndrome. You do not need to edit it severely.

> After the kick, UCLA stopped Southern Cal on their 12 yard line.

The problem, of course, is that Southern Cal is not a "they"; it's an "it." Southern Cal was stopped on its 12 yard line. Actually, the stoppage may have come at the UCLA 12; our single sentence does not make the point clear. Moving the ball to the other end of the field will cheer Southern Cal fans but will have no effect on our pronoun problem. The simplest way to straighten out our syntax is to say UCLA stopped the "Trojans" on their 12—plural noun, plural pronoun.

> The way coaches treat their players
> has a direct effect on their chances of
> later success.

The pronoun problem here arises when we use the same word to refer to two different subjects. The first "their" refers to "coaches." But you would have to guess that the second "their" refers to the players. Don't let writers get away with things like that. Take out the first "their," change the second "their" to "players'," or do something else that will not cause your readers to blink and wonder. Although we do not want to encourage reporters to use ambiguous pronouns, we may be able to forgive them. But copy editors are paid to come along and clean up such mistakes.

Unfortunately, you will occasionally run into sentences that you cannot correct without a lucky guess. Copy editors who guess a lot soon get to be former copy editors. Here is a bad sentence; all you can do is take it back to the reporter:

> Lam Jones told McTear he could
> improve his start.

You have no way to know whether Lam thinks Lam can improve Lam's start, Lam can improve McTear's start, McTear can improve McTear's start, McTear can improve Lam's start, or just what the sentence means. Is the reader likely to fathom this any quicker than you? Certainly not. You have to have the reporter clear it up.

> She challenged everyone to exercise
> their right to dissent.

I almost hate to open this can of worms. Nevertheless, we have a singular noun, "everyone," and a plural pronoun, "their." You have to make them agree. It has been customary, in English, to use "his" as the singular pronoun in such cases, even though persons of both sexes are involved. A measure of sensitivity toward the feminist movement will tell you that some people get exercised at that word choice. Quite often, you will have an easy out; in the case at hand, you could refer to "the" right to dissent. I can accept "his or her right," although I believe that is calling attention to sex unnecessarily. The "his/her" construction strikes me as cumbersome.

My suggestion is that you be aware of this problem in your writing and editing and try to go around it without being noticeable. Change "everyone" to "all students" (if students are involved), which allows you to use the plural pronoun. Or refer to "the" right, as mentioned. Be aware of what is happening around you, but don't let it force you into legalese (his/her) or other awkwardness.

> The team played without spirit,
> which irritated Akers.

Akers is probably more irritated than most copy editors, for this construction pops up regularly. It is fairly easy to understand, but it is wrong. You have no antecedent for "which." If "which" is a pronoun, its job is to stand in for a noun. What is the noun here? Not "spirit" and not "team." To ask the pronoun to stand in for a whole clause is too much; you must recast the clause:

> The team played without spirit,
> making Akers irritated.

Or "irritating Akers" or "a fact that irritated Akers." (I always edit out the words "a fact that" in favor of some less wordy construction.)

> The takeover of large copper mines,
> almost all the nation's many farms, all
> banks and most major industries have
> left the nation without a supply of
> capital.

Here is a problem of agreement. The takeover . . . have. Few editors will miss an error in agreement when the subject and verb are next to each other. Their downfall comes when other material is inserted between the two, as happened here. Copy editors have to abandon their speed-reading habits if they want to catch these mistakes. Keep your eye on the subject and don't be distracted by all those lesser attractions.

We press on, hitting some problems a solid lick and brushing lightly over others. These are problems that ensnare copy editors every day.

> Spinks said he would either fight Ali
> or Norton. Marciano not only kayoed
> Walcott but also Archie Moore.

The sentences are different but the shortcoming is the same: You need parallelism following the "either" and the "not only." Look at them one at a time. In an either-or situation, the word that follows "either" must be matched grammatically by the word that follows "or." If a verb follows "either," a verb must follow "or." In our sentence, the verb "fight" follows "either"; thus a verb must follow "or." So our sentence is wrong. We have to make it say the guy will "either fight Ali or battle Norton" (or "take on Norton" or "sign with Norton" or "go against Norton" or do some other kind of verb with Norton). And if we do not like that, we take the better way out: We go back and make a noun follow our "either." We change the sentence to say Spinks will "fight either Ali or Norton." Now our word after "either" (Ali) is a noun, and so is what we left after "or" (Norton).

As for the second sentence above, if you can handle "either-or," you can handle "not only." The part of speech, a verb here, that follows "not only" must be matched by the part following "but also."

> Marciano not only kayoed Walcott
> but also flattened Archie Moore.

If you like the noun route, you come up with:

> Marciano kayoed not only Walcott
> but also Archie Moore.

Let's try a first cousin of that problem:

> Sportswriters believe that both from
> the viewpoint of coaches and players,
> the game is changing rapidly.

You must have parallelism after "both." You could drop the word out of this sentence and still make sense, although the meaning would be changed slightly; "both" can be used to emphasize something, as was intended here. The problem is that "both" is misplaced; it is supposed to emphasize that we have viewpoints of two groups. Put it after "of." An alternative, much less attractive, would be to say "that both from the viewpoint of coaches and the vantage point of players." Now "viewpoint" and "vantage point" are parallel. Although such wording is clumsy here, this construction can be helpful sometimes.

> He said he had no plans to sell the
> Alamo.

Use of the past tense takes away some of our flexibility and our ability to be specific. Are we saying he had no plans at one time? Can't tell. We get a much better sentence with

> He said he has no plans to sell the
> Alamo.

This tells our readers that, at the moment, he has no plans to sell. If he changes his mind later today, we have a new story. But our readers have no doubt about what is happening.

We can try another sentence to show that you can be more precise when you free yourself from the past tense restriction.

> In contrasting modern education
> with that of the past, the teacher said
> students did not know how to diagram
> sentences.

This sentence would be much clearer with a "do not" instead of the "did not.'' The "did not" could refer to those of the past, and that is not what is meant.

Rule of thumb: If you are referring to a condition or observation or situation that is presumably valid now, rather than just at some specific moment in the past, use the present tense. But if you think it will change before your publication comes out, use the past tense, probably with some kind of qualifier—some date or wording like "at the moment."

A final thought: Use the present tense on eternal verities. For example, it is silly to say:

> He said the moon was made of green cheese.

Everyone knows the moon "is" made of green cheese. If you are a nonbeliever, try these:

> He said the moon was 287,000 miles from Earth.
> Jones testified that he believed a bird in the hand was worth two in the bush.

The moon is not changing distances, so we can stick with present tense: The moon is 287,000 miles away, yesterday, today and several weeks from now. Similarly, Jones's testimony refers to an unchanging maxim: the bird is worth more if you have it handy.

Remember to keep your eye on verb tenses. Normally, the context of your sentence will affect your decision. Also, you will sometimes leave the tense alone and adjust other wording in a sentence, achieving the same effect. ("He said he had no plans to sell the Alamo at the moment.") Your goal is communication.

WORD CHOICE

We now take up a few examples of faulty word choice. The main point will be to remind you that almost right is wrong and that you have to concentrate on little things as well as the big ones.

> He believes that he knows best.
> He says that he knows best.
> He thinks that he knows best.
> He knows that he knows best.
> She felt her arm, which had thrown 87 pitches, was weak.
> The company declared a dividend on the stock would not be given this year.
> She argued her reasons for the policy were sound.
> He proclaimed his love for the maiden was undying.

You no doubt recognize the problem. Take the *that*s out of the first four sentences and put them in the next four. *That* is a tricky word, often misused. You can make a mistake no matter which way you go. In the material above, the first four sentences are not wrong, but they have a needless word. The second four sentences are faulty because they lead the reader down the wrong path for several steps. Take the last sentence, for instance. The reader first thinks someone is proclaiming love. Then, at the end of the sentence, the reader learns that the lover was passing judgment on his ardor, not just proclaiming it.

Let's try some more. You will have an easy time with these for you will be expecting the kind of error (that) we have been handling. Nevertheless, you can find this work worth your time if you will learn to read the sentences both ways—and then decide whether to use *that*. When you learn how to make that decision, you can apply it to other writing.

> The dean requested student funds, previously kept in a separate account, be subject to auditing.
> We all know that the Longhorns will be back.
> As we rolled on, I clearly saw the ruts made by our wagon were nearly arrow-straight.
> He said that he could be an archbishop if he wished.
> The king revealed his underwear, which was handmade, will be on display for the first time next month.
> Many think that they should get napkins with their egg rolls.

H. W. Fowler went so far as to compile three lists of verbs affected by our friend *that*. Lists like these are of value to you mainly as suggestions, pump primers. You may want to prime your pump with the following words, gathered from Fowler and others:

Usually use *that*		Usually omit *that*	Varies
agree	indicate	believe	told
announce	learn	presume	confessed
argue	maintain	suppose	declare
assume	noted	think	hear
calculate	observe		perceive
charge	remark		promise
conceive	state		said
contend	suggest		see
			understand

Do not consider the list inclusive. All you have here is a starter. The tricky verbs are those in the right column. They do vary. Take one of the sentences we handled above: "The company declared a dividend on the stock would not be given this year." We mislead readers because the company can in fact declare a dividend on the stock, period. In another sentence, we caused readers to think our king was an exhibitionist, at least until they realize the sentence cried for a *that*. Your job as an editor is to strike the ambiguity. Make every sentence's meaning clear.

One other item while we are in this neighborhood: If you have a sentence in which one subordinate clause can do without a *that* but the other cannot, use a *that* in both to make them equal. An example:

> We were led to believe the king would appear before noon and that we could then go home.

Sometimes you can take out the *that* in one clause. More often, as here, you will need to insert one; the sentence above needs a *that* before the king. We believed that . . . and that . . . You will run into the problem often. Fix it up every time.

> He said a dog, four cats and a couple turkeys comprise the menagerie.

Couple is like *pair*. You wouldn't say someone put on a pair pants. Pair "of" pants. Couple "of" turkeys. Also, these animals do not *comprise* the menagerie. It's the other way: The menagerie *comprises* the dog, cats, and turkeys. The whole comprises the parts. The dog, cats, and turkeys make up the menagerie, or they compose it, or it is composed of them. But they do not *comprise* a menagerie.

> We were adverse to returning to our home after the storm, for we knew it had been totally destroyed.

Let us be *averse* to this faulty word choice. *Adverse* is an adjective. We lost our home in adverse weather. We must buckle down in this period of adversity. Also, *destroyed* has no degrees. Things can be destroyed or damaged, but they cannot be partially destroyed.

> We talked to her and she inferred that she would flaunt the law and attend the funeral service.

The writer of this sentence may have had in mind something that escapes us. If not, he or she erred three times. The first error was *inferred,* which should have been *implied*. If she calls for water, you infer she is thirsty. By speaking, she implies she is thirsty. The second error, terribly common, is *flaunt*; our woman *flouts* the law. Flout means to mock, to sneer at, to show disdain for. (Want a memory aid? To flout is out. Floutlaw, outlaw. The best I can come up with for *flaunt* lies in the first three letters of the word: "fla." Those are the letters in "flag," too. Flaunt the flag—wave it ostentatiously. That is what *flaunt* means— display something ostentatiously. If you've got it, flaunt it, as an ad campaign said some time back.) Finally, just call our ceremony a funeral. A funeral is a service.

> They will lay the blame on me for this.
> Now I lay me down to sleep
> She laid there for an hour before going to sleep.
> The children laid down and went to sleep.
> He laid his head on her shoulder.
> They looked sweet, with his head laying on her shoulder.

We batted .500 on those, which is good for baseball but not overly laudable for grammar. Our third, fourth, and sixth sentences were wrong. We should have said:

> She lay there for an hour . . .
> The children lay down and went to sleep.
> They looked sweet, with his head lying on her shoulder.

You are not the first person to be confused over *lay* and *lie* and *laid* (if you are confused). You are up against a tough verb. As a present tense, transitive verb, *lay* does the job. (Lay the blame. Lay bricks. Lay me down to sleep. Lay your head on a shoulder.) For a present tense, intransitive verb, you have to switch to *lie*. (Wrong: Lay here beside me; lay down and go to sleep. Right: Lie here beside me; lie down and go to sleep.)

Here is where the problem gets knotty: The past tense of *lie* is *lay*. Thus, "they lay here beside me" will do, if it means they were lying there a while ago. The past tense of the transitive verb, *lay*, is *laid*: "They laid their tools down and walked off."

> **Present tense:** I lie in the grass. You lie in the grass.
> **Past tense:** I lay in the grass. You lay in the grass.
> **Transitive, future:** I will lay my coat on that log.
> **Transitive, past:** I laid my coat on that log.
> **Intransitive, past:** I lay there yesterday.

We could do this alot better if we had less students.

You see both errors in that sentence a lot. I do not know why; maybe we can blame television. Certainly some force has led people to believe that "alot" is one word instead of two. ("A lot," even as two words, has a tinge of colloquialism and should not pop into your writing every other paragraph.)

Our sentence's second error has to do with a choice between *less* and *fewer*. Simple: If you can count it, it takes *fewer*.

> If we had fewer students, we would have less truancy.
> If we had less rain, we would have fewer mosquitoes.
> If we have fewer clouds, we have less shade.
> She has less money than I because I bought fewer drinks.
> She has done less groaning than I because she drank fewer drinks.

Greeks and jocks will be tugging war against each other.

A process called *back-formation* has produced here a new sport, tugging war. The term grates on the ear. We can say these college lads "will be tugging against each other." We can say they "will square off in a tug-of-war," or "tangle in a tug-of-war," or "match their beef in a tug-of-war." But we cannot say they "will be tugging war." Also, note that "against each other" is excess baggage. Let's just say that Greeks and jocks will have a tug-of-war.

If you will permit a spin-off observation, I will ask you to find one further lesson in that sentence. Namely, the Willoughby syndrome. People with the Willoughbys can never use the unadorned future tense. They cannot say, "Our boys will match wits with Vassar tonight." No, it is always, "Our boys will be matching wits with Vassar tonight." Or Greeks and jocks will be tugging, students will be hitting the books, the Buckeyes will be facing their sternest test. And so on into the night. The "will be" approach is one word plus a syllable ("ing") longer than the normal way. You should be avoiding this construction.

> Barbara Jordan became the first black woman elected to Congress from a southern state in 1972. Her election to the Texas Senate in 1966 marked the first black to hold that office since Reconstruction.

Usually, opening a sentence with a date slows you down. Here, however, it would have been worth the trouble. As written, this says Jordan was the first such person elected in 1972; presumably, others could have been elected in previous years without affecting our sentence. The fact is, she was not merely the first black woman elected in 1972. We should say: "In 1972, she became the first black woman elected to Congress . . ." Now, our second sentence has a different shortcoming. I find it unlikely that Miss Jordan was marked, though the experience was surely memorable. What was marked was "a time," as in this:

> Her election to the Texas Senate in 1966 marked the first time a black had been chosen for the office since Reconstruction.

You have now had a swing at a number of problems that plague copy editors. The list is not comprehensive. I hope only that you get interested in nuances, in precision, in facility of phrase. Good editing involves much more than correcting grammatical lapses. But corrections are part of your work, and you may as well start looking for errors. You can have worse habits.

Attribution

We now tackle one more major problem: attribution. Sloppy attribution often mars good writing, and your job is to clean it up. Besides, you can have fun in deciding when, where and whether to use attribution.

It would probably be good for you to learn how to spell *said*, which is clearly the most important word in the world of quotation and attribution. You will use it often as a writer and editor, no matter what your medium—broadcast, newspaper, magazine or brochure. *Said* is not the only word to use, but it is the best. When in doubt, use it.

Your thesaurus will give you dozens of synonyms for *said*. Publications get by with such things as *concluded, continued, added, indicated, went on, noted, mentioned, told, explained,* and, on rare occasions, *stated* and *declared.* All are usable at certain times, and at those times they may be better than our old, safe, neutral *said.* However, the reporter usually wants a bland word, a neutral word, a safe word, a word that carries no extra message. If you let a reporter get away with

> "I'm only 42," he chuckled.

few people will be wildly upset. Some will argue that those sounds are nothing like a chuckle. They will say we should make this change, at least:

> "I'm only 42," he said with a chuckle.

(Or "said, chuckling".) Fine. We solved a problem. But we cannot solve our problems with that step every time. Check this, for instance:

> The mayor did not have all the facts, he admitted.

That comes close to editorializing, depending on the circumstances of the statement. The word *admit* implies some sort of wrongdoing in almost every case. With it, we imply to readers that the mayor is in a corner, that he is in what one journalist calls a minus-one position, whereas he may be totally innocent. Is it the mayor's fault that he does not have the facts? We imply that it is, and it may be; but if it is not, we should not shaft him.

A similar danger lurks behind *explain.* Sometimes this word indicates that the speaker has done something that requires an explanation, when in fact he has not. The verb often describes the action precisely, and that is when you want to use it. But unless the speaker is indeed explaining, find a more accurate word.

Perhaps we need a definition of attribution. *Attribution* is the process we use to name the source of a statement. With attribution, we tell who provided the information. Like this:

> "I'm in favor of it," the mayor said.

or, without the quotation:

> The mayor said he favors the plan.

The first statement is called a direct quotation (or just *quotation*). The second is a *paraphrase,* or indirect quotation.

> *Q. Classify these sentences as quotation or paraphrase:*
>
>   *a.* "Give me liberty or give me death," Pat said.
>   *b.* Pat said he wanted to be free or dead.
>   *c.* Georgette thought of Arnie every time a mule or horse passed, she said.

    d. Georgette said, "I thought of you every time a mule or horse passed."

    e. Dandin said he had wed a wicked woman.

    f. "I have wed a wicked woman," Dandin moaned.

Easy: The paraphrases are *b, c, e.*

On to combinations. Sometimes we have a mixture of quotation and paraphrase. We usually call it a *partial quotation.* It is tricky, so we need to be moderately careful in working with it.

Let us examine a full quote and see when we should extract part of it.

> "Well, you may think otherwise, but it just doesn't seem logical to me, probably because I am a father, to let these feather merchants peddle this stuff near the schools," the mayor said.

Our reporter did a fine job in writing down all those words. Unfortunately, some of them are just wind (no offense, your honor.) The editor's job is to take out the twaddle and leave in the goodies, the pertinent information. One solution might be to paraphrase it:

> The mayor said that as a father he opposes sales of the material near schools.

That is fairly accurate. But it lacks the life that we might give it with some of the mayor's spiffy words. A partial quote would perhaps capture the best part of the wording and still economize the way a paraphrase does:

> The mayor said that as a father he does not want to let "these feather merchants peddle this stuff near the schools."

or this:

> The mayor said it "just doesn't seem logical" to permit sales near schools.

Your choice of paraphrase would be governed by the rest of the story—by what you want to emphasize. Different parts of the quotation emphasize different aspects of the situation. If our story is about an argument over quality of merchandise and integrity of the sales force, the first partial quote (about feather merchants as peddlers) is more fitting. But if our story deals mainly with the question of whether there should be sales near the schools, the second choice is more proper; it questions the logic of letting the world of commerce intrude on the groves of academe. Reporters and editors get paid to see that the right words are chosen.

Commerce may be out of the groves, but we editors are not out of the woods. We must tackle a related problem. What will happen if we use a partial quote that reads like this?

> The mayor said he doesn't want "feather merchants" to sell their products near schools.

Does the reader think that those are the mayor's words or that our publication is just quoting "feather merchants" because it is an unusual term? Editors are supposed to resolve ambiguities so readers will not have to guess. We take care of it by expanding the partial quote and making the quoted matter lap over another word that would not normally be part of the cliché or odd wording:

> The mayor said he doesn't want "these feather merchants" to sell their products near schools.

Good. The reader has no doubt that the words are the mayor's. "Feather merchants" is a strange term, an odd phrasing, but "these feather merchants" is different. The term is readily perceived to be part of a larger quotation. (One problem: The reporter can make such a change, since he knows what words the mayor used. The copy editor can make the change in the case at hand, since the original quotation, containing the word "these," was available. But if the reporter had turned in only a partial quote, the editor would not know that "these" had ever been in the mayor's mouth. Good editors do not run around sticking in extra words on whim. The point is that the reporter must do the story properly; editors cannot do everything.)

Another example may help. Here is what the mayor said:

> "I'm tired of trying to work with these commissioners. They are all fools, and we aren't accomplishing anything. I would like to see them all fired."

And here is a paraphrase:

> The mayor said the commissioners are all fools and he is tired of trying to work with them.

Some people would quote "fools." No need to. It is a common word, clearly not invented this afternoon by the mayor. That sort of word appears regularly in news stories without causing any great batting of eyelids. You could use quotation marks, of course, but you would gain little.

Do not go overboard with the above advice. You must not think we shy away from strong statements automatically. You need not cut it back to this:

> The mayor criticized the commis-
> sioners and indicated he does not like
> to work with them.

No, no, better to use the whole quotation. When you have to choose between flavor and excessive length, think twice before cutting out the flavor.

How would I do it? I would probably quote "are all fools," for reasons cited earlier.

What might happen if our mayor had had other words at his command? To wit:

> "I'm tired of trying to work with
> these commissioners. They are all clab-
> berheads, and I would like to see them
> fired."

Most writers would find some way to indicate that "clabberheads" was the mayor's word, not the publication's. Careful writers will not isolate the single word with quotation marks. That isolation indicates that perhaps we thought of the word, not the mayor.

Maybe one more sentence of illustration would help. Let's say you are editing a columnist's copy and you run across this sentence:

> Alas, the world is full of "clab-
> berheads."

Whether the columnist is talking about elected leaders, your employer, or ungrateful offspring is of no consequence. What matters is your decision about using quotation marks around "clabberheads." These marks merely call attention to the word. They say, "Hey, I know better than to use this strange word in genteel company, but I am using it to stoop to your level." If you are so self-conscious of the word that you have to protect yourself with quotation marks, for Pete's sake look around and find some other word. The dictionaries are full of them.

Rule of thumb: Either knock off the quotation marks or come up with a better word.

Well, you ask, should we have knocked the marks off "feather merchants" a few pages back? No, we used them to show that the words came from our mayor. We also put "these" inside the quotes to make the mayor's ownership clear. (As a matter of fact, neither "feather merchant" nor "clabberhead" is likely to show up unquoted in a news story. An editorial, yes; a feature, possibly; a column, sure; a news story, forget it.)

Look at this one:

> Councilwoman Emma Lou Linn
> recommended that Topeka adopt a
> lifeline charge for utility rates.

I would quote "a lifeline charge." The term is brand-new, at least to me. I would quote it and then quickly explain where the phrase came from and why it is called that. (The term has to do with lowering utility rates for retired persons and those with low incomes. It has not worked its way into the language yet; it may make it someday.)

Occasionally, you will run into a person who utters more than one sentence worth quoting. You thus have three choices of where to put the attribution: before the quote, in the midst of it, or at the end. Your choice should be based on moderately rational grounds. Normally, the weakest choice is at the beginning: *He said, "I shall return."* That is weak because (1) you run the risk of having a string of paragraphs starting with *Jones said* and *he said* and (2) what a person says ought to be more important than the act of saying. You should jump right in with interesting information, saving the attribution till later.

(Important exception: In writing for broadcast, the attribution should be at the beginning of the information. People can't see quotation marks on radio or TV.)

(Second important exception: The attribution does a good job as a transition device at the beginning of a sentence. You inform the reader immediately that you have changed speakers.)

The end of a quotation is frequently a satisfactory spot for attribution. However, it can be slightly confusing if the quotation is long; readers may be wondering who is doing all this talking before they reach the identification. You may find it best to drop the attribution into the middle, choosing a place where the utterance reaches a natural pause.

Let's look at attribution in the three spots mentioned—beginning, middle, end:

> Fox said, "They don't have the money. We have it in the bank and we propose to spend it. If they want it so badly, they can go to court after it."

> "The Canadians are running short of grain," Williams said, "but we have all we can use. If they want it, we will sell it to them for a fair price."

> "The whole idea is to bring people closer together. You can't love someone unless you know her. To know is to love," Mrs. Caffall said.

If you have time and if you are serious about writing, you might find it beneficial to mentally move the attribution around in those three paragraphs. See how it would look in different places. Decide which version you like. Decide why.

Q. *The following paragraphs have the attribution in the wrong place. Find a better location.*

    a. Some children wander into her store daily, she said, looking for a rest room.

b. "I am sick and tired," she said, "of people who track up my polished floors."

c. "The sign," he said, "is here. It's just a matter of what words they put on it."

d. The mayor asked about the bridge. He said, "I need to know the cost now, because we may have to scrap the whole project."

a. Preferably at the end, possibly at the beginning. As it stands, you have the poor woman talking while looking for a rest room; the "looking" clause modifies the nearest noun, and she is it. b. Try the end again, or the beginning if you are desperate. The middle spot, used now, misleads readers. The statement "I am sick and tired" looks like a complete offering. But then we find out that our speaker isn't just sick and tired, she's sick and tired of trackers. c. Go to the end of either sentence, or perhaps to the beginning of the first one. As it is, you are breaking up a four-word sentence, which is easier to grasp in one piece; it has no natural breaks. d. Best spot is after "cost now." Next is at the end. The idea is to slip the attribution in unobtrusively. As written, the "he said" sticks out, but in the spot suggested it will barely be noticed.

Another attribution problem is illustrated by these two paragraphs out of a news story:

> "I am amazed that people have problems with punctuation," Elred said. "It seems so elementary."
> "Nobody but a smart aleck thinks punctuation comes easy. It is fraught with pitfalls and requires great care," Mart rejoined.

I know of no research that indicates how often a reader will overlook the closing quotation marks on that first quote and continue to the second sentence under the impression that the same person is speaking. But I know it happens, and so do you. For this reason we should use attribution at the beginning of the second paragraph, despite our earlier protestation that the beginning is a weak place for it. Our goal is understanding, and we help the reader if we indicate that we have switched speakers in midstream.

By now, I hope you are beginning to figure out alternative ways on your own. You ought to be able to look at the two paragraphs just quoted and come up with another solution. You might try it this way on the second quotation:

> Mart disagreed. "Nobody but a smart aleck thinks punctuation comes easy," he said. "It is fraught with pitfalls and requires great care."

The first short sentence tells us we are switching. It would be hard to misunderstand this story.

Of course, you may have tackled the problem above without knowing the punctuation rules on quotation marks. In that case, you were at a disadvantage, and we may need to bring you up to par with everyone else. We can do that by quoting the rules about opening and closing quotations that are longer than one paragraph. Get ready; here they are:

1. Every quoted paragraph opens with quotation marks.
2. Only the last paragraph has closing quotation marks.
3. There are no other rules.

Let us make sure you have it.

Q. *Which of these two sets of paragraphs below is correctly punctuated?*

a. Elred disagreed. "I can never support you," he told the woman. "My heart is not in it."
　"And if my heart is not in it, I cannot give my all."

b. Elred agreed. "I will always support you," he told the woman. "My heart is with you.
　"And if my heart is with you, I will give my all."

b. Obviously we are on the side of true love. So it isn't elegant prose. Just note that we do not close the quotes as long as the quotation continues, even if it runs to several paragraphs. And note that the continuing paragraph gets a second set of opening quote marks.

How can you remember all this? Just remember to put quotes at the beginning of each quoted paragraph. Otherwise, use quotation marks as if the quote were all in one paragraph.

And now we come to a point many writers ignore: You should not carry a partial quotation over from one sentence into a full quotation as the next sentence. The partial quote is governed by the verb in its own sentence, and that verb cannot be responsible for the happenings in the next sentence. Therefore, that next sentence must have its own quotation marks. Let's look, starting with the original quote:

"I have been here a long time and have never seen such a strange decision," the lawyer said. "It baffled me because I didn't expect anything that odd. I really thought we would win."

If we had to summarize it, part of our summary would be this:

He called the verdict "odd."

The quotation marks, used properly here, grow out of our barrister's expression about the verdict. He "called" it something. He called it odd. We want to show that "odd" is the lawyer's word, so we quote it.

However, you will encounter a large number of writers who believe, in their unlearned state, that the following is correctly punctuated:

He called the verdict "odd. I really thought we would win."

If you encounter such a writer, shun him as an evil companion. Tell him
the lawyer did not call the verdict "odd-I-thought-we-would-win." Explain that you punctuate this way:

> He called the verdict "odd." "I really thought we would win,"
> he said.

Economy is a marvelous trait, one much to be cultivated. But the saving
produced by omitting these quotation marks is not worth the cost.

Our oddball example above is fairly easy to accept, since many
people would boggle at stretching a one-word quote across a full
sentence. The sin occurs more commonly in situations like this:

> Elred ridiculed the Bengals as "the
> league's joke. They have Clyde Camp-
> bell, and he never wins."

To reiterate: You must put ending quotation marks after "joke" and
beginning quotes before "They." That little partial quote has to be closed
so you can start a new, full sentence. In the first sentence, we are ridicul-
ing the Bengals "as" something. That something is the league's joke, not
the league's joke they have Clyde Campbell. Another wrong example:

> Ziegler termed the statement "inop-
> erative. I would never knowingly mis-
> lead the press."

The shortcoming is clear: We need quotation marks around "in-
operative," because we are singling out the word to show that it is an
unusual word our speaker chose, not our word. The second sentence has
nothing to do with the first from a grammatical standpoint; it describes
something separate. Hence the need for separate quotation marks:

> Ziegler termed the statement "inop-
> erative." "I would never knowingly mis-
> lead the press," he said.

News and feature stories almost always require quotations. Most interviews and speech stories will mix paraphrase and direct quotations
somewhat evenly. Paraphrase is often used to summarize a large part of a
speaker's talk, and then a pertinent quotation is brought in to buttress
the point. When choosing a quote, be sure it is pertinent. If it is long and
rambling, you may be better off to paraphrase or to use a partial quote.

PUNCTUATION IN ATTRIBUTION

Attribution for a full-sentence quotation is normally set off by a
comma, whether before or after the quote. Grammarians in the house
suggest use of a colon if the quotation that follows contains two or more
sentences. One respected user of the language suggests a colon if the
material runs more than two typed lines. I am not inclined to argue with
either view; however, a comma is probably sufficient for most quotations

except lengthy ones. You cannot find engraved in stone any word on how long is lengthy or why you use a comma on one sentence and a colon on two, nor can you find agreement. Maybe we can compromise: Use a colon on any quotation longer than three typed lines or at any other time the urge strikes. At all other times, use a comma.

No matter what path you take, you have to separate the attribution from the quotation. Here are some examples:

> "To know is to love," Mrs. Caffal said.
> Mrs. Caffal said, "To know is to love."

Most punctuation goes inside the quotation marks. The comma and the period always do, as in the Caffal examples. Other marks are arranged according to construction.

> Who does he think he is?" Wright asked.
> Is that a "gentlemen's agreement"?
> Singer asked, "Is that a 'gentlemen's agreement'?"
> "Are we in agreement?" the gentlemen asked.

Note that there is no comma before the attribution on the first and last items. The question mark is sufficient.

> **Q.** *A review: Punctuate these sentences. All are full quotations except for the attribution.*

> The law forbids higher rates the chief said.
> Whos going to pay for this Sharpe asked.
> Burd said I believe the job is done.
> Davis asked why did Scott call this a scrumdiddlyiscious dish.

> "The law forbids higher rates," the chief said.
> "Who's going to pay for this?" Sharpe asked.
> Burd said, "I believe the job is done."
> Davis asked, "Why did Scott call this a 'scrumdiddlyiscious' dish?"

WHEN TO ATTRIBUTE

Unless there is attribution in a story, the reader is permitted to assume that the publication stands behind the information printed. You will frequently run into situations in which the attribution can be delayed for a paragraph or so. Such a situation would arise when the source (the person producing the information) had the power to back up the statement given. For example, say Congress grants the president authority to set a ceiling on coffee prices and the president exercises his authority. We might have a lead like this:

> The price of coffee, which caused unrest in four cities last week, will be frozen at $4.25 a pound Monday.

The next paragraph would usually tell who said so (the president). The advantage of such an approach is that we cut just a little underbrush out of the lead. However, the normal attribution, "President Carter said today," is not very long, and it might indeed be beneficial here. The use of that attribution adds a note of authority to the statement. Copy editors have to look at sentence length, weigh the need for a note of authority, and then decide whether to attribute in a case like this.

We can look at another:

> Partridge was listed in serious condition in Brackenridge Hospital's intensive care unit with a gunshot wound in the chest, according to a hospital spokesman who provided information to the working press.

This has more than underbrush; it is a jungle of vines and saplings. We start hacking at the end and slash our way to the front. (1) "Working press" is a meaningless term. It generally refers to people who are at an event (say a baseball game or a political convention) to write a story, as opposed to the brass, high-level thinkers and others who are there to soak up atmosphere and background, get a feel for the situation and freeload a little. (2) The job of a spokesman is to provide information, so we need not say that. (3) We have said our victim was listed. Since listing is a form of qualification in itself, we do not need to spell out who told us unless it was the custodian.

In short, we stop this one after "chest" and we have covered it as well as we need to. If we had said he "was in good condition," as opposed to being listed, we would have to qualify it to indicate that someone else reported that to us; we didn't check his pulse and make a diagnosis on our own.

Q. *Test yourself on some sentences that may or may not require attribution. The source and action are given first, in brackets [ ]. Decide whether we can use the sentence as is or must give it attribution.*

  a. [President signs bill.] The United States is cutting its contribution to the United Nations in half.
  b. [Gallup Poll reports.] Eighty-five million Americans will vote Tuesday.
  c. [Solar heating engineer makes speech.] Half of the nation will be using solar heat by 1985.
  d. [University president speaks.] Student fees will drop from $40 to $27.50 next semester.

a. If the law says we are cutting the contribution, we do not require attribution. *b.* We must have attribution. That is the Gallup Poll's estimate. If the creek rises and the locusts hit town, we may get a smaller turnout. *c.* We need attribution. Our engineer does not have the power (no pun) to guarantee that half of us will be using solar heat. *d.* The president either has the authority or speaks for some group that made the decision. We can use this without attributing it in the lead. Later on, as a matter of tidiness, we could tell who made the announcement, but we would not have to.

We want to be quick to use attribution in paragraphs advocating a viewpoint, evaluating something, or assessing consequences of significance. Look at this sentence:

The grain deal was the best the nation could make.

It cries for attribution. Who said it was the best deal? A grain seller might be quite happy with a deal that would make a baker angry. A columnist or editorial writer can get away with such a statement, but a news writer cannot.

Q. *Here are some more. Write* NO *or* OK *after them—*NO *if the material cannot stand without attribution,* OK *if it is usable as is:*

   a. Rain is forecast throughout the state.
   b. The Soviet Union's grain purchases will have minimal effect on U.S. food prices.
   c. North Dakota has been declared a disaster area as a result of severe storms.
   d. Two hundred persons were trapped for an hour today when the upper floors of a New York skyscraper caught fire.
   e. Strands of the black widow spider's web are stronger than steel of the same weight.
   f. This country must turn to God or it will turn to dust.

Sentences *a, c, d, e* are usable as they stand. Let's take each one.
   a. OK; you do not need to attribute this to anyone. You have said rain is "forecast"; that word is sufficient qualification for your sentence. If you said the whole state is going to get rain, you would need to pin the statement to the weather service.
   b. NO; the effect is speculation in most contexts.
   c. OK; qualification has been established with the word "declared." The federal government makes an official declaration in such cases, and presumably our publication is reporting the act. (We would be improper if we based the lead on some barfly's pronouncement.) If we said North Dakota "is" a disaster area, we would have to add a source, since "is" carries no qualification with it.
   d. OK; although we did not run up to the scene and count the trapped persons, we need not build an elaborate defense of our statement by hanging it on the fire chief. Our reporter would certainly try to verify the number from several sources, both before the deadline and after, but all those sources need not be cited. If the building collapsed and the fire chief said it was empty, the story would likely say, "Fire fighters said no one was in the building."
   e. OK. Although our reporter has not gone out and tested spider webs and steel, it is not improper to report generally accepted facts without attribution. The statement is clearly testable: Tie a spider web around a piece of steel, pull them apart and see which breaks. If there is any reason to suspect that scientists who make such tests (or even more sophisticated tests) are lying, we would attribute the statement. If we were reporting some new development, something not generally accepted as scientific fact, attribution would be mandatory. ("Coffee grounds will cure athlete's foot," *two Nobel Prize winners reported* today.) However, if you have fallen behind in your reading and are

unaware of the relative strengths of steel and spider web, you answered this correctly when you said it should have attribution. I hope you do not get confused when you get one of these wishy-washy answers; the problem is that we are not after the answers but the thoughts that lie behind them.

f. NO; you need attribution. It matters not a whit whether this statement is true or even whether you can quote scripture to prove it. Without diving into the turbulent waters of theology, I will say only that an abundance of people will disagree with the statement. Since God is harder to measure than spider webs and steel, you should use some form of attribution on this statement in a news story.

[7] *Headline writing*

ALTHOUGH THE NEWS BUSINESS has its share of fierce scowlers and intemperate frowners, many people find the work rather pleasant. Few occupations outside the news business provide you a chance to bring down the government, discuss philosophy with a visiting movie starlet, analyze the world energy situation, or write good headlines. Headline writers may have the best job of all: Every new piece of copy offers a challenge and a chance to knock out a prize headline. The work provides job satisfaction seldom enjoyed by engineers, accountants, or car dealers.

Sometimes a prize headline will write itself—born of the story with but a minimum of midwifery by the editor. At other times, a short count and a long subject turn the task of writing a headline into unpleasant labor. Indeed, many people encounter great frustration in head writing, particularly in their early attempts. It is not easy to summarize in just a few words what a reporter has poured forth in many paragraphs—and make it sound interesting besides.

Easy or difficult, painful or pleasant, the headline has a number of objectives it must fulfill, all within certain space restrictions. Very simply put, the first goal, the sine qua non, is to indicate the reward readers can expect from the story. All other objectives bow down before that one. The goal is more than just to tell the story; we must also *sell* the story. We have to indicate to readers that the story contains something of interest. One more step: We also have to let readers off the hook; we have to provide enough information in the headline so that readers can decide without question that they can safely pass up a story without missing anything. Ideally, we would choose such magnificent stories that every headline would persuade the reader to go into the story. Alas, the news doesn't work that way.

It was not always thus

Newspaper headlines come in all sizes and a number of shapes, some of them peculiar. The peculiarities—that is, the great departures in style—are even more pronounced in magazines. Although newspapers are catching up and breaking new typographic ground as they take advantage of current technology, the bulk of headlines fit into traditional patterns. The most common headline format in American newspapers is called *flush left.* In this style, all lines are flush on the left margin, or just inside it, and the right ends of headlines come within two or three letters of the right margin. Some newspapers permit greater leeway on the right.

The flush left headline is relatively new, a twentieth century development. The first newspapers had no headlines at all. Ben Franklin's *Pennsylvania Gazette,* for example, had only one headline, and a purist might call it part of the flag. It said: "Containing the Freshest Advices Foreign and Domestick." (You can see that Franklin was not a pacesetter on headlines.) When newspapers finally got around to using legitimate headlines, starting in the middle of the nineteenth century, they lumped all of them at the beginning of the paper—column 1 of page 1—and ran tiny subheads, or a line of space, above the stories as they came to them. In time, major stories began getting more than one *deck* (a headline smaller than the main headline and in a subordinate position that cites a new facet of a story or expands on a facet referred to in a previous part of the headline). As often happens, someone figured that if a little bit of something was good, a lot would be better. Thus decks proliferated to such a point that the *New York Herald* used 13 of them to tell about the end of the Civil War. The poor *Herald* headline writer, having exhausted the subject in the first dozen, wrapped things up with a thirteenth deck simply reading: "&c, &c, &c." He had already written a handful of crosslines, 4 inverted pyramid decks and 4 two-line headlines with the second lines centered. It was a day's work.

The *Kansas City Star* and *Times* were the last major papers to abandon multiple-deck headlines for most stories. (The *New York Times* still uses multiple decks, but not with the vigor of turn-of-the-century newspapers. The *Times* doesn't have its heart in the effort.)

Flush left headlines are without a doubt easier to write than those old-style headlines, one column wide and in large sizes, usually all caps. The worst part of those may have been trying to remember whether the second crossline was followed by an inverted pyramid or a hanging indent. Adoption of the flush left style no doubt prolonged the life of many copy editors, or at least calmed their stomach-rumblings.

The change was welcome. But this is not to say that newspapers have abandoned or should abandon variety in their head schedules. A page full of two-line headlines would have a built-in dullness. Eight-column newspapers have some traditional patterns, however. One-column headlines are most often given three lines, perhaps two in small sizes (14 and 18 point). Two lines are common for heads of two, three, or four columns. And headlines of five or more columns most often have only one line, though it may be considerably larger than the type used in heads of fewer columns' width. The foregoing patterns should not be considered hard and fast. Dozens of exceptions can be found in any newspaper. All we have really said is that one-column headlines are not often run one or four lines; two-liners are common in heads of two to four columns; and, on the wide stuff, newspapers are more likely to run a one-line head than a two.

Other formats abound and you should at least be exposed to them. If you are lucky, you will never have to use most of them. The most common are the step, hanging indention, inverted pyramid, and combination. The combination is sort of like the Glutton's Delight at your local pizza parlor: It has a gob of everything on it.

First, let us look at the *step* head. Here is an example:

Astronauts suffer
effects of fumes;
2 go to hospital

Step headlines normally have two or three lines, all about the same length. The first line is flush left and does not fill out the space to the right. The second line in a three-line head will be approximately centered. And the third line will be indented still more and set almost flush right. If the head has only two lines, the second line will be flush right, or nearly so. These headlines are slightly more difficult to write than the customary flush left job; the count must be watched more closely. The headline's symmetry breaks up if one line's length varies quite a bit from the others. A flush left headline can get away with a bigger spread in count, because it does not depend on symmetry for appeal. You will find step headlines in New York and perhaps a few other places. They were generally abandoned 30 years ago.

Hanging indentions show up here and there. They look like this:

Hobby expected to end

dispute soon; project

not subject to review

This kind of headline is found most often in decks, the secondary parts of headlines still used in a few newspapers.

The *inverted pyramid* also shows up as a deck in big-city newspapers. This headline has nothing to do with the inverted pyramid lead you learned about in your first journalism class. The name refers to the format: a centered headline with each line shorter than the one before it, like this:

Gas enterprise
against bid
on ruling

This leaves us staring at the Glutton's Delight. The combination will include all those forms above and probably a crossline as well (the crossline being equivalent to an anchovy or jalapeño on our pizza). The *Kansas City Star* and *Times* used to offer all kinds of combination headlines. They changed format in the early 1970s and now look like every other newspaper—a pity. In the old days, Kansas Citians often got headlines like this with their breakfast:

Congress cool
to Carter plan
for energy tax

Poague says existing pacts
with mines have lost
all legal validity

Some irritation seen

Action follows rejection
of end to coal curb;
elderly are excluded

&c, &c, &c

Let us review.

Q. *Name the kinds of headlines below.*

a.
Brown to direct
arms conference
in White House

b.   **Brown to direct**

arms conference

in White House

c.   **Health care termed vital**

for nation's elderly;

costs continue rise

d.   **Brown to direct**

talks on arms

from capital

a. Flush left, *b.* step, *c.* hanging indention, *d.* inverted pyramid.

The past few pages are prologue. You are more likely to write a kicker headline than a step head with hanging indention. Usually, although it isn't a matter of law, the *kicker* head looks like this:

I'm the kicker
I'm the main headline

Kicker headlines are used to dress up a page by lending variety. The kicker itself is usually half the size of the main line. Normally, a kicker will count about the same as the headline or maybe a little less; since the type is half the main line's size, the kicker with the same count is about half as long as the main line. The resulting white space is considered attractive. Long kickers clutter thing up and steal the white space. Excessively short ones (one or two little words) get lost.

The kicker is usually in the same type family as the main headline but in the alternate face—italic if the main headline is roman and vice versa. Some newspapers do not underline the kicker, some do not indent the main headline, and some use kickers from another type family, all contrary to the headline above. There is no accounting for taste.

Closely related to the kicker are *overlines* and *underlines*. You will have no trouble with them. As with kickers, it is customary to use half the size of the main head type. Check this:

President still wants energy tax

Conservation put ahead of search for new oil

Note that the underline is about three-fourths as long as the main line. Here is an overline:

Hunt for new oil sources slighted

President pushes gas-guzzler tax

That brings us to a related, fairly uncommon kind of headline. Edmund C. Arnold, a widely respected typographer, calls it the *hammer.* (He does not claim to have invented the term and you cannot blame him for it.) The hammer is a reverse arrangement of a kicker headline. The big type is the kicker and the smaller stuff makes up the main headline. One word—two at most—will suffice for the hammer. All you are trying to do is name the subject; the smaller type tells what happened. Like this one, from England:

Blizzard
Ice buries London;
Continent isolated

Variety is the main advantage of this unusual head setup. Such an idea could pall on the reader quickly if overused. It should be used only for typographic effect, certainly no more than once on a page.

How to write a headline

You are not reading a cookbook. Recipes and formulas are in short supply here. Nevertheless, the process of writing a headline involves several definite steps. If you are a beginner, your lot will be easier if you attack a headline this way:

1. Read and understand the story as you edit it.

2. Write out a rough headline, paying little attention to precise count.

3. Look for word combinations that will form one or more lines of the headline, getting close to the proper count.

4. Substitute synonyms until all lines of the head fit.

5. Remember that you can always take a new approach if you get bogged down after writing one or two lines of a head.

The foregoing advice sounds simple. It is like the words of wisdom given by a baseball manager who instructed a batter to hit a home run—easy to say but not always easy to accomplish. Nevertheless, the copy editor can hit a satisfactory number of homers by taking a good swing at every pitch the copy chief offers. We need to look at this advice, point by point, and see if we were thrown any curves.

1. Read and understand the story. This is vital. You must understand a story before you head it up and turn it loose on the world. Inasmuch as the headline sets the tone of the story for the reader, few errors can cause as much gnashing of teeth as a headline that is incorrect. An example: The story said the judge fined 30 men after they pleaded ''no contest'' in a conspiracy case. The head said, ''30 guilty of conspiracy.'' Result: 30 instant enemies. People have filed lawsuits with less provocation. Read and understand the story.

2. Write a rough headline, paying little attention to count other than to get in the neighborhood of what you must wind up with. It does not take long to catch on to this sort of thing—a couple of weeks on the desk should have most beginners bypassing this step and composing complete headlines in their minds. Nevertheless, even the top professionals write them down before the final count. The newcomer to the desk will quickly learn to estimate the chances that the wording will fit within the prescribed limits. The learning process is speeded up if you start out by writing a rough head.

(Incidentally, the process described here is not materially changed by the move to electronic editing. If anything, having the computer reject long headlines quickly can be helpful.)

3. Look for word combinations that form one or more lines. Many headlines are written backward; the head writer discovers that a word or combination of words will just fit the given count, and those words turn out to work best at the end of the headline. For example, let us say that we have a story about a farmer who has decided to stop using pesticides and chemical fertilizers and farm the old-time way. We discover that the word ''organic'' will just about fill a line. Our newspaper is picky and will not let us put an adjective on one line and the noun it modifies on the next. Thus we are forbidden to say:

Organic

farming

planned

No; we must use "organic" as the last line if we use it as an adjective. Thus:

Farmer

will go

organic

Wonderful. Well, it may not be wonderful, but it fits and it tells the story. And in six counts, that's at least magnificent.

4. Substitute synonyms until the headline fits. (Do not take this to mean that headline writing is a matter of getting an idea and then plugging in new words until some combination fits. You may be better off to come up with an entirely new approach to the headline.) Let us take a headline and see how we can substitute synonyms:

Students shoot for headline prizes

We can lengthen it in the following ways:

Students shooting for headline prizes

Students shooting for headline honors

Students shooting for honors on headlines

Students going after headline honors

Students going after honors with headlines

Students set sights on headline honors

Headlines are more likely to trouble us by being too long than by being too short. Maybe we need to *trim* our headline. Here are some substitutions:

Students shoot for headline prizes

Students try for headline prizes

Students go for headline prizes

Students seeking headline prizes

Students seek headline prizes

This is the process that headline writers go through, although they do not always put their work down on paper (or enter it into the VDT). The copy editor, through experience, learns how to say things in different words.

5. Remember that you can always take a new approach. This is important. Don't try to solve all your problems by substituting synonyms. If the head won't work, back off and go at it from another angle. The trick is to know when to cast aside a line that fits so you can get a complete headline. After a while, the beginner learns to consider the whole headline as a unit, not just as a collection of lines.

Here is an example of change in approach. The original headline said:

Students get headline assignment

That does the job, presumably. It is dull, but it tells us what the story is about. Perhaps we can go at it from other angles, depending on the facts of the story. For instance:

Students shoot for headline prizes
Students try for headline of week
Students must work to get a head

You cannot judge these headlines without the story, of course, but you can see that you can tackle a headline from different angles.

You can develop this ability by rewriting—mentally if you wish— headlines you come across. Most people, when asked to rewrite a headline, will try to replace a weak verb with something snappier or perhaps find a better adjective. Fine. Many headlines can be sharpened quickly that way. But you must also learn to take a new approach; abandon the first headline and write something totally new. Practice.

Is that all there is to it?

Perhaps the most common sin on the copydesk is believing that a headline that fits is a good headline. More bad headlines get into the newspaper from this cause than any other. Headline writers as a group are reluctant to change a head that counts. Alas, head count is not even half the battle. You will never see praise heaped on a person just for writing a headline that fits. No—there is more to it. We can now take up other aspects of this business:

6. Get the key words, the meat of the story. Be specific.
7. Strive for snappy verbs, action verbs, colorful verbs.
8. Watch your grammar.

6. Let us start with the suggestion to be specific. All sorts of evils arise from the failure to be specific. We get wooden headlines. We get padded headlines. We get headlines that perform none of the functions a headline is supposed to perform.

As hinted earlier, a bit of experience as a reporter is desirable for a copy editor. The reporter learns early that people want to know how a story affects *them*. The reporter is supposed to tell how in the story, and the copy editor is supposed to tell how in the headline. The task is not always difficult, but it takes some concentration. The editor must examine the story to see what the key elements are, to see what makes this story different from others. Thus a story about a fire death takes on new light when we say an invalid was involved. The word "invalid" is more specific than "woman"; it describes the victim better. Here is the lead on a story, followed by a headline:

> NEW ORLEANS (GP)—At least two automobiles fell from the Lake Pontchartrain Bridge today after a freighter hit a support and left a 40-foot gap in the highway. Three Baton Rouge residents were known to have drowned in one car.

3 die in bridge accident

The headline is accurate. There was an accident. Three persons died. But the headline is too general. We get a better head if we say:

Ship hits bridge; 3 die

It would be even better to be able to say: "Ship hits bridge; 3 motorists drown." But we have to accept the limits of count. Here is another on the same story:

3 Baton Rougians
plunge to deaths
as ship hits bridge

That headline gets us a little closer to our readers, but only if we work in Louisiana.

7. In addition to being specific, the good headline writer wants to make sure that the head contains no padding. Every word, almost every letter, must carry its own weight. We might look at a specific example of padding. Let us say we are working the copydesk for the student newspaper at Notre Dame. Let us specify further that the football coach's name is Rockne. We are guilty of gross padding if our headline says:

ND president raises Coach Rockne's salary

Where is the padding? Inasmuch as it is unlikely that the president of the United States has any voice in this matter, we add nothing to the headline with "ND." The same goes for "Coach"; the Notre Dame coach's name stands a good chance of being recognized on campus. There is more: What is the point of saying the "president" raised the salary? Normally, the president is merely the person who signs the papers. It would be different if the athletic council voted against a raise and the president overturned that decision. But in that case we would have a head noting that the president had crossed the council. If we are just reporting on a pay raise, not on a council's squabbles with the brass, we drop the president. Our headline might say:

Rockne gets $4,000 raise, signs for 3 years

The headline's wording depends on facts in the story. The good editor will pack headlines with as many interesting facts as possible.

Here's another example of padding. This headline, taken verbatim from a Texas newspaper, may be the most useless you will ever run across.

School board discusses,
acts on local issues
at regular meeting

That's enough to fog your green eyeshade. It tells us that the board met. Period. Look at it. Look at all that room that could have been used to tell us that the board banned smoking in the rest rooms or instituted a dress code or threw out a dress code or decided to pay substitute teachers a living wage or bought land or fired the principal. Surely the board did something worth telling about. As for the padding, how about these ideas (not just the words):

Discusses—That's the nature of a board meeting: discuss, vote.

Local—School boards hardly ever mess with foreign policy.

Regular—We do not need to mention that all this action took place at a meeting; where else would it happen? Also, you don't put routine facts in the headline; you might mention it if this was a special meeting.

Acts—This is the key verb in the whole headline, and it doesn't give us a clue as to what happened.

In short, the writer of this headline committed a hanging offense. Besides that, it didn't count right.

Look at still another lead and headline:

> WASHINGTON (GP)—Major U.S. oil companies raised their gasoline prices four cents a gallon at the pump today in response to a production curtailment by the Arab oil-exporting countries.

Arab oil curtailment move sends
U.S. gasoline prices zooming up

Is that horrible? No, just mediocre. You have seen hundreds like it. It fits and it gives the reader some idea of what is going on. However, it is padded, it is not specific and it does not tell as much as it could in the space provided. It is a loafer, and as such it is unwelcome in these precincts. Let us look at the nature of this idleness: Although "zooming" gives readers a hint as to what will happen to their wallets, they would be better informed if we could tell just how much this will cost. We can get rid of "up," since prices never zoom any other direction. What would happen if we dropped "curtailment" or "move"? The curtailment is the move, and vice versa. So we can abandon one. Could we safely drop "oil"? Yes, because we give an indication of the subject when we talk about gasoline prices. Also, we hardly need to say "U.S. prices"; one would assume that a story in a U.S. newspaper would be about U.S. prices unless the headline specified otherwise.

If we back up and start over, maybe we can come up with an unpadded headline that tells the story. As before, we would adjust the head to fit the facts. Note that the original head started with the cause rather than the effect. We might switch angles and start with the one that hits the reader immediately.

Gasoline prices jump 4 cents

That tells the reader more than before. We have the key fact right up front. We might have approached it this way:

Arabs push gas prices up 4¢

but that has some faults. As noted, some publications object to use of the cent sign. Many balk at the use of "gas" for "gasoline." In conversation, "gas" is satisfactory. However, material dealing with the oil business can cover gas gas as well as gasoline gas, and we run a risk of confusion. (In some contexts, gas would be all right; we could use gas with mention of gallons, since real gas does not come in gallons but in cubic feet. We could probably refer to a motorist's gas bill or write: "Driving to cost more as gas prices soar.") So let us use the price jump line to start our head.

We could then offer as our second line:

in response to Arab curtailment

That will count all right, but it has a flaw—it uses almost the same words as the lead. You do want to get across the same idea as the story, but you do not want to use the same words. Try this:

Gasoline prices jump 4 cents
as Arabs cut back on production

That isn't bad. We can use it. A minor objection might focus on the "as"; some would prefer "after," as in

after Arab production cutback

That last line runs short. We can lengthen it with an "on" (cutback on production) or by making Arabs possessive—Arabs' production.

Here is my suggestion: We could use this as part of our head:

Gasoline prices jump 4 cents
as Arabs trim flow;

and go deeper into the story for something more. That's one of the good things about headline writing: You can always strive to tell more and tell it better.

Q. *Here are some sets of headlines. Select the heads that are specific.*

1*a*. **Bellow wins
Nobel prize**

1*b*. **Bellow wins
fiction prize**

2*a*. **Tomato harvest
boosted 90%**

2*b*. **Tomato harvest
shows increase**

3*a*. **Carter promises
welfare reform**

3*b*. **Carter to back
aid for elderly**

4*a*. **Parts of Illinois
hurt by weather**

4*b*. **Rain, hail hit
northern Illinois**

5*a*. **Twisters kill
2 in Midwest**

5*b*. **Ohio twister
fatal to 2**

6*a*. **GAO cites misuse of health insurance**

6*b*. **Insurance overpayments cited by GAO**

7*a*. **Red Cross: We're ready, for you**

7*b*. **Welfare group adopts slogan**

The following choices are specific. 1*a*. There are several fiction prizes but only one Nobel prize that Bellow is likely to win. 2*a*. Surely you got that. 3*b* and 4*b*. Two more easy ones. 5*b*. Ohio is more specific than Midwest. 6*b*. Not really a clearcut case. But *b* gives more indication of what this is about; "overpayments" is more specific than "misuse." 7*a*. Specific.

All of those are easy to spot. All we had to do was think. And therein lies a lesson: Somewhere, amid all the hustle and bustle and general confusion seen on the copydesk, the editor—you—ought to pause for a minute and examine each head for vagueness. Is there a more specific way to say what you want to say? If so, use it. *Think* about it.

The same thing goes for padding. You can spot padding easily if you will reflect on the headline. Sure you can.

Q. *Find the padding words in these headlines.*

Rain, hail hurt some crops in parts of Iowa

You can delete "some" and "parts of." Better yet, let the rain and hail "hurt Iowa crops." That will leave you with nearly half the headline count to add more information.

FFA plans to hold annual rodeo here

Delete either "plans" or "to hold"; they overlap each other and one is unnecessary. You could sacrifice "annual," too, although it is not a gross offender. Finally, "here" should be deleted. You could use "here" or the name of your town or of your school if the headline were about the governor making a speech, because the governor makes speeches in many places. But the only FFA that you are likely to be dealing with is the local chapter; thus "here" is not vital.

Collision of trains in Chicago kills 16 or more

Certainly you will want to knock off the last two words; most newspapers take the conservative approach and use only the known number of dead in the headline. However, if you have a solid estimate, something other than a wild guess, you may want to use the old reliable "27 feared dead" approach. That wording is normally used when you have a plane crash or mine disaster in which you know how many people are involved, though you do not have the bodies to count. You cannot delete any more words while using this headline in its present arrangement, but you can make a little shift and tighten it up: Make it say "Chicago train collision kills 16." Do not pile up modifiers and smother the noun, but you can often make this kind of shift and save some count for other information. Thus "energy plan of Carter" becomes "Carter energy plan," and "Terrorism in Uganda" becomes "Uganda terrorism." But you err when you turn "Plan for talks on Ivy League football scholarship" into "Ivy League football scholarship talks plan."

Now, all you have to do for the rest of your life is to keep a sharp eye out for padding in headlines. Belittle it in others' heads and delete it from your own.

Although imprecision, padding, and lack of action are the major shortcomings, headlines can have other faults. Many headline writers, struck by the novelty of the language employed on the copydesk, actually believe they are doing the reader a service when they refer to legislators as solons, bridges as spans, and meetings as parleys or confabs. Thus they would toss bouquets at the guy who wrote

Solons flay unit chief at span parley

This kind of nonsense is known as *headlinese.* You seldom see so much of it jammed together as in that last head, but words of this nature pop up now and then in even the best of papers. They are common in the less-than-best. Any editor who puts up with them should be dealt with severely by a committee of citizens, and the headline on such an event would no doubt say

Panel scores editor
in lingo squabble

Another term is sometimes applied to headlinese: *cripple* words. Some of these are words that the headline writer stores away and pulls out only in the direst of emergencies. Headlinese is the mark of a beginner—or a weak veteran. Leave it for the amateurs. Write your head in English.

And thus we come to the department of snappy verbs. A specific, lively headline will draw readers every time. If the headline is bland, the reader may think the story is dull. So, don't be bland. Lively, active verbs give you a head start on bagging a reader. Note these lively headline verbs:

Zoning law flattens pancake house

Back-to-back floods
stagger Plainview

House Speaker mashes 2 opponents

Look at the following list; verbs on the left side are more active than those in the other column:

traps	catches
battles	opposes
oust	remove
panting	breathing

Some headline writers could not make it through the shift if the words "set," "slate," and "meet" were taken away from them. If they do not write "Mondale set for Arab talks," they write "Arabs set for Mondale visit," or "Stanton High sets tourney," or even "Buffs set to host meet." We will no doubt someday see a poultry story headed by "Hens set to set."

Weak passive verbs take away the writer's strength. One of the weakest is the verb in this sentence: *is*. It merely shows a state of being. Seek action. "Student is happy with grades" is weaker than "Grades elate student." And "Basketball star is valedictorian" is weaker than "Basketball star posts top grades."

Of course, our drive for lively verbs cannot go on forever. There are limits on everything, including how much snappiness we ought to employ in our headlines. Many years ago a headline writer was touched by a thunderbolt of inspiration as he was working on a headline for a story about a hanging. So he wrote

Jerked to Jesus

This headline meets all the known criteria for being considered colorful. It is overflowing with action. But it has certain other flaws that outweigh the color and action. Most editors would not use it today, even if the government were still in the hanging business.

Q. *Try your hand at this. Check the more active verb in each pair.*

a. warn   say   *c.* cavort   dance

b. prevent   block   *d.* embrace   hold

The more active verbs are warn, block, cavort, and embrace.

Q. *We will put our verbs into headlines. Check the more interesting head of each pair.*

a. **Nader speaks on Corvair**
b. **Nader attacks Corvair**

c. **University standards raised**
d. **University tightens standards**

e. **3 die in fire**
f. **Fire kills 3**

g. **Students released by rebels**
h. **Rebels free students**

Surely you picked the second headline in each set: *b, d, f, h.*

Q. *Pick the head with the strongest verb.*

a. **Dry weather cucumbers are bitter**
b. **Cucumbers are bitter in drought**
c. **Cucumbers grow bitter in dry weather**

Say *c*; it has the only active verb in the house.

Q. *Of course, there's more to headline writing than just choosing the active verbs. Improve the first headline above with some stronger verbs. Take a shot at it. Write at least one full headline.*

Among the possibilities would be such things as: "Dry weather ruins cucumber taste," "Drought turns cucumber sour," "Cucumbers lose taste in dryness."

Q. *Rewrite, changing from passive into active voice:* "University tower closed."

"University closes tower" will do it.

Q. *Rewrite, using a lively verb:* "Turkey has arms aid halted by U.S."

Some possibilities: "U.S. halts arms aid to Turkey," "U.S. arms aid to Turkey stops," "U.S. ends arms aid in Turkey."

Q. *Another:* "3 are dead after bridge accident."

Three suggestions: "Bridge accident kills 3," "3 die in bridge accident," "3 killed in bridge accident."

If that story had been the one we dealt with earlier, we would have taken an entirely different approach so as to get the ship angle in it. We did do something different in the last suggestion: we used what is called an *understood* verb. Headlines are almost always written in the present tense. Normally, what looks like a past tense verb, in this case "killed," is a present tense verb in the passive voice, with the helping verb understood. So that last headline in the answer really said

3 (are) killed in bridge accident

"Are" is understood. The situation occurs often. The following heads have understood verbs, all in parentheses:

Students (are) ecstatic with grades

U.S. (is) weak, senator believes

Tennis (is) Iowa's leading sport

Aid to Turkey (is) halted

A-counting we will go

Newspaper copy editors learn early that they are hemmed in by numerous restrictions. The first and worst is that of count. Just as you cannot put six pounds of sand in a five-pound sack, you cannot squeeze six units of type into a five-unit hole. Note that the word is *units,* not *letters.* Not all letters are the same width. The *M* and *W*, for instance, take up considerably more space than the *i*. Copy editors thus use a finer counting system than one that simply counts each letter. (Actually, you will not be far off if you count each character as one unit; the average comes close to reality. However, to do that properly you need enough experience to be able to adjust mentally for an unusual number of thin or fat characters. Stick to the more precise method for your first 10 years on the desk; it's safer.)

Commonly, newspapers and magazines use what we might call the *flirt* system. In this system, the small *f, l, i, r* and *t* are counted as ½ unit. Other small letters count 1 each, except *m* and *w*, which are 1½. Caps count 1½ except for *M* and *W*, which are 2, and *I*, which is ½. Small punctuation marks count ½ each; the fat ones count 1½; and the space between words counts 1. In chart form, we have this:

1 count	*½ count*	*1½ counts*	*2 counts*
abcdeghjk	flirt I	ABCDEFGH	MW
nopqsuvxyz	,.;'!:=	JKLNOPQR	
(space)	([1)]	STUVXYZ mw	
		234567890	
		@#$%¢&? —	

You may want to write that on the back of your hand for reference, because it will come up again. Soon. You can refer to it until you commit it to memory. Letters vary from the flirt system in some typefaces. For instance, some sans serif types have a vertical *j* that counts only ½. In roman faces, the *j* has a little hook, and it gets a full count. We will use the flirt system here.

Now let us try our hand at counting a headline.

Yarber calls president a liar

This headline counts 24½ by the system outlined above. It counts 29 by the 1-for-each-character system. (The discrepancy is of no consequence; it does not mean that the headline will fit if you count it one way and bounce if you count it the other. It's like one fellow using a 5-pound sack for his sand and the other using a sack holding 2.27 kilograms. Same difference. The point: You can use any system you like, as long as the headline fits when your system says it should fit.)

Many beginners find it convenient to make marks on the copy to keep track of the count. Thus they would have a headline looking like this:

Yarber calls president a liar

Although it is against the law to turn in such chicken scratchings as a headline, you may do it this way and then rewrite it on a clean piece of paper.

The marks *under* the letters indicate full counts (19 of them here) and marks *above* the letters indicate half counts (11 of them for 5½ counts, giving a total of 24½). Use this system until you have a good idea of what you are doing, and then you should start counting in your head. (Of course, you cannot make marks on the copy when you are editing electronically. If your computer is well set up, you will be able to see the count as you work. Even so, you will need to learn to count to that you can sub a short word for a long one or do other required juggling.)

Many copy editors find a mental flagging system satisfactory for counting. Instead of mumbling "1½, 2½, 3, 4, 5, 5½, 6½, 7½, 8½, 9, 9½, 10½" for the first two words of our last headline, "Yarber calls," the mental flagger would count by ones. Each time the count had an extra ½, a mental flag would go up—one might picture a fellow on a golf course or whatever imagination permits. That flag would come down when we ran into another ½ count, and a full count would be added to the head. Thus we would do "Yarber calls" this way: 1 for *Y* (flag goes up, since *Y* counts 1½), 2 for *a*, 3 for *r* (flag comes down, since *r* is only ½), 4 for *b*, 5 for *e*, nothing for the next *r* (but the flag goes up to show us we have ½ count left over), 6 for the space, 7 for *c* (remember, the flag is still up), 8 for *a*, 9 for the two *ll*s (you could bring the flag down on the first *l* and then run it right back up for the second one, but that's a lot of needless wear on the flagpole), 10 for *s*. That's the end of the line, and the flag is still up. So we add ½ and come out with 10½.

It's easier to do than to read about.

Actually, the flirt system, with or without flags or little marks on the copy, is only approximate. Type designers do not design by halves. Normally, a cap Q, for example, will be wider than a cap L. We have already mentioned the little j. The small t and r are usually counted as ½, but ⅝ or ¾ would often be more accurate.

New types, designed for use with electronic equipment, will fit into computer programs that break a head down as fine as you want, say ¹⁄₂₅ of a unit, and keep a cumulative total on the count. But I believe you will have a better grasp of what you are doing if you learn the basics on paper and transfer that knowledge to the tube.

Each newspaper sets its own standard on how close a headline must come to filling the space available. Many newspapers require that all headlines be written within two counts of the maximum. (If you go over the maximum, of course, parts of the head will be chopped off.) Some newspapers are more restrictive, though not much, and some are considerably looser. Some experts feel that short counts make a page look ragged and unprofessional; others look at the same thing as a breath of fresh air, of casualness. I am all in favor of fresh air, but I believe it can be introduced without resorting to terribly short headlines. Many headlines are written short specifically to provide white space, that's one thing. But many are written short out of desperation or laziness, and their shortness is then rationalized by citing the need for white space. Heads done in this book must be within two counts of the maximum.

Enough talk. Let us count a few headlines. Take your time; be careful; refer to the chart if you wish. If you get one wrong, recount. The answers given are correct. You must be accurate—right on the nose—since accurate counting is part of the business. The greatest headline in the world isn't much good if it won't fit.

Q. *Count these heads, excluding the identifying letters.*

 a. **Prune pie is plum good**
 b. **Prune pudding wrinkles noses**
 c. **Pruned pyracantha shades Pecos**
 d. **Quick brown foxes jump**
 e. **Lazy dogs lie**
 f. **Stylebook's rules change**
 g. **Illicit Illinoisan is illiterate**

a. 21 on 18 and 6 (18 fulls, 6 halves). *b.* 26½ on 23 and 7. *c.* 29½ on 27 and 5. *d.* 22 on 19 and 6. *e.* 12½ on 11 and 3. *f.* 22 on 19 and 6. *g.* 22½ on 13 and 19.

These next questions presume that you must be within two of the maximum (and not over it).

Q. *If the maximum is 21 and your headline says* **Mammoth moose awakes,** *will it fit?*

No; too long.

Q. *If the limit is 25, will* **Quick brown foxes jump** *fit?*

No; too short. Get within 2 of maximum.

Q. *If the limit is 23½, will* **Somebody ate my porridge** *fit?*

Ah, just right.

Don't fence us in

At some point in your life, you may find yourself confronting a teen-ager ready to use the family car on a date for the first time. You will no doubt be willing to provide bushels of driving tips and wise counsel on what to do (and not do) and what time to come home. A parallel situation lies before us now. You are eager to jump in and start writing headlines, and I am standing here telling you what not to do, generally spoiling your fun. As noted, many newspapers have strict rules on headline construction, while others have few rules or none. We are going to go with strictness ("Be home by 11, don't go over 40 mph, and keep both hands on the steering wheel"). If you can write heads under severe rules, you can surely write them under relaxed rules. On the other hand, if you learn your craft with no restrictions, you may be in for a shock when you move to a publication that has tight rules.

Let us look at some common restrictions, all of which are in force from now on in this book.

1. Put modifiers and words modified on the same line
2. Put all parts of any verb on the same line.
3. Do not end a line with a preposition.
4. Generally, do not repeat words within a headline.
5. Do not use the word *is*.
6. Do not use initials to identify obscure groups.
7. Do not use abbreviations standing alone.

We could probably scrape up a few more commandments, but seven is a satisfactory number. (Ten would be pretentious, wouldn't it?)

We will examine these one by one. The first rule: Do not split modifiers and the modified words on multiline headlines. For example, these headlines break that rule:

Pair of wealthy   **Smith barely**
lawyers indicted   **beats Williams**

The thinking behind this rule is that readers will assimilate one line at a time and may be thrown off by certain divisions.

Here's a better illustration:

Greek melon

That looks like an adjective and a noun, "Greek" and "melon." Presumably, the rest of the headline will tell us that it tastes good, that is it expensive, or that it has just won a spot in the *Guinness Book of World Records*. Alas, our diagnosis is wrong. Here is the full headline:

Greek melon
dealer sued

For the flicker of an eyelash, readers will have been misled. Of course, they will zip right down to the second line, which will make sense, and they may not even frown. However, they will have been misled for an instant. The Greek melon will have turned into a fruit dealer. Although this is less worrisome than a carriage turning back into a pumpkin, most newspapers operate on the principle that headlines should not give readers even the slightest feeling of being taken down the wrong path.

> **Q.** *A similar problem occurs in some of the headlines below. Which headlines are acceptable under our split-head criteria?*

> *a.* **Coffee house**   *b.* **Coffee house**
>   **sale brewing**   **stirs realtors**

> *c.* **National Guard**   *d.* **National Guard**
>   **callup planned**   **to be called**

> *e.* **Town has no**   *f.* **Town removes**
>   **parking meters**   **parking meters**

> *g.* **University drops**   *h.* **University taxi**
>   **proposal for taxi**   **proposal dropped**

We accept *b, d, f, g*; the others have modifiers on one line and modified words on the next. Note that only one line of each of the first three headlines was different. In the first pair, we turned "coffee house" into a noun instead of an adjective. In the second pair, we did the same for "National Guard." And in the third pair we kept the bottom line as it was and rewrote the first line to eliminate the modifier on the end.

Our second rule says we do not split verbs. Thus

Mayor says he will
reveal plans today

is objectionable as a split head. The two parts of the verb, "will" and "reveal," are on separate lines. We have to revise our wording. Perhaps one of these (it depends on the nuances of the story):

**Mayor will reveal
plans for campaign**

**Mayor will reveal
decision on party**

Q. *Which headlines are unacceptable under this rule?*

a. **Lawyer is
indicted**

b. **Lawyer
indicted**

c. **Board plans
labor talks**

d. **Board to
hold talks**

Headlines *a* and *d*; some people will not believe this answer—because they didn't read the instructions. They didn't note that we switched from acceptable to unacceptable as our guideline. (If you got both heads wrong for that reason, you are good on heads but bad on directions. If you read the directions right and still missed both, better plan on marrying wealth.)

Our third rule, a related stricture, forbids the use of prepositions on the ends of lines, like this:

**2 held for
jaywalking**

**Carter goes to
London talks**

Where did we get such a rule? Maybe it came from the ancient practice of not using a preposition to end a sentence. That rule has been cast aside by almost all grammarians; I can find no one who considers it ironclad, though it makes sense much of the time. More likely, prepositions were forbidden on headline ends because they looked peculiar sitting out there with a lowercase letter at their beginning, back in the days when most major words in heads were capitalized. The alternative, then, would have been to capitalize a preposition on the end of the line but not in the middle.

Would the headlines above cause subscribers to throw rocks at your building? Probably not. The sin is slight, and you can argue that readers will never notice. However, I would like to operate on the premise that there is a little bit of artist in all of us and that a line ending with a preposition is slightly less artistic than one that ends another way. The Egyptians of 50 centuries ago produced some magnificent art, but at one stretch they had great trouble with perspective. They indicated distance by placing one figure above another. The shortcoming is not ruinous, but it is noticeable. Same goes for prepositions on the ends of headlines.

Q. *Which heads here are acceptable under the preposition rule?*

a. **Barbers go onto
welfare rolls**

b. **Barbers go
on welfare**

  c. **Teachers punished**   *d.* **Teachers stand in**
   for shortcomings   **classroom corners**

  e. **2 shot down in**   *f.* **Bowery bar gunfight**
   Bowery bar   **leaves 2 dead**

  g. **No love lost in**   *h.* **Mayoral foes**
   race for mayor   **slugging it out**

Heads *b*, *c*, *f*, *h* satisfy the rules. You may be unsure about *h*. If "in" is a preposition, isn't "out"? Not here; it's an adverb under the normal definition or part of an idiomatic verb under another. The idiomatic verb's infinitive form would be "to slug it out."

Q. *Glance back at the list of restrictions. Bearing them in mind, let's rewrite these headlines with the same number of lines and approximately the same count. Do not be overly concerned about general quality.*

  a. **Mayor, melon**   *b.* **3 die as ship**
   dealer argue   **hits bridge on**
             Louisiana lake

  c. **Seven killed in**   *d.* **County shocked by**
   Mexico quake   **Carter aid plan**

Here are some suggestions:

Melon dealer,   **Melon dealer**
mayor argue   **battles mayor**

3 die as ship   **Ship collision**   **Bridge struck**
slams bridge   **with bridge kills**   **by ship; 3 die**
in Louisiana   **3 in Louisiana**   **in Louisiana**

Mexican storm   **Storm kills**
leaves 7 dead   **7 in Mexico**

Carter aid plan   **Carter aid plan**
shocking to county   **surprises county**

If you look at the suggested revisions, you will have a great truth revealed unto you: It is difficult to write a headline without some access to the facts. For instance, in the Louisiana bridge story we could have written a far better headline if we had been able to use the facts given early in this chapter. The word "motorists" would have made it clear the dead were not ship crewmembers. Or we might have noted that the three died in a plunge into the lake. Nor did we know about the Mexican storm. Was it a windstorm, a rainstorm, a hailstorm or perhaps a storm of abuse? We have to be specific. Similarly, we might have had a better headline if we knew what our melon dealer was beefing about in his row with the mayor.

At any rate, we have come to grips with a problem and vanquished it. We will meet this dragon in many other heads, and if we pay attention to our sword work, we will slay it just as quickly.

I once worked on a newspaper that forbade the use of any major headline word more than one time on a page. This restriction was often considered to be an underlying cause of the dyspepsia common on the rim. Copy editors are quicker to perceive hardships than are the people who make the rules, the latter generally being people who do not have to labor under those rules. Nevertheless, the evil that led to the restriction, our fourth rule, was real. For confirmation, look at the sports page some Saturday morning in October. Friday night's football games are reported under headlines like these: "Buffs nip Steers," "Tigers nip Bulldogs," "Eagles nip Broncos," "Maroons nip Rebels." Nip, nip, nip. Other pages are seldom as bad. But a front page with two of its seven headlines using "chop" as the main verb, for example, is hard to defend. The solution: Be alert and don't let yourself get into the habit of repeating words. Look at this one:

Ford welcomed in Japan;
second welcome planned

It leaves the reader with a feeling that the copy editor operates with a limited vocabulary.

We have discussed the restriction on our fifth rule, regarding the word *is*; you will be hard put to find a weaker headline word.

Our seventh commandment prohibits abbreviations standing alone. It is meant to bar such things as these:

Gov. flying to Japan

Prof. to retire

Okla. braces for Huskers

Cal. governor renominated

Miss Miss. missing

A hasty examination of daily newspapers will show you that this rule is bent more than some others. One might guess that a majority of newspapers will accept "initial states" as adjectives. To wit:

N.J. theaters closed

N.M. senator gagged

N.C. farmers smoking less

Some newspapers will accept almost any abbreviation as an adjective:

La. man hurt trolling

Penn. senator gagged

Wis. chicken plucked

We narrow the list of newspapers somewhat with the following, which only those with strong throats can take without choking:

Crowd jubilant in Ariz.

Girl hikers head for Minn.

Neb. will vote today

You will probably see the wisdom inherent in this prohibition, but you may question it when you are assigned a 12-count headline about some occurrence in Massachusetts. At that point, you will have to decide whether it is better to sacrifice location or break a rule. Truly skilled copy editors can usually write around such problems; they might locate the event in Boston, for instance.

We have gone through the rules. Review the material in this section. The stuff is important, and you need to be doubly sure you have it nailed down.

A tense situation

The practice of using present tense verbs in newspaper and news magazine headlines lends an air of urgency and freshness to the news—makes it up-to-date. Past tense headlines make it seem the publication is reporting history. Also, use of the present tense for most headlines frees the other tenses for special purposes.

One difference between a headline and a news story is that the story contains a time element, usually a day. The story says "London welcomed President Carter" and then tells us he was welcomed "today" or "Friday" or whenever; we get more than a simple declarative sentence. In the headline, we get a special summary, covering the latest news.

Q. *Which of these headlines is in present tense?*

   a. **Carter chose envoy**
   b. **Carter chooses envoy**

Headline *b*, of course. The word "chose" would be appropriate for a story about an event that happened some time ago. Also, it could go in a headline on a secondary story used to support a story about something an envoy had done. ("Envoy" is the head writer's all-purpose word for ambassadors, some civil servants and most plenipotentiaries.) One remaining possibility: The word "chose" puts emphasis on Carter, sug-

144

gesting there was some debate about whether he or someone else selected an envoy. You avoid the hassle by using the present tense, letting your verbs make clear statements.

Another advantage of present tense verbs is that we can now switch to passive voice on certain heads and shorten our count by dropping the helping verbs. That is,

Elred named envoy

means that Elred is an envoy now, not that he named/chose/selected the envoy. Since most of our readers know we do not use past tense on normal headlines, they will not be misled; they will know Elred has been chosen. We have dropped the *has been* (or *is* part) auxiliary verb, the understood verb.

Q. *What is the normal meaning of the head below?*

Doctors often called in middle of night

It means that doctors' phones ring in the night, not that old-time docs woke people up with midnight telephoning. Frankly, this is not a good headline either way. You would run less risk of misunderstanding with "Doctors often get midnight calls."

Other peculiarities can be found in our tense situation. Since the present tense is for events past, we may wonder what to use for the future or the present. Present tense news *stories* are rare in print. Even a story occurring as the magazine is being printed will usually be written in the past tense, referring to some starting point. For example, the president might at this moment be on a nonstop flight to Japan. But the story would say he *left* Washington at 8 A.M. The headline writer would probably peg the head to the event that occurred at a specific time: "President leaves for Japan."

However, an alternative is available. If we want to describe action going on right now, and at the moment the reader is likely to pick up the paper, we say, "President flying to Japan" or "President on way to Japan." We have left out the *is* in both cases, but our headline is clear.

We can find other uses for the present tense in a headline. Until someone comes up with a better term, let's refer to our next subject as the *durational present* (a term just coined). We can define it as a situation that exists from now until sometime in the future. In light of this definition, the following headline,

Need for copy editors growing

means the need for copy editors is growing today, will be growing tomorrow, and probably will be growing for a while.

We might touch on that again. Here's a lead:

> The Class A Stanton Buffaloes meet the
> favored Class AAAA Big Spring Steers

tonight in the finals of the Odessa High
School basketball tournament.

Assuming that sportswriters have not abandoned several decades of tradition, this story should contain information justifying a headline that says

Buffs hoping for upset

or perhaps even

Buffs facing sternest test

The headline word ''hoping'' means that the Buffs hoped it yesterday, they
hoped it this morning, and they will continue hoping it, no doubt, until the
game ends.
    The cagey headline writer will perceive that this durational present can
apply to some present tense headlines. The headline here,

Buffs hope for upset

does not mean that the Buffs sat down, took a deep breath, and collectively
hoped for an upset. Instead, it means they hoped and are still hoping. What
we have done, then, is increase our options. We can use ''hope'' or
''hoping.'' The difference in count is 1½, which can be just enough in a
tight squeeze. Sometimes the difference is more.

Q. *Count these headlines:*

a. **Buffs seek victory**   b. **Buffs seeking victory**
c. **Buffs go for title**   d. **Buffs going for title**

a. 16, *b.* 18½, *c.* 14½, *d.* 17. You pick up 2½ counts on each headline.

Future tense in headlines is handled three ways:

1. Simple future tense: ''Carter will go to Japan.''
2. Infinitive: ''Carter to go to Japan.''
3. Present tense with a time element: ''Carter goes to Japan Sunday.''

The future tense can be used in headlines. However, the infinitive is
called on more than future tense; it is shorter. That is, ''to go'' is shorter
than ''will go.'' Also, some veterans argue that ''to'' has more snap than
''will.'' Snappiness is often in the eye of the beholder; use the one that fits.
The third option, present tense with time element, lets you specify when the
action will take place. Headline writers should note that the date can also be
used on simple future tense and on the infinitive (. . . to go Sunday), if
space permits.
    Since a date and a present tense verb indicate a future event, headlines
on events that have already happened must not carry a time element. This

situation occurs occasionally on smaller, more hurried newspapers. We get such headlines as "Albert Williams dies Tuesday." This headline is no good unless Mr. Williams is a candidate for capital punishment; the headline says the fellow is going to die next Tuesday.

Here's a lead. Read it, and then we will do some heads on it.

> President Carter left Andrews AFB at 8 a.m. today for a 26-hour jet flight to Tokyo. He will be the second U.S. president to visit the country.

Q. *Write three headlines, fitting them within these counts: a.* 18-20, *b.* 21-23, *and c.* 23-25.

Among the possibilities: *a.* "President off to Japan" or "Carter flying to Japan." *b.* "President flying to Japan" or "Carter takes off for Japan." *c.* "President leaves for Japan" or "President on way to Japan." You could get variety with a different approach:

Carter begins trip to Japan
Carter begins Japanese trip
Carter leaves on Japanese trip
Carter on jet for Japan
Carter heads for Japan
President departs for Land of the Rising Sun

The last one must be on a wide space or in small type.

We take one final look at tense—a fourth option that can be used in special circumstances. In this one, we would say: "President going to Japan."

"Aha!" you protest. "We have already covered this." Not exactly. This headline is good only for the initial announcement of the trip. Furthermore, most verbs do not work in this arrangement. A person can say, "I'm going to Denver," as soon as the decision to travel has been made, long before anyone hits the road. But your headline cannot say, for example, "Moynihan working for U.N.," until he is on the job. Common sense will carry you through on this sort of thing. You must think about what you are doing.

Qualification, attribution

One simple rule guides you in matters of qualification and attribution: If the story is qualified, the headline must be qualified.

Go back to the headline we counted, "Yarber calls president a liar." In that one, we attribute the charge to Yarber. The headline thus contains attribution. It also contains *qualification,* which is the term we use when we show that a statement was made by a source other than the reporter.

A headline saying "Fire hits store" would be unqualified. It would not need qualification, because the smoke and flames that the reporter could see would be a pretty good indication that a fire had indeed hit the store. But if we have a headline saying "Store blaze caused by arson," we are saying we know it for a fact, that perhaps our reporter saw the town pyromaniac heave a torch into the building. That's unlikely, so we shy away from such a head; we need to qualify our headline. We got our information secondhand, probably from the fire chief, so we should say

Arson blamed in store blaze

Now we have put the burden of proof on someone else. We have reported a fact: Someone did say arson caused the fire. Pay attention now: We *qualified* the statement but did not *attribute* it. If we want attribution, not just qualification, we would say

Arson caused store fire, chief says

See the difference? This head credits the fire chief as our source. We have attributed the information to a specific source. The headline is still qualified, since attribution is a form of qualification. (But qualification is not always a form of attribution.)

Q. *Which of these headlines do not have qualification but need it?*

a. **President is a liar**

b. **Sadat termed tough cookie**

c. **New rules to help U.S. auto builders**

d. **New rules considered a boon to automakers**

e. **Vance says Sadat is a tough cookie**

f. **R.T. Ache funeral to be held Tuesday**

a, c. Although we have had a president or two lately who might qualify for the term used here, the newspaper should not make the charge except in its editorial pages or under certain circumstances we will deal with elsewhere. Headline *c* could probably go unchallenged most of the time, depending on the full story. If there is no controversy and everyone agrees that the new rules will help automakers, we can probably get by without qualification. But if the story is about someone saying the rules will help, we have to qualify it. As for item *f*, we are safe even without qualification; death is a fact.

Q. *Recall the bridge story (page 128)? Let's say the ship's captain has been arrested and charged with negligence. Rewrite this headline and get in the required qualification:*

Ship captain arrested for causing accident

That head says ol' Cap *caused* the accident. Could be, but he will get a hearing, and he may prove he was blameless. We cannot say he caused it. We have to qualify our statement. These headlines might do it:

**Ship captain arrested
in bridge collision**

**Ship captain arrested
in fatal bridge crash**

**Ship captain blamed
for bridge accident**

The problem is that our original first headline goes too far. What we mean is that the captain has been arrested on a *charge* that he caused it. We can say that he has been arrested, for he has. Thus our next two headlines are accurate. In the fourth head, we say he has been blamed for the accident. He has; someone swore out a paper blaming him, accusing him of causing the accident. Thus we put the onus on the blamers, not on the newspapers.

In some situations, headline writers convict somebody before the case gets to court. If someone robs a delicatessen, roars away in a car, and then wrecks the car two blocks down the street in the view of the robbery victims, most newspapers and radio stations will name the person as a criminal. The danger is slight. But if the robber gets away and the police later arrest someone on a tip, your libel antennas should pick up some dangerous waves: qualify head and story. (We deal with this kind of thing at greater length in Chapter 9 on libel.) In the meantime, learn to confine your errors to the side of conservatism. If you call a robber a suspect, you have done no great harm to the suspect or to society. But if you call a suspect a robber, you may be in hot water.

The qualification issue goes beyond libel to other problem areas. In our next work, you will first see headlines. Then come some brief summaries of stories—leads, if you want to call them that. Your task is to decide which headlines require qualification. Some of the heads require qualification but do not have it; some have it but do not require it. And some either have it and require it or do not have it and do not require it.

After you determine the situation, write a proper headline. We will disregard count, since you do not have all the story to work with. If the headline is all right as it is (if it neither has nor needs qualification or if it properly has it), say so.

Q. Mayor says he opposes porno sales near schools.

Mayor Martin Elred said today that, as a father, he opposes the sale of pornography near the city's schools.

You don't need to say he *said* it; by merely saying what he did he has voiced opposition to porno sales.

Q. Fenlaw calls commissioners a pack of fools.

> Saying the four county commissioners have wasted taxpayer money for six months, County Judge Rick Fenlaw called them a pack of fools today and said they should be fired en masse.

This one is all right. He did it, clear and simple.

Q. Snowplow operators prefer benefits to pay raise.

> Councilman VanSteenkiste moved to block a pay raise for snowplow operators today. He said they are more interested in free insurance, vacation time and free gasoline than in a wage boost.

We need to qualify this headline. If the head is accurate, VanSteenkiste must be the spokesman for snowplow crews—but we have no verification of that in the amount of story before us. If the story says he was reporting results of a poll (and, again, the story we have does not say that), we might get away with an unqualified headline. As the story stands, you must come up with something as a replacement for the headline offered. Perhaps

Road crews prefer benefits to pay, VanSteenkiste says

Plow crews prefer benefits to raise, council told

Plow crews' preference of benefits claimed

The middle offering is probably the best of this sorry lot. We are handicapped by the length of the councilman's name. It does not give us much trouble on a long one-liner, but such names are the bane of the desk on two- and three-line heads.

Q. Waste, mess cut off City Hall coffee.

> The city council pulled the plug on coffee sales in offices at City Hall today. Council members said city employes have been wasting time and money and have created a difficult cleaning situation.

Can't use this. One man's mess is another man's pudding, or something like that. The council may have given that as an excuse, or it may truly have perceived a mess. Either way, *we* cannot call it a mess. We can either play this one straight ("Council bans office coffeepots") or we can show that the council is the source of messy thoughts ("Council sees mess, bans coffee" or "Council messes with City Hall coffee").

Q. Soviet grain purchase won't affect U.S. food prices.

> The Soviet Union's purchase of American grain will have no effect on food prices in the United States this winter, the secretary of agriculture said today.

We must qualify our grain head. Maybe one of these: "Secretary: Prices to hold despite Soviet grain deal" or "Grain sale's effect on food prices downplayed." Note that the second headline did not mention the purchaser. If the grain deal has been in the news, you have no trouble at all with such a headline. If the sale has not received prominence lately, and thus readers are not likely to pick up on the story immediately, you have an imperfect headline—usable, but imperfect.

Q. Farm laborers riot in Mexico.

> LOS MOCHIS, Mexico (EP)— Rioting broke out in this West Coast tourist stop today when agriculture workers marched into town to demand higher wages. Police spokesmen said a group of nearly 1,000 cane field workers tore up the town's two main shopping areas before they were dispersed with tear gas.

You probably accepted this headline. It is all right with this story, although prudence (nurtured by hindsight) might cause you to read deeply into the story before forming a headline. If the story is accurate, the headline is accurate.

Q. Police break up Mexican labor march.

> LOS MOCHIS, Mexico (OP)— Federal police with tear gas, guns and billy clubs broke up a peaceful demonstration by cane field workers today. They chased the 1,000 marchers through the city's two shopping areas, which suffered heavy damage from bullets and rocks.

If you read the story first, you probably approved the headline offered. Fine; it fits the story, and all we have to do, again, is hope the story is accurate.

You will not get a dose of ideology in this book, but you will get an occasional reminder that different sides sometimes tell different stories. Our reporter, who called the demonstration peaceful, was obligated to tell us why the *federales* broke it up. Did the police act first?

We cannot produce answers here. All we can do is remind you that there are always questions. Unlike our Chicago fire chief, our Mexican police source has something to lose if the story is told from the wrong viewpoint. So would the marchers' leader. Therefore, we offer special incantations to ensure accuracy by our reporter. And, to help the gods along, we qualify story and head in some cases.

Before leaving this general area, we need to touch on one other aspect of qualification that has to do with the kicker headline. Kickers are often ignored by readers, who do not appreciate the amount of work or native intelligence required to produce a headline. You, as a headline writer, must plan for the possibility that your finest work will go unnoticed when kickers are involved. You have to write the kicker head so that the main head can stand alone in case a reader doesn't see the kicker. (Sometimes, moreover, kickers are removed by accident or design in the composing room; a tight story may squeeze in if the kicker is killed.) The main headline—the big type—must contain the key facts, and it cannot depend on the kicker. Instead, consider the kicker's job to be amplification or clarification. It should add something. Let's look at one.

Q. *What is wrong with this headline?*

FBI believes
Kennedy assassin had help

The qualification is in the kicker. Main head cannot stand alone.

Q. *Try another. What is wrong?*

Grower's forecast
New tomato variety sure to hog market

Same thing. The headline makes a flat statement, but the kicker shows that we are only reporting someone's guess.

Let me summarize the thinking here. If we read the headline carefully, we see clearly that the story is qualified. The story is not reporting that this new tomato has the market nailed down; it is saying a grower believes or predicts it will do that. If the forecaster says it will snow tonight, we do not write a story saying it will snow; we write one saying the forecast is for snow. It may be wrong. You must understand the difference between reporting something as fact and reporting that someone said it.

Editorializing

It is but a short hop from the cane fields of Los Mochis to our next problem, editorializing. The problem arises most often when we apply words of value judgment. The reporter should do the first screening, making sure the story indicates that we are reporting something, not necessarily endorsing the source's views. Take this lead:

> Gov. Jerry Brown of California blamed his showing in public opinion polls this week on "a very negative press."

If we use a headline saying "Biased press hurts Brown," we have told the reader that *we* have confirmed that the press is indeed biased. That is editorializing.

Q. *Rewrite the Brown headline, ignoring count.*

"Brown says press bias hurt him" would do it. So would "Brown blames press for poll showing." Ditto "Brown says press bias did him in."

Q. *Here are more headlines. Some, even without the news stories that prompted them, can easily be seen to contain editorializing or some other flaw that requires qualification. Check those that should be revised. Tell what the problem is.*

a. **Nixon looks better in latest interview**
b. **Carter worrying businessmen**
c. **Carter excesses worry businessmen**
d. **Oil producers call proposal outrageous**
e. **Oil producers agitated over proposal**
f. **'Outrageous' oil proposal under fire**
g. **State bar criticizes Michigan D.A.**
h. **D.A. criticizes bar's double standard**
i. **D.A. says bar uses double standard on him**
j. **Brazilians plan to jack up coffee price**

You should have checked *a, c, f, h* as the transgressors. We will look at all:

a. The word "better" is judgmental. You need to tell who thinks Nixon looks better in this interview. If you are dealing with a columnist—and our problem noted that we were working with news stories—you need some clear indication that the piece contains opinion.

b. Assuming that this story expresses results of interviews with, or a poll of, businessmen, we can use this. We were reporting worry, which is reportable. (However, if our head had said "Carter threatening businessmen," we would need to indicate that businessmen were "perceiving" Carter as a threat. Since any threat is from without, the businessmen are not the final authorities.)

c. This one contains another value judgment: excesses. We cannot say the program has excesses. We can say someone perceives excesses. But that's all.

d. Again, not guilty. It does not matter whether the program is outrageous or magnificent; people can call it anything they wish. We don't even need quote marks on this one, since it's a normal word.

e. Ditto. Granted, "agitated" is a fairly lively word, but we can trust our reporter to use an accurate label. This is less trite than saying they are up in arms.

f. You will find some people who think that quotes around a word are the only qualification necessary. They are wrong; if the reader does not pick up the quote marks, and many do not, the headline has passed judgment on a proposal. Get a little clearer qualification.

g. Nothing wrong here.

h. Here is another example of my easy grading policy. You can accept this one if you believe a true split-level standard has indeed been set up and the story brings it out. Normally, however, "double standard" is strictly a pejorative term, strictly an attack on some source of criticism or other judgment. (If we change the word to "hypocrisy," we cannot accept it. For us to say he is criticizing the bar's hypocrisy, the bar has to have a supply of hypocrisy, which means we could have written a story earlier and said the bar was a den of hypocrites. Although I would hesitate to accuse a lawyer of being more honest than good sense required, I would not write a news story saying one or more was a hypocrite.)

i. Nothing wrong here. He says they laid for him and bagged him.

He could say they cheated him or lied to him or tricked him. If he says it, we can say he said it. We can't say they did, but we can give his side.

   j. "Jack up" is a first cousin of slang, or perhaps a member of the immediate family. Still, it is accurate, and thus it is usable. And so is the headline. If we said "Brazilians plot to," we would have a coffee bean of a different color; "plot" is a judgment word.

Punctuation problems

Punctuation rules change a bit when we get to headlines. Here are the most common departures:

1. Periods are used only in abbreviations.
2. The semicolon replaces the period; it indicates a complete stop.
3. Quotation marks are trimmed in half (', not ").
4. The comma indicates a pause.
5. The comma can be used to replace the word *and*.
6. Exclamation points should be banned or used sparingly.
7. The dash can be used on occasion in a headline to show a quirk, a twist of thought.
8. The colon can replace a verb in some instances.

Beginners have more trouble with the comma and the semicolon than with any other headline punctuation.

   The comma serves a useful purpose in replacing *and*. Here are some typical uses:

**Carter, Nixon   Carter promotes
talk briefly   Jones, Smythe**

The first headline was a compound subject, Carter and Nixon. The comma substitutes for the *and*. The second headline has a double object, Jones and Smythe. Again, the comma replaces the *and* properly.

**Carter promotes Jones,
downgrades Williams**

Here the comma replaces *and* in a compound sentence. Note that the headline has only one subject, Carter. Carter promotes and Carter downgrades. (If you're thinking about *giveth* and *taketh away,* forget it. It's dirty pool. May be sacrilegious. Besides it won't fit; I tried it.) With a headline that has only one subject, as this one does, you will almost always use a comma. If it has two subjects, each with a predicate of its own, you will probably use a semicolon:

**Carter promotes Jones;
Williams downgraded**

Jones promoted; Carter
downgrades Williams

In both cases, we introduce a new subject for the second part of the headline. The comma would be proper with only one subject in a headline, like these:

Ford pardons Nixon,
sees key aide quit

Raiders win conference,
begin Super Bowl work

The comma normally replaces *and,* true, but it does not do so in all cases. Many times a headline will sound better with the word *and.* The headline writer develops an ear for such instances. One might be:

Moses reaches land of milk, honey

Some readers might think you were using sweet-talk; others, more astute, would realize that the full idiom rings truer to the ear:

Moses reaches land of milk and honey

The first headline, with the comma, is technically correct. But it breaks the land of milk and honey down into a land of two specific things and that was not what was meant in Exodus 3.

Let us recap: The comma indicates a pause. The semicolon indicates a stop, a headline period. One subject, one verb: comma. Two subjects, one verb: comma. One subject, two verbs: comma. Two subjects, two verbs: semicolon, probably.

Q. *Are these headlines punctuated correctly? Why are the wrong ones wrong?*

a. **Carter praises 2; promises moon trip**
b. **Viks nip Jets, bag first place**
c. **Angola violence renewed; toll soars**

Only *a* is wrong. To test that view, note the semicolon and then try to find a subject after it. None there. *b.* The Viks nip and the Viks bag, a case of a simple subject and a compound predicate. *c.* We have two sentences, two complete thoughts; use a semicolon.

Q. *Some more of the same:*

a. **Inflation rips U.S., Mexico**
b. **Inflation belts Mexico, crime rate soars**

  c. **Inflation belts Mexico, causes misery, crime**
  d. **Mexico belts inflation; gets grip on peso**

a. The first one is all right. Inflation rips two objects. That's one subject, one verb, and two objects. *b.* You have two distinct sentences here. One mentions inflation and the other crime. Use a semicolon. *c.* This one is technically correct—that means it meets the requirements but has a flaw. It is correct because it uses a comma on the one-subject-two-verb arrangement, as is proper. But the second comma throws things off. Readers will find this multiplicity of commas slightly confusing. You would be better off with "Inflation belts Mexico; misery, crime growing." Even this has a little too much punctuation, though it is technically correct. You can only hope the reader will come to a dead stop at the semicolon and then tackle the second part as a separate unit. *d.* The semicolon tells the reader to stop and start a new sentence. But our second sentence has no subject; we have a single subject with a compound predicate: Mexico belts and gets. Use a comma. If you keep the semicolon, make "peso" a subject and find a verb.

The decision to use single quotes in headlines was made purely to save space, as far as I know. That means I do not know where to go to look it up and can't find anyone who does. The saving of space can be of moderate value; it amounts to one count per headline. On occasion, the use of single quotes can cause problems. This headline appeared over a story about a team called the Longhorns:

' 'Horns will come back'

The newspaper had to have one mark for the opening of the quote and another next to it to show that "Longhorns" had been abbreviated. Looks odd. I would drop the apostrophe in the abbreviation.

If you disagree with this advice or even with the whole thought that single quotes are better, you may be right. Try to persuade the person in charge that you are right.

Guideline 5 deals with the exclamation point. Not much to it. The exclamation point, sometimes called an astonisher or the "mark of self-admiration," seldom contributes much to a headline. If you like it, use it. The mark was quite popular around the time of the Spanish-American War.

That gets us to the dash. Generally, the dash should be used to indicate a twist, a change of direction.

Farmer prefers organic methods—naturally

This magnificent headline must be filed away until we find a story it fits. Note that the dash sets the reader up for the little twist, the little play on words that brightens a headline.

Compare that last headline with

Farmer prefers organic methods, naturally

This is not fair, of course, since no headline is going to be as bright on the second reading as on the first. Still, I argue that the dash does a slightly better job. Bonus thought: You can get a similar effect with ellipses (. . .) as with the dash. Try it sometime.

The dash has two other assignments—as strong parentheses to set off part of the head and as an attribution mark. The parenthetical part goes like this:

24 Ridley's turtles—the rare ones—found on Padre Island

We could use parentheses, but the dashes are a dab stronger. Ellipses would not cut it here.

As for attribution, some newspapers use the dash at the end of the headline to name the speaker.

Turtle colony grows at snail's pace—Ridley

Such a headline would indicate that someone named Ridley has expressed himself about turtles. The advantage for a headline writer is that "Ridley" and a dash are shorter than "Ridley says."

Some newspapers prefer the colon to the dash in questions of attribution. They would say

Turtle colony grows at a snail's pace: Ridley

A newspaper reader who realizes that the dash stands for attribution probably will understand that the colon does the same thing. The advantage of a colon is in count: ½ for a colon and 1½ for a dash. I once worked on a newspaper that used the colon for attribution at the beginning of a headline and the dash for attribution at the end, thus:

Ridley: Turtle colony grows at snail's pace

Doesn't matter. But your newspaper ought to be moderately consistent from day to day.

Many good publications forbid the use of colons or dashes to replace verbs. Such a prohibition can be defended readily. At best, the colon and dash are shorthand and require cooperation from the reader.

However, we should not auction off our supply of headline colons. Forfend. The colon can follow a noun and replace the predicate. In that spot, it indicates that the headline is a statement about the subject. Some examples:

Havasupai harvest: a feast or famine

Alaska pipeline: coldest job in the world

Sumo wrestling: survival of the fattest

We have replaced the verbs with colons, but no one will misunderstand these heads. This headline trick can be worn thin in a hurry. It is not a desperation shot to be saved for a tough headline, but it is enough out of the ordinary to prevent our using it more than once or twice a day.

Our typewriters contain a few top-row characters that we might mention. Some of them are proscribed by various publications. You must learn which way the wind blows at your place of business and set your sails accordingly. For instance, this headline,

Ali defeats Foreman
& gets his title back

would never make it at the *New York Times.* It could easily pass muster across town at the *New York Daily News,* where some rules are more relaxed. (The *Times* has a circulation of less than 1 million; the *News,* more than 2 million. The ampersand probably has little influence on circulation figures.)

Some publications forbid the use of the percent sign, the cents mark, and perhaps some others. Spelling out *percent* in a headline leaves you with little room for other goodies, it seems to me, but this is a local decision.

Though I would go with the symbolists on %, I side with the conservatives on abnormal use of the dollar sign. It's fine on $10 or $10 million, but all the cleverness long ago dripped out of this kind of use:

World Serie$ great for Mets

Every headline writer should be permitted to write one such headline. After that, the offense would be grounds for instant dismissal, including forfeiture of pension funds and back pay.

Only slightly less heinous is the crime in which the headline writer offers this:

Mets have eyes for Series $$

or, heaven forbid:

It doesn't make ¢

Eschew such vulgarity.

Capitalization

You can find just about any style of capitalization you want in American newspapers. The trend is toward downstyle, in which only the first word and proper nouns are capitalized, as in sentences. The traditional newspaper capitalizes all words except prepositions in the middle of a line. A few newspapers still cap every word.

We have used downstyle headlines in this book because of the nationwide move to that style. I was opposed to downstyle headlines not long ago, but a little moonlighting on a downstyle desk, coupled with observations of others who have used both styles, has changed my mind. The extra count and the aesthetic appeal of downstyle offset a century or two of tradition. And some research (inadequate, to be sure) indicates that people can read downstyle heads as well as any other, particularly if adequate spacing is maintained between words. So we will use downstyle. You will have no trouble converting to any other style if you go to some publication that requires it.

Putting it all together

We might devoutly hope at this point that all the rules and regulations and guidelines we have bitten off so far will not choke us here on the threshold of victory. We are getting ready to put into practice all the things considered to date in this rather long chapter. We are going to write headlines. We will do it step by step. Here is a story we will use for our first headline. Read it and then follow instructions.

> EAST LANSING, Mich. (GP)— Tomato harvests increased by 90 percent in three Michigan counties where growers used a new Mexican watering system, scientists from Michigan State University reported today.
>
> Growers flooded their fields with irrigation water equal to six inches of rain every other week. Comparison plots were irrigated the usual way, with an inch of water once a week.
>
> Dr. N. O. Picre of MSU said the dramatic increase in yield caused no loss in quality. He said the idea may mean economic salvation for hard-pressed growers.

You are on the copydesk of the *Detroit Free Press,* and the copy chief tells you to write a headline on that story. Let's say he calls for a 3–30–2, and the head chart tells you to write two lines, flush left, each with a maximum count of 27 (and thus a minimum of 25).

We will walk through it.

Q. *What words or phrases are most important to this story—the keys to an enlightening headline?*

"Tomato," "harvest," "watering," "increase." It will be nice if we can use the percentage, too, but it is not mandatory.

Q. *Do we have a verb? Active voice? Present tense? If not, list one.*

We used "increase," which can be a verb or a noun. (We will get others on this next question.)

Q. *Provide synonyms for all your key words.*

We do not have a good synonym for "tomato." Although your grand-mother may call it a love apple, we had better stick with "tomato." But for "harvest" we have crop, yield, output, production, . . . , the list can go on and on. And for "watering" we offer irrigation, flooding, soaking, or even just water. If we want to be less specific, we can refer to a plan, an idea, a system, a trick. Our verb of increase can be almost anything: jumps, rises, boosts, soars, goes up, leaps, swells, blooms, grows—choose whatever fits the story best.

Q. *Now, write a sentence of sorts, using the material just covered. Make sure the sentence does these things:*

a. Focuses on the most important item(s).
b. Uses present tense verb, preferably in active voice.
c. Keeps modifiers and modified words on the same line.
d. Does not editorialize or omit necessary qualification.
e. Fits the prescribed count of 25–27.

Instead of giving you an answer right away, I want to look at a mediocre head and see how it might be shaped into something better. Check this first:

Mexican gardening idea helps
harvest in U.S. tomato fields

Is that a good headline? It's so-so, and you have seen hundreds like it. The headline lacks specificity: it does not zero in on the subject. It is pad-ded. Why use the word "gardening"? It adds nothing. Why "helps"? It is vague. And why "fields"? The bottom line would give us just as much information as now if it said "U.S. tomato yields" or only "tomato yields." So we might try something like this:

Tomato growers boost yields
with Mexican idea on watering

The top line passes at first glance, but it might be tightened. "Growers" is not really vital here; we would not expect anyone to have a tomato crop except people who grow tomatoes—the people we call growers. The bottom line is passable. "Mexican watering idea" would be better, but it's short. Let's see what else we might do, what we might use to replace some of the count we are saving.

Tomato crop increased 90%
with biweekly flooding

Aha! Now we tell the reader the size of our increase. Good. Still, the top line has a minor flaw; it is not fatal, and it is fairly common.

Q. *What is the flaw in the top line?*

Check item *b* in the previous question for the answer.

Q. *That brings us to the counting problem on the bottom line: We're too short. Count both lines. What do you get?*

The counts are 26 and 19½.

The veteran copy editor would know by looking that the second line of the head is short, and you will develop that ability before long. At any rate, we have to have 5½ more counts, and we can take as many as 7½. That gives us ample room to maneuver. Might try this:

with biweekly 6-inch flooding

Such a line would fit. If it were short, we might use "floodings." We might spell out "6," although some newspapers do not give copy editors leeway on low numbers. If the head proved to be long, *biweekly* could become *"regular,"* or *"6-inch"* could become *"deep."*

Have we produced a perfect headline? No. We might push for something livelier in the top line. Maybe:

Tomato output jumps by 90%

The problem—a borderline problem—is that *jump* is almost an editorial word. We must realize there is a difference between "going up 10 percent" and "soaring a whopping 10 percent." Nevertheless, an increase of 90 percent can probably be called a jump without alienating too many readers. You decide.

We might worry about our lack of qualification. We are taking the word of our scientists that this has happened. The story mentioned a comparison plot, so this was more than just a chance operation. However, if you believe the headline should be qualified (I do not, but some astute people will), you might offer something like these:

Floods boost tomato harvests
90%, Michigan scientists say

90% boost in tomato yields
reported in MSU experiment

(In Michigan, "MSU" is perfectly acceptable; elsewhere, it is borderline or improper.)

We have covered some of the normal avenues for headlines on this story. We have not dealt with the little word plays that sometimes distinguish good headlines (or the sadness that occurs when someone pushes too hard for cleverness and looks silly). The last paragraph of our story mentions economics. That prompts this characterization:

Flooding boosts tomato yields,
may help growers keep afloat

One caveat: The word *may* gets too much work in publications everywhere. It lacks strength, since almost anything *may* happen. Use it sparingly.

Q. *We need to do another one. Here's the story:*

> Thomas A. Murphy, chairman of
> General Motors Corp., said today the
> coming model year will be a boom
> year for new car sales, even if sticker
> prices increase and gasoline climbs to
> 90 cents a gallon.
> He said higher prices may stimulate
> sales by forcing motorists to buy
> more fuel-efficient cars.

Your copy chief, an inconsiderate chap, tells you to write a three-line
head with lines of 11–13. Please do so.

Some possibilities:

a. **GM chairman**
    predicts boom
    in auto sales

b. **Big sales year**
    in cars seen
    by GM head

c. **GM chairman**
    sees big year
    despite prices

d. **GM forecast:**
    big sales year
    despite prices

e. **Prices to be**
    no sales bar,
    GM predicts

f. **Sales to boom**
    despite prices
    Murphy says

Six perfect headlines? Hardly; they have flaws, just as almost any head
will when the writer is hemmed in by such a tight count. Let's look at
them:

Our *a* is probably the best of the lot. Its major drawback is that it
opens with the chairman rather than with the sales boom. Still, it uses active voice and comes on straightforward and clear. Something like this
would be acceptable on most desks.

Headline *b* puts the emphasis on the big year, but it has to fall back
on the verb "seen," which is imperfect. That is not a horrible substitute
for "predicts," especially since it fits, but it falls short of being wonderful. Also, it uses passive voice. And we had to cut our officer's title down
from "chairman" to "head." ("Head" and "boss" are slangy, too informal for some people. They may be used, but better words should be
chosen when the count permits.)

In *c*, we use "see" in active voice, and we introduce the price angle.
The headline is acceptable.

We get another acceptable headline in *d*. You might argue that Murphy, not GM, is the speaker, but that's a minor objection. Presumably,
GM's chairman has some say around the place and can pass as a
mouthpiece. (The danger of taking an officer as the official voice of the
whole organization is greater in governmental contexts than in corporate
ones. You go overboard if your headline says "U.S. supports"
something just because the secretary of state or some ambassador made a
speech supporting it.) This headline packs in quite a bit of information,
including identification and action in the top line.

Our *e* tells quite a bit, but it does not mention the boom. It could be read as saying that if there is a sales barrier, it won't be prices.

One flaw in *f*: Murphy has yet to achieve worldwide fame. Some people will not know who he is. Use of the name preceded by the identifying "GM" would be fine; readers may not know who he is, but they will know he speaks for the company. "GM's Murphy" counts 12½ and could replace "GM chairman" in the two headlines that use that term. I prefer "GM chairman," however, since it is specific to readers who do not recognize Murphy except as the name of a woman who uses overalls as a chowder base.

Q. *We'll try another. Here's the first part of the story:*

> Fact: You need help desperately with a dangerous and unhealthy flooding condition in your apartment house in the middle of the night.
>
> Fact: In a city with a quarter-million employees—half of them supposedly working for the health and well-being of the city's inhabitants—you can't get help. These two facts added up to one more for Edward Rose: "Nobody cares."
>
> Rose, 46, made his complaint as he dumped a 10-gallon barrel of water into the sink in his apartment at 152 W. 143rd St. It was 2 a.m., and Rose was standing in two inches of water.
>
> The flood that came to a crest early yesterday started with a simple drip in April. Rose's story of beating his brains against city and private bureaucracy began at the same time. . . .

This story from New York ran considerably longer, but you have the gist of it. Try your hand with another two-line head, 23 maximum.

Here are some possibilities, with comments:

Leak becomes a deluge
but renter can't get aid

This fairly straightforward headline does the job. The headline contains some action, and the reader gets a fair picture of the situation.

Renter up to his ankles
in floodwater and despair

We are almost guilty of joking about the fellow's plight in this one, and that's dangerous. The "up to his ankles" bit is the sort of wording normally used on something humorous. Furthermore, "his" could be called padding. However, the headline has a better sound with it. Next, we get to "floodwater." How did we decide between floodwater and plain H$_2$O? Floodwater fits the count. You are always in danger when you force something like that. You may want to call it drip water. Finally, we used a word you may consider unnecessary: "and." I defend it; it goes well here. The "and" strengthens the head. We have put this guy in up to his ankles literally (in water) and figuratively (in despair). The "and" helps readers distinguish between the literal and the figurative.

Renter dips into despair
as leak turns into deluge

Here we have used another play on words—"dips" goes well in a flood story. The head does not poke fun at our renter, so it is usable. We might have had him sinking into woe, but "despair" is better.

And that brings us to the one that appeared on this story, which is from the *New York Daily News*. It said:

He has a flood of gripes,
but no one gives a dam

Perfect? No, but not bad. Some people would argue that "he" is vague; it is, a little. (If you get fired from enough copy editing jobs, you will eventually land on a newspaper that will forbid such an approach.) The word "he" is better and shorter than "man," and it is nearly as specific as "renter." The articles ("a") pad the head, in one sense, but they also make it more euphonious. The second "a" is almost mandatory; we would have awkward reading with "nobody gives dam." If we put an "a" there, we can balance things nicely with the other one in the top line. You will note that the play on words works out all right: In a flood, you need a dam.

You have completed a tough chapter. You may want to go back over it from time to time as a refresher course. Or you may want to burn it as a symbol of hard work. Headline writing can indeed be hard work, but it can also be fun. Here's hoping that your headlines turn out to be fun—and that they all fit.

[8] *News from the wire services*

ONE DOES NOT DISCUSS handling of wire copy in the electronic era without trepidation, because today's clever methods and solutions quickly become outdated. New technology accounts for much of the obsolescence as more functional machines are invented to meet editing needs. But despite vast changes, the basic organization and goal of the wire services remains the same. The services still gather information with telephones and shoe leather and still send it to newspapers and broadcast stations. How they send it is another story.

Neither of the two major news services in this country, United Press International (UPI) and Associated Press (AP), uses the word *customers* in referring to people who use their material. AP has members; UPI has clients. The difference is significant. AP, the older of the two services, is a cooperative. News organizations that get the service are members of the cooperative, and they are obliged to furnish their news for AP use. AP often sends a member's story out on the wire, unchanged, directly to other members. UPI, on the other hand, works on a straight sale basis. You pay your money and UPI sends you the news. You need not give UPI your stories.

Rates for the two services are substantially the same, despite AP's news-sharing requirement. The requirement is not truly onerous; you are not compelled to give AP your exclusive story in advance and thus let news outlets in your area beat you to the newsstand with it. However, nothing prevents a competitor from using your work as a great big news tip and preparing a story to match it. You cannot copyright facts; you can copyright only the method of presentation.

The Associated Press in its present form began in 1900, although it can trace roots to 1848 in a New York group. United Press was founded by E. W. Scripps in 1907, primarily in opposition to AP policies, although the thought of profit may have crossed Scripps's mind. The Scripps-Howard organization still owns a majority of UPI stock. The *I* in UPI comes from International News Service, founded by William Randolph Hearst in 1909. INS was absorbed by UP in 1958.

The UP-INS merger reduced the field to two major services, but an abundance of lesser creatures remained to nibble at specialized parts of the pie. The *New York Times* has long maintained a news service that concentrates on think pieces—analyses and other heavy material—leaving the daily run of catastrophes and minor triumphs and tragedies to AP and UPI. The *New York Daily News* and *Chicago Tribune,* connected by family ties and editorial page kinship, have a news service that runs toward columnists and opinion pieces. The *Washington Post* and *Los Angeles Times* teamed up in 1962 to exploit their strengths—West Coast and Asia for the *Times,* politics and government for the *Post*—and have done well. They started their news service with 45 clients and are now pushing 450.

Reuter's, a London organization, challenges AP and UPI on fast-breaking news more than any other service. The news is ordinarily of international import.

To supplement these services, we have syndicates, a plethora of syndicates. Syndicates are news and feature organizations that will send you just about any kind of feature you want. You can get Beetle Bailey, B. Jay Becker on Bridge, and Hints from Heloise from King Features. You can get Dennis the Menace, Ann Landers, and Food and Your Health from Field. You name it: some syndicate has it. Some live and die with one feature. Some offer the works, including news interpretation.

Normally, syndicates work by mail, although increased transmission speeds have led the wire services to move their material electronically. UPI Data News, for example, moves material from a couple of dozen organizations, including direct competitors King Features and United Features. Data News zips textual material from a New York computer directly into a newspaper's computer. Saves stamps. At the moment, transmission is limited to words, but you may safely mortgage the homestead and bet on transmission of photos and line art (cartoons) in this generation.

Working by mail, syndicates have not customarily had the timeliness or urgency of wire services. Most syndicated material has a long shelf life; a great amount of it is prepared and sent out as much as six weeks ahead of release time. I used to talk the amusements editor of the *Houston Chronicle* into letting me check my favorite comic strips ahead of time. I enjoyed reading six weeks of Pogo at a whack, though it took some of the shine off the comic page for the period.

Some comic strip artists cut it closer. Garry Trudeau, who does Doonesbury, tries to cut the time to a couple of weeks. His Universal Press Syndicate is set up to handle the strip under those conditions and can do so by concentrating its energies on getting it out.

So what does all this mean to you? That depends on what kind of work you do. If you are a reporter for the *Caliche County Mud Dobber,* you are unlikely to be wooed by the syndicate sales people. But if you are the managing editor or features editor of the *Louisville Courier-Journal,* your mailbox will never be empty and you will eat a lot of meals with people who want to sell you something. (Incidentally, the managing editor is normally the final authority on the purchase of a syndicated feature, although department heads tell the managing editor what they want.)

If you work on the copydesk, you will become intimately acquainted with wire copy. You may even become the wire editor, the person in charge of all news service material. In some places, the wire editor is called the telegraph editor. (Many of us old-timers prefer this term from another era because we believe it has a faintly romantic ring to it.)

The handling of wire copy has changed drastically in the past decade, in the past year, maybe even in the past month. In the old days, the news clattered in at 66 words per minute on the Teletype machine. Now it comes in 20 times that fast, without the clatter. Their computer talks to your computer, and you sort of listen in on the side.

You no longer see the complete version of every story. Instead, the wire services send what they call "abstracts," (the lead and a note on the length of each story). AP calls its system DataStream; UPI, Data News. The wire editor examines the abstracts and decides what stories to look at in their entirety. He calls them up on the video display terminal and makes a further decision on running them.

If the wire editor (or news editor or whoever else is in charge) chooses to run a story, it will be sent back to the computer and a copy editor will be told to call it out, edit it, and head it up (put a headline on it). Here's what you, the copy editor, will do:

First, you will enter the typesetting codes, probably the most difficult-to-learn part of electronic editing. (The difficulty comes in remembering all the requirements for printing and all the signals to the computer that you must use to get what you want.) The computer has to be told how wide a column is going to be. Newspapers usually use two basic column widths, one for eight-column and one for six-column pages, but they may use any variation in an effort to improve their layout. Then you must tell the computer what size type you want. Again, newspapers have standard sizes. The most common size type in this country is 9 point (⅛ inch) with a point of space between lines. The headline will be of a different size, of course, and sometimes you depart from the normal size body type. Cutlines are usually different in size and also in typeface. You next have to tell the computer what typeface you want. As before, one face will be standard; you must specify it, and any departures must be noted for the computer.

Newspapers have a slight advantage over magazines when it comes to printing codes: They use much more material in a standard format. Consequently, they can make an agreement with the computer to get the standard size and face with a single command. One equipment manufacturer sets up the system so that "[uf131]," for instance, means, "Use format 131," which is 9 on 10 News Roman, set 10 picas wide.

After you have mastered the coding business, you are ready to get into the work. Remember that what appears on your screen will also appear in the newspaper. Spelling, organization, grammar, facts—these are your responsibility, as noted in the chapter on trimming.

Wire copy

In theory, wire copy should be handled the same as local material; in practice, it isn't. For one thing, a typical newspaper will use less than half the wire service material it gets every day—but this is much better than having only half enough to fill. (If you threw away half of your locally produced copy, you would need a new platoon of reporters.) As for trimming: Copy editors do not boggle at turning an AP opus into a two-graf short; wire service reporters write stories that are designed to be cut from the bottom, usually at the end of almost any paragraph. These stories are written for news outlets all over the country, with the assumption that someone will want the full length and everyone else can trim as necessary. Local stories, on the other hand, are written for your specific audience, and drastic changes are sure to stir the wrath of the author. While I do not suggest that you make your news decisions on the basis of how much harm will be done to a reporter's fragile ego, I will point out that feedback will be forthcoming much sooner on local copy. That is, a wounded reporter will squeal much quicker when his or her copy is butchered by someone on the same payroll than will a wire service reporter who sends you material from across four state lines.

The trick is to edit every story as if your best friend had written it and would examine it after you finished. You do your friend no good if you let sloppy work go by. However, you also do your publication, yourself and your friend no good if you reduce the story to a bland, understated mess of porridge. The good copy editor has to be tough enough to edit sharply without worrying about bruising someone's psyche and without becoming a butcher.

Wire copy differs from local news in another way: It is more likely to be changed before the story is complete. A metropolitan newspaper will have five to seven editions a day—five to seven deadlines. But a wire service will be trying to meet deadlines in four time zones in the continental United States, others for Alaska and Hawaii, and still others around the clock throughout the world. (Indeed, a book about UPI was entitled *Deadline Every Minute.*)

The wire services, particularly AP and UPI, are fiercely competitive. They keep logs on how often they beat the competition to a story, how many minutes they were ahead, and how many newspapers used their stories. In that sense, they have a deadline every minute. However, the wires also have slack times; few reportable events of importance take place between midnight and dawn. In those quiet hours the wire services flesh out their reports with lengthy stories (called *advances*) for later use. Their nature and release time is clearly indicated at the top and bottom of the copy. It is considered improper for you to run on Wednesday a story that everyone else is holding for Thursday, or even to run at 10 A.M. a story embargoed until noon. (Users can be cut off the service if they continually violate release dates. Abuse of release dates is not widespread.) Advances are not sent at the busiest times, between 6 A.M. and noon and between 6 P.M. and midnight. At 66 words a minute, a normal, three-page story would take 8–10 minutes, and a big investigative or contemplative piece might take upward of 20. The wire services do not like to tie up their circuits that long. The problem has diminished with the introduction of computer-to-computer links, of course, since a story that now requires a minute for transmission is a whopper.

The wire services strive to keep you posted thoroughly on what is coming up and on the status of developing stories. An item called the *budget* provides your first clues as to what is in store in your news day. The budget is a digest of the 8–12 major stories that are already prepared or are known to be coming up. From the budget you learn how good the story is, how long it runs, whether it will be topped, and anything else the wire service can pass along to help you decide where to place the story, if you use it. (Clarification: A story that is topped is one that gets a new lead, a new top. Let's say the story is on the agriculture secretary's meeting with disconsolate farmers. The wire service will send you an early story saying they will meet and telling what they will discuss; you can use this in your early edition or in your only edition if you have to go to press before the meeting. The wire service will cover the meeting and will send a new top that reports what happened at the meeting. The top will pick up a large part of the early story as its bottom part.)

Wire services try to move some kind of story as soon as they learn of an event. On a major event, they may move a single sentence as a lead—usually called a *bulletin*. (A *flash,* the highest priority item, is rare; it is reserved for something like a presidential assassination.) The bulletin may be followed in a few minutes, or even immediately, by an *add*, perhaps one or two paragraphs. The add may be marked as a bulletin, too, though it is more commonly termed *urgent*. As more details come in, another add will follow. Maybe this sort of thing would be easier to show than to tell about. So let us show:

```
    a249
        r a byluivqyv a656
    AM-Presley,110
    MEMPHIS, Tenn.  (AP) --
Elvis Presley was taken to the
emergency room of Baptist
Hospital in serious condition
Tuesday afternoon, suffering
from what hospital officials
said was respiratory distress.
    Maurice Elliott, the hospital's
vice-president, said the singer
and entertainer was in the
emergency department.
    "He is being treated," Elliott
said.  "I can't tell you much
more than that."
    Presley was taken from his
Graceland mansion to the hos-
pital in a fire department am-
bulance.
    He has been hospitalized sev-
eral times in recent years for
rest and for eye problems.
        --------
08-16-77  17:15edt
```

At left you have a verbatim transcript of a developing AP story. The "a249" at top left is the story number—"A" wire, story number 249. The letters in the next line are coded information for people who handle Teletypesetter tape. The "AM-Presley, 110" line tells you this is for morning papers, the story is slugged Presley, and it is 110 words long.

The long line tells you the story has ended. The numbers after that give the date and time.

```
     a251
          e: a bylwyfzvt a661
    AM-Presley, 1st ld, a249,40
    BULLETIN
MEMPHIS, Tenn. (AP)--
Elvis Presley, the Mississippi
boy whose country rock guitar
and gyrating hips launched a
new style in popular music,
died Tuesday afternoon at Bap-
tist Hospital, police said.  He
was 42.
    --------
0 8-16-77  17:17edt
```

An unrelated story moved as a250, and then AP came back with this one. The slug line indicates that this is a new lead (ld) on material already sent, namely story a249. The word "BULLETIN" indicates the story is of unusual importance. (On those old slow printers a bulletin was accompanied by five dings of the bell. Today's VDTs don't even hum. A pity.)

Note that the bulletin moved two minutes after the initial story.

```
     a252
          u a bylwyfbyl a663
    Presley, 1st led, 1st add, a251,
170
    URGENT
MEMPHIS: was 42
Presley, who parlayed a $4
trip to a recording studio into a
multi-million dollar business,
was taken to the emergency
room of Baptist Hospital in
serious condition Tuesday after-
noon, suffering from what hos-
pital officials said was respi-
ratory distress.
    Presley was taken from his
Graceland mansion to the hos-
pital in a fire department am-
bulance.  He had been hospi-
talized several times in recent
years for rest and for eye prob-
lems.
    Presley's gyrating hips were
only mildly suggestive com-
pared to most of today's rock
performers.  But when he ap-
peared on the Ed Sullivan Show
in the late 1950s fears about
his sexuality seemed so overt
that he was shown only from the
waist up.
    His shake, rattle and roll
showmanship--with such mil-
lion sellers as "You Ain't Noth-
```

Now we get an add to our 1st ld (bulletin). The number 170 is an approximate word count. "URGENT" is one step down from a bulletin. The "MEMPHIS: was 42" gives us the first and last words of the story as we have it so far.

Here the writer, or perhaps an editor, went into the file and fished out background. Wire services, which don't like to get caught off guard, keep material like this on a great number of newsworthy persons. You may want to consider how much of the rest of this story could have been written months ahead of time.

ing But A Hound Dog," Heartbreak Hotel,"· "Blue Suede
Shoes" and "Love Me Tender,"
kept teen-age girls sighing.

He performed with slicked
back hair, sideburns and a perpetual sneer.

MORE

08-16-77   17:26edt

a255
        r a bylwyfwyf a667
AM-Presley, 1st ld, 2nd add,
a251-a252,150
MEMPHIS: perpetual sneer.

Presley went from driving a
truck to driving the girls crazy
in the mid-1950's. They
screamed, jumped and hollered
as Elvis gyrated about the
stage in sequined skin-tight
outfits.

Frank Sinatra had had that
impact on females a decade before, but with a different style.
No one else did until the Beat-
les came along almost a decade
later.

He once asked his mother:
"Momma, you think ahm vulgah on the stage?"

Elvis said his mother replied:
"You're not vulgah, but you're
puttin' too much into your sing-
in'. Keep that up, you won't
live to be 30."

Elvis Aron Presley was born
in a two-room house in Tupelo,
Miss., on Jan. 8, 1935. During
his prime in the 1960s he carried about 175 pounds on his
six-foot frame but in recent
years was plagued by weight

The word "MORE" tells us that AP
plans to keep sending. The word usually is
not all caps, in case you are looking for a
trivia question.

Two stories on other subjects were
slipped in after the last take. The slug is actually AM-Presley, 1st ld. We are now getting the second add. It goes after the words
"perpetual sneer," as you see.

problems as well as fatigue.
    Elvis didn't smoke, didn't
drink and didn't drive a car.
    More

08-16-77   17:36edt

        a257
            u a bylwyfeev a672
AM-Presley, 1st ld, 3rd add,
    a251-252-255,110   MEMPHIS: a
car.
    Although he didn't drive, he
had a generous habit of giving
cars away, to friends, police-
men and admirers.
    He had more than 30 gold
records--million-sellers.
    His popularity made him a
movie actor, too, and he appeared in about 25 films.
    Thousands of his followers
were proud members of the
Elvis Presley National Fan
Club, which once had 400,000
members in the United States,
Canada, Mexico, Cuba, England, France and Australia.
    At its headquarters in Madi-
son, Tenn., as many as 4,000
letters a day poured in. Each
was processed by one of Presley's disciples.
    Anyone who wrote in was
sent a free membership card--
and an invitation to purchase
autographed photos of the singing star.
    More

    By Les Seago
Associated Press Writer

08-16-77   17:43edt

A single story, a256, got on the wire
before AP came back with more Presley.
The string of numbers tells you what takes
precede this piece of copy. The 110 is for
wordage, and we again have the first and
last words of our material to date.

Note that we have a shorter dash than
usual. That is in case AP has some unusual-
ly dense member who cannot see that the
next words are a by-line, meant for the top
of the story. Then we get the dash to end
that take.

a260

u a bylvyxczc a675

AM-Presley, 2nd ld, a251 et seq,280

URGENT

By LES SEAGO

Associated Press Writer

MEMPHIS, Tenn. (AP)--
Elvis Presley, the Mississippi boy whose rock and roll guitar and gyrating hips launched a new style in popular music, died Tuesday afternoon at Baptist Hospital, police said. He was 42.

Presley, who parlayed a $4 trip to a recording studio into a multi-million dollar business, was taken to the emergency room of Baptist Hospital, suffering from what hospital officials said was respiratory distress.

His physician said he may have suffered a heart attack.

Presley had been a frequent patient there over the past two years.

Robert Walker, director of the fire department's services division, said Presley was unconscious when a department ambulance arrived at Presley's Graceland mansion. The call for the ambulance was received at 2:33 p.m. (3:33 p.m. EDT).

When the ambulance arrived, with a driver and a paramedic, there was a doctor with Presley and he accompanied the singer on the seven-mile trip to the hospital.

When Presley was rumored to be suffering from various incurable diseases, his physicians had blamed his hospitalizations on eye trouble, a twisted colon and on exhaustion.

After a time-out for a258 and 259, AP is back with a new top for this story. It should be somewhat better organized than the original, with smoother transitions. In addition, it will have any new information brought to light. If you are wondering whether Les Seago was writing under pressure, check the times on our different takes. He finished his first story at 5:15 P.M., had the death bulletin at 5:17, and is back with a full new lead that has gone from Memphis to New York and then to the world by 6:01 P.M. Most of us have trouble just typing that fast.

Here's the first mention of heart attack; a respiratory problem was mentioned earlier.

Earlier this year, he cancelled several performances in Louisiana and returned to Memphis where he was hospitalized for what his physicians said was exhaustion.

He had rarely been seen in public recently, and his weight was said to have ballooned.

Presley's death was confirmed by a police department spokeswoman shortly after 4 p.m.

"I can confirm his death, but not the time or the cause," the spokeswoman said.

Presley's gyrating: 4th graf, which was 3rd graf a663.

08-16-77   18:01edt

a261

    r a bylvyxzvt a678
AM-Presley, 1st ld, 4th add, a251-252-255-257-230
  MEMPHIS: star.

The first album to sell one million copies was an Elvis Presley record. Even more astonishing was the fact that the magic mark was reached in only six months.

Although only half of Elvis was shown for the first Sullivan appearance in 1956, the show was watched on a single network by more people than President Eisenhower drew when he made his acceptance speech on three networks.

A television rating service gave Elvis 82.6 per cent of the nation's TV audience to 78.6 per cent for Eisenhower's speech.

His career was interrupted in 1958 when Presley was drafted for a two-year hitch in the Army. It was written in 1960

Something new: a pickup line indicating that previous material received is to be attached here. Start counting grafs with our bulletin (a251) and 1st add (a252). Go to the fourth paragraph. It starts with the words given.

AP is now sending an add to the old lead. The numbers tell us which takes have been sent, with the last number telling us how many words we can expect. The pickup line reminds us that the third add ended with the word "star."

that upon his discharge, Elvis
talked about girls only half of
the time instead of all the time.

Mr. Swivel Hips, as he was
often called at the time, said
that if there was one thing the
Army had taught him it was
that "you can't please everybody."

Presley stuck to singing, the
movie and lucrative appearances in Las Vegas, shying
away from television after he
made it big. He said television
restricted him.

"The music moves me and
that's why I jump around. I
can't do that in television," he
once said. "As soon as I do
they got the camera on my
face for a closeup. Anyone who
sees me on television isn't getting their money's worth like
they are in person."

08-16-77   18:06edt

As of the moment, this is the tail end of
the story. We will have an add shortly.

a269
    u a bylvyzgyv a690
AM-Presley, 3rd ld, a260,440
URGENT
        By LES SEAGO
    Associated Press Writer
    MEMPHIS, Tenn. (AP)--
Elvis Presley, the Mississippi
boy whose rock and roll guitar
and gyrating hips launched a
new style in popular music,
died Tuesday afternoon at Baptist Hospital, police said. He
was 42.

Presley, who parlayed a $4
trip to a recording studio into a
multi-million dollar business,
was taken to the emergency
room of Baptist Hospital, suffering from what hospital offi-

AP has decided to send a new version of
the story, tidying up loose ends. An editor
who has invested time on the other version
many stick with it if it is ready for the
printer and the deadline is close.

The first two paragraphs of the two
stories are the same.

cials said was respiratory distress.

Dr. George C. Nichopoulos,
Presley's personal physician,
said that a heart attack was a
possible cause of death, but
that he could not be sure until
after a post mortem.

A spokeswoman for the Memphis police department said
that detectives were in-
vestigating "the strong possibility that death was a result of
an overdose of drugs."

Hospital officials said the entertainer was found unconscious at his home by his road
manager, Joe Esposito.

Esposito began resuscitation
efforts and called a fire department ambulance. Emergency
medical technicians with the
ambulance continued cardio-
pulmonary resuscitation efforts
on the way to the hospital.

Nichopoulos halted resuscitation attempts at about 3:30
p.m. (4:30 p.m. EDT), according to the hospital.

Presley had been a frequent
patient at the hospital over the
past few years.

When he was rumored to be
suffering from various incurable diseases, his physicians
had blamed his hospitalizations
on eye trouble, a twisted colon
and on exhaustion.

Earlier this year, he cancelled several performances in
Louisiana and returned to
Memphis where he was hospitalized for what his physicians
said was exhaustion.

He had rarely been seen in
public recently, and his weight
was said to have ballooned.

This paragraph names the doctor. The next one brings in the drug angle.

Here are some new details on the chronology.

Nichopoulos's wife said Presley was due to leave Tuesday night on an 11-day tour to begin Wednesday in Portland, Maine.

Presley's gyrating hips were only mildly suggestive compared to most of today's rock performers. But when he appeared on the Ed Sullivan Show in the 1950's, fears about his sexuality seemed so overt that he was shown only from the waist up.

"Everytime I move on television, they write that I'm obscene," Presley once said. "I've seen a lot worse movements than mine every night on TV. Look at all that modern dancing. If I did those movements, they'd want to lynch me. Yet I never read anything criticizing modern ballet."

His shake: 13th graf.

08-16-77 18:37edt

Go back to a260. Count down 12 paragraphs and you will be at the pickup line we had before: Presley's gyrating. Since we have that idea in the lead now, AP goes to the next paragraph for a new pickup.

a274
    u a byleevuiv a710
AM-Presley, 3rd ld, 1st add, a269,240
MEMPHIS: in person."

Earlier this year, there were published reports that Col. Tom Parker, Presley's business manager for 22 years, would leave that job. The report was quickly denied. Presley often said Parker "made me everything I am."

Presley and Priscilla Beaulieu were married May 1, 1967, in Las Vegas, where the music star was performing. The marriage followed an eight-year courtship that began when Presley was stationed with the Army in Germany.

Here is an add for the end of the story. It is marked "1st add" because the whole story, pieced together, makes up the "3rd ld." Note that the pickup line includes the closing quote marks.

They were divorced in 1973.
They had a daughter, Lisa
Marie, now nine years old and
in the custody of her mother.

Presley's love life generated
many rumors, and a recent one
had it that he planned to marry
a 20-year-old beauty, Ginger Alden. She was reportedly spotted
wearing a $50,000 diamond en-
gagement ring from Elvis.

In 1975, Elvis tried to purchase the lavish Boeing 707 jet
once used by fugitive financier
Robert Vesco, but the deal fell
through.

In 1976, while on a two week
vacation in Denver, Elvis
bought at least nine luxury cars
as gifts, dispensing four of
them to city workers. The
city's board of ethics later
ruled the three police officers
and the city doctor could keep the
$13,000 autos.

Last year he made 100 ap-
pearances before about a million fans. At an appearance in
Hollywood, Fla., last February,
one fan was asked whether a
paunchy, 42-year-old Elvis
could still be sexy.

"It doesn't matter," she said.
"He's Elvis."

08-16-77 19:10edt

Here's the new end of our story.

a282
        r a bylryrbyl a732
AM-Presley, 3rd Ld, Correc-
tion, a269,50
  URGENT
  MEMPHIS; To correct that police are NOT investigating a
possible drug overdose, sub 4th
graf; A spokeswoman....of
drugs."
  Capt. John McLaughlin of the

Someone erred. You have the choice of replacing the faulty paragraph with this or of just killing the offending material. Sometimes, if libel or other gross offense is involved, AP will send a "Mandatory Kill." Contract terms require that you make such a deletion.

178

Memphis Police Department
denied an earlier report that
detectives were investigating a
possible drug overdose.

We are not investigating the
use of drugs." said
McLaughlin. "I don't know
where that information came
from but it's not so."

Hospital officials: 5th graf

08-16-77 20:09edt

        a296
          u a bylqvvyx a750
AM-Presley, 4th Ld--Writethru,
3 takes, 480-1,210
    Wirephotos NS2, NY36, NY42,
J02
        By LES SEAGO
        Associated Press Writer
    MEMPHIS, Tenn. (AP)--
Elvis Presley, the Mississippi
boy whose rock 'n' roll guitar
and gyrating hips changed
American music styles, died
Tuesday afternoon after being
found unconscious at his mansion.

The 42-year-old entertainer
was declared dead at 3:30 p.m.
(4:30 p.m. EDT) at Baptist
Hospital, where he had been
taken by a fire department ambulance.

Dr. George Nichopoulos,
Presley's personal physician,
said a heart attack was a possible cause of death, and hospital officials said Presley was in
"respiratory distress" when he
was brought into the emergency room.

Capt. John McLaughlin of the
Memphis Police Department
denied an earlier report that
detectives were investigating a

Things have settled down a little now and
Seago has brought everything together.
The "Writethru" designation tells us this is
a straight shot—no inserts or other little
pieces to be pasted up or merged electronically. The story will be sent in three
segments, indicated by the "3 takes" line;
if sent in one take, it would tie up the line
for about 19 minutes at a fairly busy time,
9 P.M.

After "3 takes," we are told this take is
480 words and the whole story runs 1,210.

Finally, we learn that AP is sending four
Wirephotos with the story.

possible drug overdose.

Memphis Police Director E.
Winslow Chapman said Presley's death would be routinely
investigated by the medical ex-
aminer's office, because there
was no obvious cause of death.

Presley's unconcious form
was discovered at his white-columned Graceland mansion by
Joe Esposito, his road manager. A Baptist Hospita4
spokesman said Esposito began
resuscitation efforts and called
for Nichopoulos and an ambulance.

News spread that Presley
was seriously ill, and radio and
television stations were in-
undated by telephone calls.
Hundreds of people gathered at
the hospital and at Presley's
home. Scores of police were
sent to both sites.

Presley, who had rarely
emerged from his mansion
grounds in recent years except
for performances, had been
hospitalized at Baptist in April
when he cut short a tour in
Louisana and returned to Memphis.

At that time, he was said to
be suffering from exhaustion
and intestinal flu.

In the past two years, he had
also been hospitalized for eye
problems and for what doctors
described as a twisted colon.

Earlier this year, he cancelled several performances in
Louisiana and returned to
Memphis where he was hospitalized for what his physicians
said was exhaustion.

He had rarely been seen in
public recently, and his weight
was said to have ballooned

This paragraph has two typographical mistakes. Neither is horrible. They are mentioned to remind you that even the top-flight pros make mistakes—and copy editors have to read every letter of a story to catch them.

from the 175 he weighed as a
young man.

However, Nichopoulos's wife
said Presley was due to leave
Tuesday night on an 11-day
tour to begin Wednesday in
Portland, Maine. The Cumber-
land County Civic Center in
Portland announced it would
refund the 17,000 tickets that
had been sold for two performances.

Dr. Elias Ghanem, friend of
the Presley family, said in Las
Vegas that he had talked with
Presley's father, Vernon, and
that the elder Presley was taking his son's death "very badly."

More

08-16-77 21:15 edt

a297
      u a bylqyveev a75i
   AM-Presley, 1st Add, 490
   MEMPHIS: very badly
Elvis Aron Presley was born
in a two-room house in Tupelo,
Miss., on Jan. 8, 1935.

He was working as a truck
driver after graduating from
Memphis' Humes High School
when he walked into Sam
Phillips' office at Sun Records
in 1955.

He went from driving a truck
to driving the girls crazy.

Phillips, who recorded such
stars as Johnny Cash, Jerry
Lee Lewis, Rufus Thomas,
Charlie Rich and Carl Perkins,
allowed the 19-year-old singing
guitar player to cut a personal
record.

The song was "Blue Moon of
Kentucky," and the recording

shortly became a hit.

Then followed the million-sell-
ers, "Heartbreak Hotel, "You
Ain't Nothing But a Hound
Dog," "Blue Suede Shoes," and
"Love Me Tender." His career
ended with more than 30 gold
records.

After Col. Tom Parker be-
came his manager, Presley
made his famous appearances
on the Ed Sullivan show.

His gyrating hips were only
mildly suggestive compared to
many of today's rock per-
formers, but when he appeared
on the Sullivan show fears
about his sexuality were so
great the cameras showed him
from the waist up.

"Everytime I move on television, they write that I'm obscene," Presley once said.
"I've seen a lot worse movements than mine every night on
TV. Look at all that modern
dancing. If I did those movements, they'd want to lynch
me. Yet I never read anything
criticizing modern ballet."

He performed with slicked
back hair, sideburns and a perpetual sneer. Women screamed,
jumped and hollered as Elvis
gyrated about the stage in sequined skin-tight outfits.

Frank Sinatra had had that
impact on females a decade before, but with a different style.
No one else did until the Beat-
les came along almost a decade
later.

He once asked his mother:
"Momma, you think ahm vulgah on the stage?"

Elvis said his mother replied"
"You're not vulgah, but you're
puttin' too much into your sing-

in'. Keep that up, you won't
live to be 30."

In the 1960s, Presley's career
continued to climb, despite a
two-year Army tour which sent
him to Germany.

In Germany he met the
daughter of an Air Force officer, Priscilla Beaulieu. They
were married in 1967 and divorced in 1973. They had one
daughter, Lisa Marie, 9.

Although Presley didn't drive
a car, he occasionally made
headlines by giving away expensive automobiles. He gave
Cadillacs to two Denver police
officers who were assigned to
his security details during a
concert there, and he surprised
a hospital nurse with another
Cadillac two years ago.

He occasionally delighted the
fans who crowded around his
Graceland gates by zooming
through their ranks on a mo-
torcycle or three-wheeled vehicle powered by a Volkswagen
engine.

More

08-16-77 21:23edt

a299
    u a bylqyvqyv a753
AM-Presley, 2nd Add,240
MEMPHIS: Volkswagen en-
gine.

Presley's popularity made
him a movie actor, too, and he
appeared in about 25 films.

His fan club once had 400,000
members in the United States,
Canada, Mexico, Cuba, England, France and Australia.

Although only half of Elvis was shown for the first Sullivan appearance in 1956, the show was watched on a single network by more people than President Eisenhower drew when he made his acceptance speech on three networks.

A television rating service gave Elvis 82.6 per cent of the nation's TV audience to 78.6 per cent for Eisenhower's speech.

But Presley stuck to singing, the movies and lucrative appearances in Las Vegas, shying away from television after he made it big. He said television restricted him.

"The music moves me and that's why I jump around. I can't do that in television," he once said. "As soon as I do they got the camera on my face for a closeup. Anyone who sees me on television isn't getting their money's worth like they are in person."

Presley's love life generated many rumors, and a recent one had it that he planned to marry a 20-year-old beauty, Ginger Alden. She was reportedly spotted wearing a $50,000 diamond engagement ring from Elvis.

Last year he made 100 appearances before about a million fans. At an appearance in Hollywood, Fla., last February, one fan was asked whether a paunchy, 42-year-old Elvis could still be sexy.

"It doesn't matter," she said. "He's Elvis."

08-16-77 21:29edt

The story ends here, as a previous one did.

184

```
    a302
           r a zyvczbyl a765
    AM-Presley, 4th Ld-Insert,
    a299 etc,20
    MEMPHIS, to include mother's
death, insert after 14th graf:
Dr. Elias ..."very badly."
    Presley's mother, Gladys,
died almost exactly 19 years
ago, on Aug. 14, 1958. Like Elvis
at his death, she was 42.
    Elvis Aron: 15th graf, which
was 1st graf a297.
    ---------
08-16-77  21:46edt
```

Someone noticed that a mention of the father alone might raise a question, so this insert told of Elvis's mother's death. It got her age wrong, and AP did not correct that mistake until the next day.

```
    a307
           a a zyvczceev a769
    AM-Presley, 5th Ld, a296,260
    Wirephotos NS2, NY36, NY42,
J02
           by Les Seago
    Associated Press Writer
    MEMPHIS, Tenn. (AP)--
Elvis Presley, the Mississippi
boy whose rock 'n' roll guitar
and gyrating hips changed
American music styles, died
Tuesday afternoon of heart fail-
ure.  He was 42.
    Dr. Jerry Francisco, medical
examiner for Shelby County,
said the cause of death was
"cardiac arrythmia," an ir-
regular heartbeat.  He said
"that's just another name for a
form of heart attack."
    Francisco said the three-hour
autopsy uncovered no sign of
any other diseases, and there
was no sign of any drug abuse.
    Presley was declared dead at
3:30 p.m. (4:30 p.m. EDT) at
Baptist Hospital, where he had
been taken by a fire depart-
ment ambulance after being
found unconscious at his Grace-
land mansion.
```

Ordinarily, a writethru will stand up. However, after an autopsy, a statement on the cause of death prompted AP to revise the 4th ld.

Dr. George Nichopolous, Presley's personal physician, said Presley was last seen alive shortly after 9 a.m. Nichopoulos said Presley had been taking a number of appetite depressants, but he said they did not contribute to his death.

Francisco said there was no sign of any drug abuse.

Gossip reporter Rona Barrett had discussed on ABC Television Tuesday morning a book in which former bodyguards alleged that Presley had been using drugs.

Presley's unconcious form was discovered at his white-columned mansion by Joe Esposito, his road manager. A girl friend, Ginger Alden, 20, was at the mansion, Nichopoulos said.

A Baptist Hospital spokesman said Esposito began resuscitation efforts and called for Nichopoulos and an ambulance.

News spread: 7th graf.

08-16-77 22:12edt

This is a little more genteel than previous handling of the drug angle, in which AP raised the question by denying it. This version acknowledges that a question was raised and then gives a doctor's answer.

    a327
        r a zyvbyleev a787
    AM-Presley, 5th Ld-Sub, a307-a296 etc,30

    MEMPHIS, to include Presley's whereabouts in house, sub 8th graf: Presley's unconscious ... Nichopoulos said.

    Presley's unconscious form was discovered in a bathroom at his white-columned mansion by Joe Esposito, his road manager. A girl friend, Ginger Alden, 20, was at the mansion, Nichopoulos said.

    A Baptist: 9th graf.

08-16-77 23:42 edt

Here is the last take, completed at 11:42 P.M. It was a long day for reporters and editors.

Back in the old days and in some shops today, a story like the Presley obituary would cause the paste to fly and gentle curses to tumble from the lips of copy editors. Although the wire services give clear directions on how the pieces fit together (as you see), the physical act of pasting makes for an imperfect process. Nowadays the services can do the piecing together electronically, and UPI favors that approach. The wire services have the ability to send your computer a new version as the story grows or requires revision. No paste, no gentle curses; not much fun, but a lot easier. The drawback to this method occurs when a new version appears after the copy editor has fished the story out of the computer and edited it. If you edit a story with some effort, have it set into type, and get it pasted up, you do not want a whole new story. You want only the paragraph or two necessary to update the story, to correct an error.

However, a completely new story, called a *writethru* (or write-through), is an advantage for those who have not yet handled the original version. Consequently, the wires frequently go through several versions, consolidating the pieces, inserting the corrections, easing the copy editor's work. Wire services worry—with reason—that something will go wrong when editors have a dozen leads, adds, changes, subparagraphs, and such things to wrestle with. Still, the danger of having paste splashed into your coffee has diminished, and the list of copy editors who prefer the old way of handling wire news is small or nonexistent.

We have heretofore discussed the wires as if they operated as monopolies, one to an outlet. Not so; about 500 daily newspapers carry both AP and UPI, and some carry several others. (The number of dailies trying to operate without any wire service is minute.) Double coverage keeps you from missing some stories, but it occasionally hands you another problem: What do you do when you get conflicting information? It happens, to a degree, every day, fortunately not on major stories. In 1961, however, when U.N. Secretary-General Dag Hammarskjöld was killed in a plane crash in Northern Rhodesia, UPI filed the story. An AP reporter saw a passenger at an airport in a nearby country, took the man to be Hammarskjöld, and reported that the secretary-general was alive and well. And when civil rights activist James Meredith was wounded in the head on a protest march in 1966, a reporter thought he heard an official saying he was shot "dead," and AP carried the news; but the official had said Meredith was shot "in the head." UPI is fallible, too; it managed to end World War I a week ahead of everybody else.

[9] *Libel*

LIBEL LAW bears a great resemblance to Kansas weather: If you don't like it, wait a minute and it will change.

Perhaps that is an exaggeration; instead of waiting a minute, you may have to wait as long as a Supreme Court term. Nevertheless, changes do occur regularly, and some of them are as effective as a Kansas cyclone in upsetting things. The *New York Times* v. *Sullivan* case, which we will examine later, was particularly disruptive. *Times-Sullivan* was the watershed case in a long series of court decisions that have shaped libel law.

Journalism schools customarily require—or at least strongly recommend—a course in law. Such courses used to be called "Law of the Press"; but changing times, changing methods and a trend toward verbal niceties have caused us to call the course "Media Law" now, or perhaps "Media Law and Ethics." The title does not matter; the main concern is what you can write without putting yourself and your publication in danger of a libel suit. Properly taught, the course will also remind you that ethical considerations may persuade you not to run some things that you could legally print. (That is, you are not required to give your readers all the dirt you can dig up, even though it may be legally safe to offer it.)

Although I applaud the law class requirement, I would quickly warn you that the course, no matter how wise the professor or eager the student, will not answer all libel questions. It will only point you in a general direction and perhaps give you a straw to fend off the sword thrusts of those who believe they have been unjustly aggrieved.

Such a course may bring you into contact with something you would otherwise pass by—the joy of reading law cases. Although this joy is not universally recognized, particularly by students facing a long night with the books, exposure to study of the law may do you good. You may become a better person.

In all seriousness, I would argue that your education is incomplete until you have some appreciation of the legal system and a modest knowledge of the development of a free press in this country. It is not vital that you know John Peter Zenger was tried for libel in 1735 for calling the governor of New York a fee splitter, which he was. Nor must you know the wording of the Sedition Act of 1798, under which a couple of dozen newsmen were prosecuted. You can cover the courthouse or the White House adequately without knowing much about Milton's famous defense of free expression of thought, given in *Areopagitica*. No, you do not have to know those things. But they are part of the journalist's heritage; they are behind the law that bears on most writing, and you might find them interesting.

Of course, if a semester of libel law is insufficient protection, the lone chaper in this book will be even less of a shield. True. But it is probably wiser to send you into the jungle with a straw—as long as you know it is a straw—than to send you forth full of confidence that you know all there is to know about law, only to be cut down before your time. Your straw can protect you if it is used to tickle your sensors, to warn you of danger.

Danger comes when you write something that hurts someone else without good cause. The basic principle in U.S. libel law is the same as in other laws: People have a right to be secure in their possessions, including a good name, and nothing can be taken away unjustifiably without recompense. If you sully someone's reputation, you are obligated to make it up. It is difficult to restore luster to a tarnished name. Consequently, you may find yourself standing there and throwing money at a libel victim until the pain subsides. Many libel victims require a prolonged massaging with greenbacks before they begin to feel better.

Let's start at the beginning. Try this for a definition of libel: *Libel is defined as the publication of any representation that tends to hold a person up to hatred, contempt, or ridicule; that causes him to be shunned or lose respect; or that harms him in his occupation.* You will not have to look far for variations on that definition. A simpler version might say only that libel is any written defamation. The basic point remains: You libel the person whose name you tarnish in print. In that sense, you commit libel every time you run a story about someone being arrested. However, it is easier to understand libel if you think of it as *unjust* defamation.

(Let me briefly take up a problem in definitions. We have two kinds of libel to examine: civil and criminal. Discussion to this point has dealt with civil libel, an offense against someone else. Criminal libel, much rarer, is an offense against the state, a crime. Criminal libel is almost extinct in this country. If you published a story calling for sabotage or mob action—some offense against pubic order—you might be hauled up on a criminal libel charge. But you would be a rarity.)

Turning to our definition, we focus on the first condition required for libel, that the material be published. Publication occurs when you write something about someone and cause one or more outside parties to see it. If you and your sweetheart have a falling-out and you write this person a letter detailing his or her faults, you have committed no libel. But if you write a denunciatory letter to a former business associate and have your secretary type it, you have fulfilled the first condition for libel—publication. (You don't even have to mail it.) A third person fulfills the legal requirement, normally. Although the damage is less than it would be if the material were published in a magazine, the principle is the same.

Incidentally, spoken defamation is called *slander.* It was originally put in a different category because the spoken word could not travel as far or last as long as something in print. Broadcasting has changed that, and the courts are still grappling with the question of whether defamation on the airwaves is slander or libel. Rulings vary from state to state. If there is any thread of consistency, material read from a script is likely to be called libel, while ad lib comments can go either way.

Libel refers to *any representation.* Thus a headline, letter to the editor, cartoon, photo, or what have you, as well as regular stories, can produce a lawsuit. Words cause more trouble than the others (mainly because we have more words than artwork, particularly in areas that are likely to involve libel). Besides, persons prominent enough to be subjects of cartoons may have thrust themselves into the public light and consequently have shed their protection. Also, words are more explicit, and a person wounded by a cartoon will have more trouble articulating the injury than will someone claiming a clear defamation with words.

And that brings us to the next part of the definition—dealing with "a person." From a legal standpoint, this means groups, associations, even corporations. Similarly, injuring a person in "his occupation," a phrase from our definition, can be extended to include injuring a company in its pursuit of a dollar. How? Simple; let's say you write a story saying the Elred company's canned aloe vera soup has been found to contain botulism spores. Inasmuch as botulism is an often fatal disease, the company may encounter a measure of buyer resistance. If you are wrong, your story has unjustly hurt the company, and you can prepare to pay up.

Although you can libel a group or even a class of people, it is moderately difficult to do so. Or at least it is difficult for members of a sizable group or class to collect. They seldom do. A person would normally have to prove he or she had suffered identifiable damage. If a writer were to charge that all Americans are racists, a person would have to show how he or she had been lowered in the esteem of others and individually had been held up to hatred, contempt, or ridicule before collecting in a libel suit.

One case, *Neiman Marcus* v. *Lait,* provides guidelines on both ends of the numbers issue—high and low. A writer said the store's models were high-priced call girls, its salesmen homosexuals, and its saleswomen lower-priced call girls. All 9 models sued. They won. Fifteen of the 25 salesmen sued. They won. Thirty of the 382 saleswomen sued. They did not win; the court held that their group was too large for individual identification. But libel has been ruled in other groups as large as 100 people.

The bad things we say about people are customarily broken down into two categories: libel *per se* and libel *per quod.* The former is libel of itself, libel on its face. If you say in a newspaper story that a person is a thief, for example, he or she will sue you (unless of course, the statement is true).

Libel per quod is libel by implication, libel in certain circumstances, inferential libel. For example, it is not libelous to say that a person has bought a $100,000 house or taken a trip to Europe, even if the person earns only $15,000 a year. But if you put forth this information in a story about a shortage at the local bank, and if our big spender is a bank employee, some people will put two and two (or $100,000 and $15,000) together and decide the person has had one hand in the till. A normal reader would probably suspect the employee, whose reputation would thus be damaged. If the employee happens to be especially thrifty or has another source of honest income, you probably need to see your lawyer. Also, it isn't libelous to say a woman has had a baby, even if she has not. But if she is unmarried and has *not* had a baby, and you say she has, you may be guilty of libel.

The chances are that you cannot imagine yourself committing such a blunder. You know you are fair-minded, maybe even scrupulous. Alas, the court dockets are full of people who think they are fair-minded. The trouble is that you and I cannot resist temptation. We act like everyone else: We put two and two together and report it. We forget there might be a good reason for some sinister-appearing action. Maybe we have seen too many detective shows on television and think we need only follow the clues and we will find the guilty party by 10 p.m. (9 Central). Life does not necessarily work that way, and a libel suit can be a forceful reminder that we should not get carried away.

Let's have some questions.

Q. *If you telephone a bank teller and call him a thief, a cheat and a scoundrel, is that libel or slander?*

Neither one. Look back to see what is the first requirement for libel.

Q. *What is the difference between civil libel and criminal libel, and which is more common?*

Civil libel is a transgression against someone else, whereas criminal libel is a crime against the state, such as sedition. Civil libel is far more common.

Damages

If you lose a libel suit, you will have to pay out some money. It may be a great amount or it may be only a small bit. (Henry Ford once sued the *Chicago Tribune* for calling him an anarchist, and he wound up with an award of six cents. The *Tribune* got off light—except that it spent $303,968.72 in its defense.)

Damages are awarded in one or more of three categories: (1) general, or compensatory; (2) special; and (3) punitive, or exemplary. People who have been libeled may ask for all three. Normally, they get general damages, for which they need prove only that you committed a libel and damaged a reputation. A jury will set the amount, making some kind of calculation as to what a damaged reputation is worth. Recent decisions prohibit recovery for libel per se in some cases. (This refers specifically to plaintiffs who sue under guidelines set up in *Elmer Gertz* v. *Robert Welch, Inc.*)

In the second category, special damages, the libel victim has to show the specific loss (for instance, the loss of a job or a drop in sales) and try to prove that the libel caused the loss. If a company can prove that sales dropped only because of your libel, it will be able to collect the amount lost. (It is often difficult to show that libel is the sole cause of a loss. Sales sometimes fall for unlibeled companies, too. Nevertheless, people do prove losses on occasion and get special damages.)

The third kind of damages, punitive, is something the jury throws in to remind you to be more careful next time. If the jury finds that you have generally done a sorry job as a journalist, that you are full of malice, or are extremely careless, it can award punitive damages.

Defenses

What do you say when someone accuses you of libel? The first question your lawyer asks is this: "Is it true? Did the guy do what you said he did?" Moreover, the lawyer does not want to know if you are sure, if you are positive, if you know in your heart you are right. No, to a lawyer, *true* means something you can *prove* is true. And in some states—Colorado, Indiana, Missouri, Nebraska, New Mexico, North Carolina, South Carolina, and Vermont at last count—truth is a complete defense. But if you cannot prove the accuracy of your statements, you have a problem.

A few other defenses will help, even if we cannot document truth. We now examine them, starting with the less dramatic defenses and working our way up to the good stuff.

1. Statute of limitations
2. Consent or authorization (direct or indirect)
3. Self-defense or right of reply.
4. Privilege
   (*a*) Privilege of the participant—absolute privilege
   (*b*) Privilege of reporting—qualified privilege
5. *New York Times* v. *Sullivan* rule
6. Fair comment and criticism

The *statute of limitations* is a simple limit on how long a person can wait before deciding to sue you. Generally, the countdown starts with the most recent publication or republication of a libel. A one-year limit is common.

If a person gives you *direct consent* to publish something, you are home free. You have no worries if that person has a change of heart on seeing the material in print and decides to sue. It helps if the consent is in writing, since juries are easier to convince in such a circumstance. Even more common is *indirect consent,* which the reporter secures by asking a person to reply to a libelous charge. The legal assumption is that a person grants consent to print the original charge by responding to it. A response of "No comment" leaves the reporter without a consent defense.

The response has a bearing on our third libel defense, the *right of reply*. If a person is attacked in print, that person has a right to reply with as much fire and brimstone as the original attacker, but not more. If the first attack is not libelous, the reply cannot be libelous without running the risk of a suit.

Now we bring out the heavy artillery, the best defenses—after truth, of course. They are, again, privilege, *Times* v. *Sullivan,* and fair comment.

Privilege. One of the bedrock assumptions in this country is that we should do all we can to encourage the flow of information about—and debate on—public policy. Our laws normally protect major governmental figures from libel actions in the official performance of their duties. For instance, a congressman on the floor of the House or Senate can say anything at all that comes to mind—true, false, or ridiculous. He can lie about anyone, and the victim has no legal recourse, no comeback, except denial. The late Senator Joseph McCarthy used to make strong charges about many people, and he wound up being censured by the Senate. But he was immune to libel suits as long as he did his talking in the Senate or in other official surroundings. Senator McCarthy had *absolute privilege,* privilege of the participant. Absolute privilege is also granted witnesses at trials, if they stay on the subject at hand. (They cannot volunteer derogatory information about people unrelated to the case.) The thought is that witnesses ought to be able to say what they want without having to prove every scrap of information they offer. (If they are shown to be lying, they get a perjury charge. Lying is not the same as being mistaken about facts.)

What does all this have to do with news reporters? They have a kind of privilege called *qualified privilege;* it concerns their reports of public proceedings and is granted by laws. Although the statutes vary from state to state, the general rule is that a reporter can report any official action and not be sued for libel. This means, for example, that a reporter can tell what a witness testified, even if the witness is a registered liar and sworn enemy of the subject of the testimony. One of the requirements for the retention of privilege is that the reporter give a full and fair report of the proceedings. (If you report only the liar's testimony and do not hint that the opposing lawyer destroyed him as a credible witness, that he was cited for perjury, and that he was contradicted by two saints and a schoolteacher, you may have to go back to court as a leading character in a libel suit.)

The reporter's qualified privilege also extends to documents filed in connection with a case. In some states, you can report on documents as soon as they are submitted. Generally, however, you must wait until a judge has taken some action—made some acknowledgment that the papers have been filed—before a reporter is protected. (It behooves you to know the law in your state.) Once the matter is officially entered into public records, you can report it at length, including the substance of any documents introduced.

At another level, you can commonly report any official action taken by a governmental unit. As a rule of thumb, you should see it in writing so that you can easily prove an action was taken. In fact, official actions are almost by definition those that have been recorded. Although what a sheriff tells you in the course of duty is usually privileged, and thus reportable, we sometimes have a thin line between official statements and unofficial elaborations. Some states limit what officials can reveal—usually the charge, the circumstances of an arrest, and such things are allowed but the existence of a confession or details of evidence are not allowed. The goal has been to forbid law officials to say things that might never get to the jury, thus making sure the case is tried in the courtroom and not in the media.

However, reporters are not forced into silence until after the trial. Hardly. The charge is always privileged, and that is the first big source of news. The charge is an official accusation that a person, perhaps even a person whose name is not known, has violated a particular statute. It tells when and where the deed was done and, to a degree, just what happened. A typical charge would say that a person had broken statute number so and so, and then would add wording something like this: ". . . in that he did on September 4, 1979, drive an automobile while in a state of intoxication."

Read this next part carefully: You are entitled to say the person is charged with this violation, the person is *accused* of doing it. You are entitled to say the police report, to use a loose term, says so. But you are not legally entitled to say or imply that the person actually did it. You are not entitled to call the person a drunken driver. You may go as far as the charge goes *and no farther*.

We will look at another case for an additional development: If the police arrest someone for bank robbery, the suspect will have a chance to get a lawyer, will go before a magistrate to be told about the charge, and then will be allowed to make a plea. If a man says he was out for a stroll in the woods and someone came along and thrust a sackful of money into his hands and then the police grabbed him, he remains a suspect. But if he says that, yes, he committed the holdup, he pleads guilty; he becomes a robber.

An element of common sense must come into play here. If a person holds up a bank but stumbles while running out and is collared on the spot, we are in little danger if we call that person the robber. If a person hijacks an airliner or a bus and is talked into surrendering after a couple of tense hours, we can call that person a hijacker without any great worry. But as long as there is any legal question of whether the person did the deed, we should shy away from convicting the suspect.

That brings up a major new subject: Can a person get a fair trial in such circumstances? Well, yes and no, depending on what you call a fair trial. If you mean the suspect has an even shot at getting off free, the answer is probably no. The situations just cited are not good examples for a fair trial-free press debate, since the culprits would probably not contest the charges. Of greater pertinence is something like the Son of Sam case in New York, in which a suspect's life was very thoroughly washed and hung up for public drying. The suspect, David Berkowitz, was in for a rough time of it, assuming that most potential jurors would have seen, in the media, assorted bits of evidence that he committed the murders of which he was accused. Although we will not go into the subject further here, it is a vital topic that news reporters and editors have to consider.

Q. *Let's approach privilege another way now. Here is the lead for a story. Could we use it? Why or why not?*

Two brothers were arrested at their home early

this afternoon, shortly after they held up Abe's

Delicatessen, at 50th and Guadalupe. The two, Sam

and Sydney Sims, were charged with armed robbery.

In all likelihood, no. Although we do not have enough information here to permit an ironclad ruling, this looks like an easy call. The danger sign leaps out of the second clause: "they held up." This wording says flatly that these are the villains. It is conceivable that we could use the wording if Abe and the police and maybe some irate customers chased the brothers down.

Q. *We will say the Sims boys deny they were involved. Just what are the ascertainable facts? That is, what actions occurred and can be reported without fear of a libel suit?*

The deli was held up. Police arrested Sam and Syd after the robbery. Sam and Syd have been charged with armed robbery.

We need to examine our answers. First, we can properly assume that the delicatessen was indeed robbed. (The chance that Abe is working an insurance scheme—though it exists—is so small that we waste time trying to construct the story to allow for such a possibility.) If Abe was alone (no customers) at the time of the robbery, we might handle the story just a little differently. (If Abe is fooling us, we will someday have another story pointing that out.) We know the police made an arrest unless some bizarre circumstance has caused the police to say they have made an arrest that they have not really made. Reporters do not normally have to go into the jail and count prisoners. Finally, the record clearly says that these two fellows are accused of a certain kind of crime, armed robbery.

Q. *Bearing these facts in mind, how would you edit the lead to keep us out of a libel suit?*

You might try something like this:

> *gunmen*
> [Two ~~brothers were arrested at their home early this afternoon, shortly after they~~ held up Abe's
> *early this afternoon.* ~~The~~ two *(brothers)*
> Delicatessen, at 50th and Guadalupe. ~~The~~ two *(* Sam
> *[arrested a short while later and]*
> and Sydney Sims, were charged with armed robbery.

And if you do not like that, you could approach it this way:

> *charged with armed robbery*
> [Two brothers were ~~arrested at their home~~ early
> *a holdup at*
> this afternoon, shortly after ~~they held up~~ Abe's
> Delicatessen, at 50th and Guadalupe. The two, Sam
> *arrested at their home.*
> and Sydney Sims, were ~~charged with armed robbery.~~

The difference in leads, one focusing on the holdup and one on the arrest, is considered at greater length elsewhere. The main point is that we protect ourselves from a lawsuit—and treat the Simses right at the same time—by not reporting anything we cannot back up or trace to an official source, a privileged source.

Generally, anything that is part of an official record is likely to be privileged, although laws vary from state to state. Newswriters work under the protection of privilege in dealing with such things as court documents, testimony, judicial comments, police charges, open deliberations of public bodies, official rulings (from a justice of the peace's verdict in a suicide to the Securities and Exchange Commission views in a stock fraud, and then some), and, in some states, even comments made at an open, public meeting. Remember that you are obligated to provide a full and fair account of the events and proceedings.

Let us consider fairness at this point. Fairness can affect your treatment of a story even when you face no danger of a libel suit. For example, you are free to print the SEC charges in that stock fraud case, but fairness requires that you attempt to get the other side from the accused, even though it is not part of the record.

Another example: If the General Accounting Office issues a report saying a cannery has overcharged the government in sales of soup to the army, we can run the story at length. We have no legal obligation to present the company's rebuttal, no matter how cogent—or lame—it may be. But several reasons for running the company's views come quickly to mind. (1) The GAO may be wrong. Our public watchdogs catch bushels of offenders and save the country a great deal of money, but they do not claim infallibility. (2) The GAO report may be only partly right; the soupmakers may be able to offer something to take some of the onus off their shoulders. (3) The American people, your readers, want a measure of fairness in their news coverage, and they may think you are trying to shaft the company if you don't give it a say. (You can discover two more reasons in John Stuart Mill's *On Liberty,* should you find yourself interested in the philosophical bases for getting both sides of a story.)

Times v. *Sullivan.* The Supreme Court of the United States overturned in 1964 a decision awarding $500,000 to the commissioner of public affairs in Montgomery, Alabama, in a libel action against the *New York Times*. The commissioner, L. B. Sullivan, had sued, because in his view, an advertisement in the *Times* accused him of running a police department that spread a wave of terror among civil rights activists at a Montgomery college. The advertisement contained some factual errors.

The Supreme Court took some giant steps in this case. First, it held that erroneous statement is "inevitable in free debate," and it must be protected if freedom of expression is to have the breathing space it needs to survive. Therefore, public officials in this country must learn to put up with occasional hard knocks, even unfair hard knocks. The court recognized "a profound national commitment to the principle that debate on public issues should be uninhibited, robust and wide open." In other words, it is better to risk wounding a public official unfairly now and then than to inhibit debate on public issues. If we have to choose a risk, the court sides with debate.

The second giant step dealt with the case's definition of malice. The court defined malice as knowledge that a statement is false or reckless disregard of whether it is false. Previously, malice had been defined in many ways, from ill feeling toward the subject of the story to "an intent to do harm."

Later cases have refined some of the definitions of *Times-Sullivan,* but the central idea remains: You can safely make practically any assertion against a public official as long as you do it without malice, as defined above, and as long as the person is acting in an official capacity—has not temporarily become a private citizen. (In one case, an official sued successfully when a newspaper carried comments about work that he had done when not on his government job.)

Here's a *Times-Sullivan* example: Your story indicates the sheriff is using county prisoners to paint his farmhouse and repair his fences. After the story runs, you learn that the painters and fence menders are upright citizens and that all the prisoners are accounted for in the lockup. The sheriff sues. If you plead *Times-Sullivan,* the sheriff must prove knowing falsehood or reckless disregard for the truth of your statements.

To summarize: *Times-Sullivan* is the defense you offer when you make a defamatory factual statement about a public official and it turns out not to be factual after all. *Times-Sullivan* gives you something to fall back on in case you foul up. It should not be used as a crutch for a lazy reporter. The reporter—and editor—should continue to try to nail down all facts and, in my view, should not run a story containing an unsubstantiated accusation just because they know the wounded party is a public official and cannot sue.

You may have concluded that *Times-Sullivan* is a simple case. Wrong. Although the case offers news reporters a broad umbrella, it does not end the threat of libel from public officials. (1) The problem of malice remains. The burden of proof is shifted to the plaintiff (the official), but some plaintiffs may be able to handle it. (2) We have to get a good decision on who is covered under the court's verdict. Traditionally, public officials are such people as congressmen, legislators, mayors, police chiefs, and school board members. At one time, it appeared that the courts would become more and more lenient and broaden "public official" to mean "public figure." (I thought the courts were going to take in enough latitude to cover the ultimate Catch-22 situation: A person would become a public figure, and thus be immune to libel, if his or her name was in the paper.)

The Supreme Court had other thoughts, which it expressed in the Gertz case. In that case, Chicago lawyer Elmer Gertz sued Robert Welch, founder of the John Birch Society, for unkind statements in his magazine, *American Opinion.* Welch argued in defense that Gertz, as a lawyer for several celebrated persons, was a public figure and was thus covered by the *Times-Sullivan* ruling. At that point the court stopped its plunge toward a free and loose definition of public figures. It held that Gertz had not thrust himself into the vortex of this case, that he was just a private citizen doing a job in a public setting. The definition, buttressed by others, thus moved us back to a tighter definition of public people.

Times-Sullivan has not received universal acclaim. And not all criticism has come from wounded officials. I appreciate the ruling's contribution to debate, but I fret now and then that it encourages slothfulness or at least inattention to detail by reporters. The good reporter will still make every effort to get all the facts straight, umbrella or no umbrella. Although *Times-Sullivan* may protect you from a lawsuit, it does not protect you from righteous employers, subscribers and colleagues who do not like to see errors in the publication under any circumstances.

Fair comment and criticism. Our third major protection against a libel suit, called fair comment and criticism or just *fair comment,* has two conditions: It must be fair and it must be comment.

Times-Sullivan dealt with facts; fair comment deals with opinion. This opinion can appear anywhere—news columns, editorials, advertisements—you name it.

Laws governing fair comment vary from state to state, but their general idea is that we all have the right to criticize those people who offer themselves or their products for public consumption. In particular, such laws support the right of the governed to make assessments of their governors, the people they have hired to handle public business. Fair comment applies to officials, agencies, candidates, artists, speakers, writers, athletes and other entertainers. Persons who ask you to buy tickets or spend time to see them perform, or to spend time or money reading their books, are presumed to invite criticism.

(A reminder: If you call a person a thief, you are making a statement of fact. If you call a person a nincompoop, you are asserting an opinion, since the criteria for nincompoopism vary from observer to observer.)

We detour here for a swing by that journalistic edifice known as the Cherry Sisters case. (You may have taken this trip already, and you surely will again if you stay in this business.) We review a 1901 Iowa Supreme Court ruling that said the following criticism of a new dance act in town was fair comment without malice:

> Billy Hamilton, of the *Odebolt Chronicle,* gives the Cherry Sisters the following graphic write-up on their late appearance in his town: "Effie is an old jade of 50 summers, Jessie a frisky filly of 40, and Addie, the flower of the family, a capering monstrosity of 35. Their long skinny arms, equipped with talons at the extremities, swung mechanically, and anon waved frantically at the suffering audience. The mouths of their rancid features opened like caverns, and sounds like the wailing of damned souls issued therefrom. They pranced around the stage with a motion that suggested a cross between the danse du ventre and fox trot—strange creatures with painted faces and hideous mien. Effie is spavined, Addie is stringhalt, and Jessie, the only one who showed her stockings, has legs with calves as classic in their outlines as the curves of a broom handle."

Such ungentlemanly prose upset Effie, Jessie and Addie (the flower of the family). They sued. But the court held that the newspaper, the *Des Moines Leader,* was within its rights. Said the court:

> One who goes upon the stage to exhibit himself to the public, or who gives any kind of a performance to which the public is invited,

may be freely criticized. He may be held up to ridicule, and entire freedom of expression is guaranteed to dramatic critics, provided they are not actuated by malice or evil purpose in what they write. Fitting strictures, sarcasm, or ridicule, even, may be used, if based on facts, without liability, in the absence of malice or wicked purpose. . . . Ridicule is often the strongest weapon in the hands of a public writer; and, if fairly used, the presumption of malice which would otherwise arise is rebutted, and it becomes necessary to introduce evidence of actual malice, or of some indirect motive or wish to gratify private spite.

What that means is that if our drama editor got turned on by old Jessie's broom handle underpinnings and if she rebuffed his advances, she might argue that he used those nasty comments to get back at her. And she might collect. But it is up to her to do the proving.

You can see from the Cherry Sisters case that fair comment does not have to be nice; it can be exceedingly rough and still fall under the court's protection. However, the comment must be based on a full and reasonably accurate report of facts; and it must deal only with the subject's public life, not private life, unless the private side of a person's life bears on the public side under discussion.

In one celebrated case, the *New York Sun* lambasted a teacher for his attack on Shakespeare. It ridiculed him effectively and said that he would no doubt take this sentence from the bard: "Night's candles are burnt out, and jocund day stands tiptoe on the misty mountaintops," and rewrite it into a version more to his liking: "I hear the milkman."

The court had no quarrel with that jibe, but when the *Sun* added that the professor was so addlepated that he took a year to name his child, the situation changed. That was personal. It made the whole article indefensible. The *Sun* had to pay up.

[10] *Type*

YOU HAD A TASTE of typography in the headlines chapter. Now we will bite off a larger chunk. We will look at typefaces first and then at the point system—the printer's peculiar method of measuring.

Typography is the art of arranging printing elements on a page so as to achieve the greatest effectiveness in communicating a given message.

In newspapers, the bulk of communication is done by words—your writing. In magazines, typefaces carry a little more of the load. You have more typographic freedom in magazines, ads and brochures than in newspapers. Your newspaper limits itself to one or two type families for 90 percent of its headlines, and properly so. Newspapers maintain typographic stability because they want to present a consistent, stable image to readers. Even so, you will on occasion soup up a layout with a special typeface or some other typographic maneuver. This does not mean you drop an oddball headline in among the regular stuff on whim. No, you are more likely to use it on a special full-page layout or a half-page that is limited to one story, or something of that nature.

In magazines, you make more of an effort to match headline face to story content. You are trying to enhance the message of the words with a message from the typeface.

To understand that, perhaps you need to have a look at what is available in type. Type comes in many categories. These are commonly given, in order, as race, family, face and size.

Race. Some people say we have 13 races of type; some may claim more. I say we have 5, and maybe only 4, depending on how you count; however, I recognize that we have to stretch some of these categories to cover all the families in a race. I would list these races: roman, monotone (or sans serif), text (old English), written, and decorative and novelty. Some people would divide the romans into old style, modern and transitional; they would split square-serif types out of the monotone race, and they might even create a new category for newspaper faces. Fine. However, we will stick with the five above, inasmuch as they are about all most people can remember.

More printing is done in roman typefaces than any other. This book is set in a roman face, English Times. Body type for almost all news-

B.C. by permission of Johnny Hart and Field Enterprises, Inc.

papers is roman. Generally, roman faces are more legible than other faces, particularly in a large block of type. When you have only a few words to examine, as in a headline or a telephone directory, monotones work all right, but for general, all-purpose reading, romans do the job.

The chief distinguishing mark of roman type is the serif, the little fancy finishing stroke on the ends of a letter. Look at this capital *T*, for instance:

$$T$$

Note those little hangey-down things on the ends of the arms; those are *serifs*. Note the bottom of the letter; more serifs. For contrast, look at this monotone:

$$T$$

No hangey-down things. No feet. No serifs. Got the difference? Now check this pair of *N*s:

N   N

Note that the roman's vertical members are considerably thinner than the cross member, the slant. This type, Bodoni, is a modern roman, designed by a lad named Giambattista Bodoni in Parma, Italy, in the middle of the eighteenth century. That's modern? Well, sort of. It differs from the old-style romans mainly in that its serifs are thin and flat; old-style serifs are thicker and bracketed into the main part of the letter. This tapering was once necessary because metals used in casting type were not strong enough to handle the required pressure on the press when serifs were thin. Modern romans came along after metals got stronger. Art followed science.

We have looked at a big monotone letter. I call this race *monotone* because all the strokes of the letter are the same thickness. The term *sans serif* is probably more common, and you may use it. If you use *monotone,* however, you do not have to change when you look at square serif types like this:

Karnak

You cannot call that a roman, though it has serifs. You need not lose any sleep over this problem; just realize that these types have different appearances.

You will not be using a great deal of text type, our next race, although you will see it on occasion, particularly in newspaper nameplates and on wedding invitations. Behold:

Cloister Black

Ask around and find out whether your publication has a typeface like this. You may never need it, but you may find a need for it if you have it.

Following are two specimens of type from the written race:

Kaufmann Script

Coronet Bold

The first is a *script*; the endings on one letter appear to touch the beginning strokes on the next letter. The second face, the Coronet, is a *cursive,* which differs slightly from the script. Although it also looks much like handwriting, a closer examination shows that the letters are not joined. (My memory aid: I say that you *curse* about *cursive* type because someone broke the letters apart.) We have a number of typefaces in this written race, but few are used as everyday headline material.

These types belong in our last race, decorative and novelty:

Amelia

Legend

FOURNIER

You can readily see what kinds of special uses they would have. I ask only that you not get hung up on Amelia and use it every time you have a feature that mentions computers.

Families. The next type breakdown is by family. Families are commonly named after the people who designed them, as in Bodoni, mentioned earlier. We have a great number of families in every race; more than 20,000 typefaces exist. The counting has become more difficult lately, as slight variations of a face are run up by new companies (and old ones) for use in photocomposition equipment. If someone tells you we have 40,000 faces (or 5,000), do not argue. Do not worry, either. Almost all the nation's printing is done with fewer than 200 families, I would guess. (Two hundred families might include 1,000 faces.) You can be grateful that you will work regularly with only a handful, often only two on newspapers, plus one for body type.

Let us see what we have in the way of families in the roman race. We have already met Mr. Bodoni's effort. Now meet these noble romans:

Cheltenham
Goudy
Century
Garamond

Each of these is a family name. Same goes for the monotones:

Futura

Franklin Gothic

Helvetica

Univers

Faces. Each family has a number of offspring called faces. They bear a family resemblance, so you can almost always tell which family they are from. Most families have one or two faces that get the most use—Cheltenham bold and bold italic below, for example. Some families are quite large, and some have only one member. Take a look at a large family:

Cheltenham Old Style

Cheltenham Old Style Condensed

Cheltenham Wide

Cheltenham Medium

Cheltenham Bold

Cheltenham Bold Italic

Cheltenham Bold Condensed

Cheltenham Bold Condensed Italic

Cheltenham Bold Extra Condensed

Cheltenham Bold Ext.

Sizes. Our last category is size of type. You will run across the word *font* in crossword puzzles and typography articles. A font is all the characters of one size of any single face. Years ago, a font was a drawer of type in a cabinet. Printers set type from the cabinet one letter at a time, holding them in a metal device called a *stick*. Then Ottmar Mergenthaler invented the Linotype typesetting machine. For three-fourths of a century we used hot metal slugs from Ottmar's wondrous equipment. A font to a Linotype operator was a large metal case containing, again, all the characters in one size for one face. A change in font—to 9-point type instead of 8 or to italic from regular—involved cranking the new font into place. And if the required font was not among the few that could be kept on the machine, a change meant the operator had to remove one 50-pound case and get the correct one from storage. Printers have been known to utter expletives in such circumstances.

The point system

Johann Gutenberg is the person most often credited with the invention of printing with movable metal type. Gutenberg was born in Germany about 1397. His father was named Friele zum Gensfleisch. Johann took the name Gutenberg, presumably after his mother's birthplace, because he preferred to be known as "Good Mountain" instead of "Goose Flesh." I consider that a sign of intelligence. We do not really know that he invented printing with movable type, but we know he was involved in lawsuits with an employer who had paid for tools. These "tools" could have been used for the printing that was done at Mainz, Germany, in 1448, the time and place often given for the first movable-type printing.

Gutenberg unquestionably was not the inventor of printing or the printing press. He was one millennium and two or three centuries behind the Chinese, who were apparently printing on paper by A.D. 105. They did not have movable type, in which individual characters could be rearranged and reused, but they were printing.

Although Gutenberg advanced the art of printing greatly, he did not eliminate its problems. One problem was a lack of uniformity. Inasmuch as every printer cast his own type (or whittled it), types were not uniform in size. Type from one shop was not interchangeable with type from another. There was no standardization. A person who wanted a flyer printed had no way to specify what size the type should be. It was the size the printer had. Period.

Enter Pierre Simon Fournier, who devised a standard system in 1737. He split an inch into 72 parts (0.013837 inch) and that is the division we have used ever since. I would not be astonished to see a move to millimeters (a millimeter is about 3 points). The computer can adjust to points, millimeters, furlongs, or whatever you want with very little trouble. Metal type is somewhat less flexible.

You are familiar with the point system from writing headlines. You learned that points are used to measure how much space a letter takes up vertically on a printing surface. (Width is usually measured in picas.) You know that headlines come in a fairly consistent list of type sizes. The most common ones are 14, 18, 24, 30, 36, 42, 48, 60, 72, 96, 120 and WAR! Note that after 14 we increased by 6-point increments to 48, then by 12 twice, and finally by 24 to 96 and 120. The latter size, 96 point, is big type. You will not often see this size in most American newspapers, although those with heavy street sales competition do resort to it.

The main thing you need to know is that 72 points is an inch; you can get your bearings from there by figuring that 36 points is ½ inch, three lines of 24 is 1 inch, and so on. (Headlines usually take a little extra space between lines, often 6 points. In that case, a three-line 24 pointer would take up 1⅙ inches if space were used only between type lines, or 1⅓ inches with space between the lines and above and below the head. The space between lines is called *leading,* pronounced ledding. Generally, large headlines have more leading than small ones.)

In hot metal composition, leading was accomplished by actually inserting slugs between lines. In photocomposition, you lead headlines in one of two ways: (1) Set the typesetting equipment to drop space in automatically. (2) If you do not like what the machine does (meaning your headline is not deep enough to fill all the space you have), you can simply have the lines cut apart and positioned to suit your wishes. (Normally, this work is done by the composing room crew. You keep your hands off the type.)

We encounter a slightly different—and more difficult—situation when we move to horizontal measurements. Excessive horizontal spacing between letters in a headline word is readily apparent, not to mention ugly. You usually achieve proper horizontal spacing by rewriting the headline.

Horizontal measurements are usually given in picas. A *pica* is ⅙ inch, or 12 points. This rule is 1 pica thick:

Newspaper pages come in assorted widths, but the trend is toward narrower widths for economy. The *New York Times,* for example, spends more than $75 million a year for paper. The *Times* can save more than a million dollars a year by trimming ¼ inch off each page. The days of wide margins are gone. And some newspapers will probably reconsider their use of 18 points of white space between columns and think about using a hairline rule and 6 points of space, as the *Times* does. This idea will probably not overcome the trend toward white space anytime soon, but it will lurk in the back of many publishers' minds, especially when they get a bill for $350 for every ton of newsprint they buy.

A typical small newspaper runs a single page 14½ to 15½ inches (87–93 picas) wide. We will disregard the margins, which are ¼ inch to ½ inch. If you use 87 picas for the printing surface (the part that has ink on it), if you have a six-column page, and if you use 18 points (1½ picas) between columns, you will come up with a column 13¼ picas wide. (Get this: One-quarter is ³⁄₁₂; we write our number as 13.3 picas. It means 13 and ³⁄₁₂, not ³⁄₁₀.)

Let's look at the math. Five spaces between the six columns gives us this:

5 × 1½ picas = 7½ picas (write it 7.6)
87 picas (page width) — 7½ = 79½
79½ ÷ 6 columns = 13¼ (13.3)

Have a look at it graphically, though not full size (see Fig. 10.1).

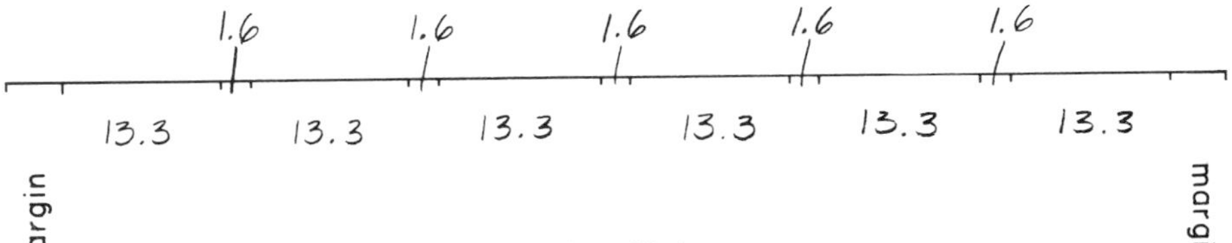

Fig. 10.1

See if this helps:

$$5 \times 1.6 = (5 \times 1) + (5 + 6) = 5 + 30$$

We multiply the two figures separately: 5 times 1 is 5, and 5 times 6 is 30. One is picas; the other, points. So we have 5 picas plus 30 points. Since 30 points divided by 12 (12 points in a pica) is 2½, we are back to 7½ picas for the space between columns. Next, we have 13.3 times 6 = 78 picas plus 18 points, or 79½ picas. Add the 7½ picas to 79½ and you have 87 picas, the width of your printing area. Add some for your margin and you have the page.

You must learn the point system and be able to handle pica measurements. Write down those tricky figures. Fortunately, most news publications use regular, specified widths for the bulk of their body type, such as the six-column page we just dealt with. For odd-measure type (the tricky stuff), most publications keep a chart that tells them how wide to set type. Should you be asked to make up such a chart, or should you decide you want to run some odd-measure type tomorrow, here are the steps you go through to calculate the setting:

1. Determine the width, in picas, of your printing space.
2. Determine how many legs (columns) of type you want.
3. Decide how much space you want between columns.
4. Multiply the number of spaces (one fewer than the number of columns) times the width of each space.
5. Subtract that from the space available.
6. Divide this new space available by the number of legs of type.
7. Adjust as necessary to pick up odd remnants.

Let's run through that with some real figures. Say we have our six-column page. We want to run a one-column picture and, beside it, a story in five columns of space. We want to set our type in four legs to fill five columns. Now we will calculate, using an 87-pica page.

1. Five columns of type at 13.3 is 65.15, or 66.3. Add some for the four spaces we had between those five columns: At 1.6 picas each, four spaces are 4.24, or 6 picas. Add that to our 66.3 and we have 72.3 picas available. (You could have gone in the back door by adding 13.3 and 1.6—a column and its space—to allow for the photo, and subtracting that 14.9 from 87.)
2. We chose four legs of type.
3. Choose any amount of space you want. We can try 2 full picas, since we are going to use fairly wide lines. You usually choose 1½ or 2 because they are easy to work with. If you go much over 2 with regular-size body type, your page is going to look gappy.
4. Four legs of type will have three spaces between them. Multiply three spaces by 2 picas each, giving us 6 picas of space.

5. Subtracting 6 from 72.3, we find we have 66.3 picas for our type, not counting space.

6. Divide that by 4. Wait: Round 66.3 off to 66 by setting the 3 points to the side. Four into 66 gives us 16½, which we write as 16.6, with 3 points left over.

7. Since we have three spaces, we can add a point to each and come up with four legs of 16.6, separated by three spaces 2.1 picas wide, totaling 87 picas.

To run three legs in that space, you go through the same process, using only two spaces. If you do much of this fancy stuff, you will find a chart worthwhile. Final hint: If you have problems, take a minute to ask a printer for help.

Now we will review.

> **Q.** *How deep is* 30 *points?*   *a.* 30 millimeters, *b.* one-quarter inch, *c.* nearly one-half inch, *d.* two-thirds of an inch, or *e.* two picas?

Thirty points is *c*, nearly half an inch; it's ⁵⁄₁₂ inch, to be more precise.

> **Q.** *How long in picas is a* 10-*inch line?*

At 6 per, it's 60.

> **Q.** *How do you write* 7¾ *in picas?*   *a.* 7.34, *b.* 7.6, *c.* 7.¾, *d.* 7.9, or *e.* 7 & *three-fourths?*

In picas, 7¾ is *d;* that's 7 and ⁹⁄₁₂, or 7.9.

Although your first encounter with Fournier's brainchild may be difficult, the system is not hard to grasp if you work on it. And when you work with it on a regular basis, it will come to you as naturally as the letters of the alphabet. While waiting for that time of nirvana, spend a moment nailing down the two basic measurements in this system. With them in your pocket, you can work everything else out. They are:

You have 72 points in an inch.
You have 12 points in a pica, ⅙ inch.

[11] *Newspaper layout*

THE ELECTRONICS PEOPLE have flushed us out of this final fortress of pencil-and-paper editing. The rout is not complete, but old-style layout work is in its last decade. *Pagination,* the electronic era term for page layout on a video display terminal, has gone beyond the dreaming stage and crept into newsrooms. The equipment is expensive, it is imperfect and it is best suited to tabloid-size newspapers, but publications are buying it.

Pagination, when used with other electronic editing and printing equipment, offers a number of advantages. You can arrange a page as you want it—you see body type, headlines, cutlines, boxes and blanks for photographs. When you press the *go* button, the page zips through the computer and comes out full size, ready to be photographed in the plate-making process. The day is coming, shortly, when your page-size VDT will be connected directly to the press, and any change on the VDT image will result in an immediate change on the printed page.

In such a system, the computer will be able to tailor any paper, or any page of it, for a special audience. If you like sports, whiskey ads, ballet stories, and international news, the computer can be programmed to load your newspaper with such material. The only problem is that the newspaper carrier—the kid on a bicycle—cannot be programmed. If the carrier picks someone else's paper out of the bag, you may wind up with a newspaper laden with stock market reports, extra comics, and two pages of think pieces.

Let's go back to a quieter time and see what was happening then. We will work our way up to the present, and as we do so, we will learn how to make up newspaper pages. We stick with pencil and paper, for two reasons: (1) The old way is much cheaper and more convenient for learners. (2) Pagination equipment has not yet achieved prominence in the field.

Layout, or makeup, is the arrangement of headlines, body type, photos, and other elements on a newspaper page.

Although Benjamin Franklin averaged about one idea a week for the benefit of mankind, from bifocals to electricity to wood stoves, he wasn't much on newspaper layout. Newspapers in his day (he became a publisher in 1729) may be said to have had no makeup. Most were about the size of a sheet of writing paper, 8½ by 11. They had two columns of type, usually topped by an arrangement of bigger type giving the name of the paper. Headlines were unknown. Readers started at the beginning and consumed the whole thing, front to back. Then they sold it, or loaned it to someone, or memorized it, or gave it to the person who helped them pay for it, or put it back on the wall at the tavern where they were reading.

We could say these early sheets had vertical makeup. The reader's eye went from top to bottom, a straight drop. This general pattern stayed with us for decades, though the newspapers grew in all directions—wider, deeper, and fatter. We had vertical makeup for more than a century. A hairsplitter could say we have had only two kinds of makeup: vertical makeup and postvertical (everything else).

Instead of splitting hairs, we might benefit from splitting our layout discussion into five categories:

1. No makeup, as in colonial times
2. Vertical makeup
   a. All headlines in the first column
   b. One-column headlines sprinkled throughout
3. Incipient horizontal makeup—basically vertical but with a scattering of headlines two or more columns wide
4. Horizontal
   a. Traditional
   b. Extreme
5. All others
   a. Magazine/modular
   b. Tabloid
   c. Weirdo

Colonial newspapers had no need for makeup. It was only when page sizes grew that the masses of type began to look gray and forbidding. Despite the grayness, full-size newspapers stuck with the no-makeup format. They evolved into vertical sheets with few or no headlines of substantial size. Eventually, headlines were used to appeal to a growing market for street sales. With the advantage of a century or two of hindsight, we readily see—and marvel at—the pioneers' slowness in moving toward more presentable makeup. Remember that printing was a painfully tedious job in the first place; a great amount of work was required in putting together a story one letter at a time—a separate piece of metal for each letter and space. Printers had no time to loll around and dream up modular layout. Consequently, the practice of piling up headlines in column 1—headlines for all the issue's stories—was viewed as progress. (Maybe it was.) The reader could check all the headlines at one shot and then start reading where the headlines ended in column 1. At the end of a story, a small crossline announced the arrival of a new story, and the normal reader began that one. I suppose a few perverse souls started at the back of the paper, the way some people read magazines today. It made little difference.

This all-vertical, lumped-head arrangement was supplanted early in the nineteenth century by vertical makeup with separate headlines for each story. The arrival of two-column headlines was delayed by a technological improvement—the Hoe type-revolving press. This press, invented by Richard Hoe and first used in 1846 to print the *Public Ledger,* had a pair of wedge-shaped rules between columns. The wedges were mechanically pushed together from the ends, tightening them against type in the columns. Type forms thus were made tight enough to be attached to a cylindrical press, which rotated and printed a page each revolution. The press boosted printing speed to about 1,500 papers an hour. Newspapers could not use multicolumn headlines because the wedges had to go between all columns.

On rare occasions a piece of type worked loose. And when one piece fell out, the whole thing came unglued, spraying type the width of Manhattan and causing great outcries from printers and others who had to pick the stuff up and start over.

The problem was overcome in 1854 with the use of stereotyping. In stereotyping, the page, in a form, was used to make an impression on a piece of heavy cardboardlike substance, and that in turn was curved and had hot lead poured onto it. The lead cooled and left a curved printing plate that was put on a rotary press and revolved at unheard of speeds of 10,000 copies per hour.

Did editors nudge each other and say, "Ah, now that we have stereotyping we can have modular layout"? No; old habits are hard to break, and it took the Civil War to generate enough excitement to cause someone to start regular use of spread heads. Maybe that's an exaggeration; at any rate, multicolumn headlines and tentatively horizontal makeup were slow in gaining prominence.

Even the Spanish-American War, which produced giant streamers in the Hearst-Pulitzer press, did not cause a permanent shift away from a basically vertical layout. A number of newspapers stayed with vertical layout into the second half of the twentieth century. The *Kansas City Star* and *Times* were among the last to give up; they did not abandon their one-column, multideck headline approach until 1970. Tears fell. The *Times* and *Star* were no longer distinctive.

The loss may have been more apparent to nostalgia buffs than to Kansas City readers. Surveys indicate that newspapers with vestiges of vertical makeup are perceived as being less alert and even less credible than those with a more modern appearance. The main objection is their grayness, their failure to offer a headline that catches your attention. Proponents would argue that readers should be interested in the words and not in the packaging. That is true, but we have to recognize that at some point the reader's desire for knowledge is deadened by the unrelieved ugliness of masses of gray type.

Is the answer a switch to horizontal makeup? No, not totally. Extreme horizontal makeup exists, but it is rare. It has no vertical elements—nothing more than six or seven inches deep and the whole page broken into three or four horizontal bands. Reminds me of a layer cake, but layer cakes are pretty cohesive and layered newspapers aren't. I like a vertical element in there somewhere, a good, strong, half-page deep vertical element to tie the layers together.

Newspapers with one or two horizontal elements mixed with nonhorizontal elements are more common. That is, a newspaper may run one story all the way across the top or bottom (or both) but treat the rest of the page differently.

Only two of the terms used to describe particular kinds of makeup—*vertical* and *horizontal*—are significant. We have a large number of terms, but they are seldom useful except for academic discussions. Newspaper layout people do not sit around talking about brace makeup, circus layout and modules. If I had to pick one term to describe layout in U.S. newspapers today, it would be *informal balance*. Most newspapers have horizontal tendencies marked by informal balance. In this kind of layout, strong elements on one side of the page, perhaps near the top, are offset by strong elements on the other side, perhaps low or near the middle. (Formal balance, stressing symmetry, is passé. In that kind of layout, half the page folds over and matches the other half. Looks forced.)

Look at some of the other terms used to describe makeup. Bear in mind that they are just names to help in discussions.

Brace makeup focuses all the attention on the upper right corner. Some say the name comes from the similarity in appearance to a closet-shelf brace, the thing attached to the wall to hold up a shelf. This style is extinct.

Magazine makeup appears regularly because it can be effective at times. It is most likely to be found on the front pages of inside sections. The *New York Herald Tribune* made a big splash with magazine makeup in the 1950s, but the beauty was only skin deep and was not enough to save the newspaper. I think magazine layout took unfair criticism in that situation. The *Herald Tribune* won many typography awards, and the typical question was, "If magazine layout is so great, why didn't it save the *Herald Tribune*?" Maybe magazine layout kept it alive longer than anything else would have.

Circus layout is characterized by large headlines, colored type, big art, contest notices, and assorted other bells and whistles in the top half of page 1. It draws its name from the three-ring circus, where something exciting is happening wherever you look. I contend that all display is no display, that circus layout overloads the reader's circuits and causes some stories to be overlooked despite a screaming headline.

Modular layout puts each story into some sort of rectangle and fits rectangles together on the page until they fill it up. Modular layout differs from other kinds in that the pieces are not knitted together at all. One story never wraps around another or around a picture unless they are related and separated into their own module. Modules must be flat-bottomed, meaning that all legs of type must be the same length, unless they are shortened by something within the module. You can get attractive layouts with modules, but copyfitting is troublesome unless you are permitted to jump stories from one page to the next.

Tabloid is the only kind of layout that has come to include a philosophy. Tabloid newspapers are typically about half the size of broadsheet publications, like regular newspapers printed sideways. Tabloid papers quite often have nothing on page 1 but a nameplate and a giant headline, with a reference to a story inside or perhaps a picture and a slightly smaller headline. The practice of choosing the story that will appeal to the most people that day and the act of splashing it all over the front page has produced the view that tabloid journalism leans to the sensational.

Tabloid newspapers include the *New York Daily News,* which has the largest circulation of any general daily in the country. The *News* has a conservative editorial page and a serious approach to its work, but it is nevertheless much more likely to play a good murder story than the latest report on the economy. The *Daily News,* the *New York Post,* the *Chicago Sun-Times,* and other general circulation tabs are cut from different cloth than the *National Tattler* and a dozen emulators who thrive on sordid sex and sundry sensational sins.

We have reviewed Benjamin Franklin's quiet, no-makeup approach to the tabs' deafening shout. What difference does it make? Or, to put it another way, what is layout supposed to do? Layout has several functions, from grading the news to dressing your newspaper in attractive clothes as it faces the public each day. Grading the news is the main function. Before dealing with that, we need to examine layout's function of image-making, for it is through layout that the public gets its first impression of your publication and through layout the impression is reinforced or torn down.

Ideally, readers will consider your newspaper to be their newspaper. If you have a bright, lively appearance in your pages, readers will detect it. *Image* has to do with the way people perceive you; it is what they think you are. Makeup has an immediate impact on image. Depending on layout (and on many other things), a newspaper can be considered lively, serious, mature, dull, happy, capricious, unsettled, sober, perhaps monotonous. College newspapers, often marked by experimentation, are likely to be livelier than most, probably on the side of capriciousness. Some of their gamboling can be attributed to the variety of people doing layout and a desire to try something new; it is common for several persons to handle layout on a college paper, sometimes as many as five a week for page 1. Continuity is hard to maintain in those circumstances. But this does not mean that makeup has less effect; makeup still provides an image for your publication.

As part of the image-making process, layout reflects the newspaper's approach to news. A newspaper with 18–20 stories outside is taking the bulletin board approach. It offers everything on page 1, believing, perhaps properly, that a small headline on page 1 is worth more than something larger inside. Such a paper must necessarily resort to a multitude of one-column headlines and masses of gray type. Photographs are small—and rare. Many stories are short, and the long ones jump to inside pages to spread their grayness across more space. (I once counted 18 jumps off page 1 of the *New York Times*, but the number has diminished lately.)

A newspaper with three to seven stories on page 1 has to handle its work differently. Stories obviously run longer. The paper does not have little stories to sprinkle around the page, getting many names on page 1 but playing hell with layout aesthetics. Longer stories call for more creative packaging, usually including art and sometimes including boxed quotations or lists and special headline treatment. A newspaper that demands longer, more thorough stories is likely to give reporters more time to produce them and editors more time to dress them up. Such newspapers are also likely to believe that a sedate layout is proper with a kind of journalism that goes beyond what radio and television do with the news. These newspapers will not try to outshout the broadcasters on traditional news and instead try to whip them with stories that broadcasters do not have or cannot cover in satisfactory depth.

Newspapers moving to a total design approach, will lay aside the makeup that was designed primarily to attract street sales. Except for a handful of major cities, direct competition at the newsstand is rare, anyway. The need for big headlines and top-heavy pages (laden with eye-catchers) has passed. Journalism educators, myself included, have done students a disservice by instilling in them a belief that every page 1 should be laid out as part of a continuing battle between William Randolph Hearst and Joseph Pulitzer.

One of the reasons we continue, I suspect, is that memories of such competition are truly pleasant. One of my fondest recollections, of no consequence whatever, dates to the morning the *Houston Post* ran an eight-column banner saying

Who Killed Fred Tones?

My newspaper, the *Houston Chronicle,* had an hour-later deadline and a reporter in New York to interview the two suspects. Our Blue Streak edition, racked side by side with the *Post*'s Five Star, had a headline saying

'I Killed Fred Tones,'
Leslie Ashley Says

That's when you would love to live forever. Such competitive opportunities are nonexistent on most newspapers nowadays, and we need to recognize the change.

My call for a switch to a quieter approach should not for an instant be considered a call for the abandonment of traditional news values. The things that have been news in the past—things of interest and importance to readers, including the Fred Tones killing—should not be ignored. But the packaging of such news will be different as newspapers expand their service functions in new competition with the broadcast media. Remember that layout cannot do the job by itself. Layout is a vehicle for getting news and other information to readers; it is format, not substance, and image-making is only one of its functions.

The primary function of makeup is grading the news. Makeup is what you use to tell the reader what you consider the leading stories (not story) of the day. Good layout tells which story is the most important and subtly categorizes all other stories on each page. It ranks stories against each other in a given day's run and against other stories from other days. Readers are seldom aware of it, but newspapers perform a continuous symphony of ideas as headline sizes go up and down and italic heads team up with round-cornered boxes and underlines and kickers and railroad gothics to show how today's news is different from yesterday's. I suspect I am making that somewhat more romantic than it really is, but newspapers do play their layout game under certain rules that make it an intellectual exercise.

Some newspapers approach the news differently, using substantially the same layout every day. The *Chicago Tribune* used to lead with an eight-column streamer in black 96-point caps on every edition. I was once in a small group that interviewed the *Tribune*'s editor, then Don Maxwell. Some cheeky lad amongst us asked Maxwell why the *Tribune* employed the same layout every day and just what the newspaper might do if some really big news came along. To be specific, he asked how the *Trib* would play the Second Coming. Maxwell, a gentleman if not a theologian, replied softly that all news is relative and that the *Tribune* gives the most important story in the world an 8–96 each day. He implied, but did not say, that, should Jesus put in a reappearance, the *Tribune* would cover the event with an 8–96, probably with a sidebar.

The *Tribune* was not unique. I sadly recall participating in an ignominous event with the *Galveston Tribune* that had a similar policy. The *Galveston Tribune*, an afternoon paper, competed with two Houston newspapers, and the management required that the street sales edition be led with an eight-column, 120-point banner. As the telegraph editor, I was the instrument through which this policy was carried out. The deadline was bearing down on us one day when the managing editor, noting my distress, asked what was wrong. I replied that the entire civilized world had been unable that day to produce a news story worth an 8–120 headline. "Damn," he said, heading for the Teletype printer. He looked through my discards and in only 60 seconds was back with a story to stun the multitudes. On that day, the *Galveston Tribune* went after the citizenry's nickels with

Grasshoppers Plague Colorado

And that is the kind of corner you can paint yourself into when you set up rules and put them in concrete.

By-products of grading the news include (1) facilitating the reading of the newspaper and (2) attracting attention to main stories.

In facilitating readership, layout helps the reader go through the newspaper quickly and find stories of interest or skip those with no appeal. Proper makeup, in this sense, includes a big dose of what we used to call "good editing." It includes grouping by subject or geography, perhaps, and arranging the pages in some orderly progression from one kind of news to another.

The good news editor will capitalize on reader habits. Indeed, the news editor (the layout person, whatever the title) will help instill certain habits in readers. Consistency is the first element to have a bearing on habits. The reader must come to associate certain things with certain kinds of layout. For instance, the reader must learn that the largest and boldest headline on page 1 is on the day's top hard news story if your publication uses that system. Similarly, readers come to expect that stories enclosed in boxes are something special. Some newspapers box stories because of importance, some box them because of approach (they are either humorous or bizarre), and some, sad to say, box them for no known reason beyond the need for a box to dress up a page. Obviously, you are able to communicate more to readers before they read a single word if you box a story and they know what sort of story they are likely to find with such treatment. The same thing goes for various other layout maneuvers.

In helping readers find what they want quickly, we reduce their effort. In Chapter 2, we discuss the fraction of selection, in which the expectation of reward is divided by the effort required. Your goal as layout chief is to reduce the amount of effort. You have a split goal here: You want to enable readers to go through the newspaper quickly, and yet you want them to spend more time with your product. You accomplish both by putting forth a great amount of interesting and important information and arranging it attractively so that the reader can see all the goodies you have available.

This coin has another side. You do the readers a service if you help them make a decision to skip a story. Not all readers will skip the same stories, of course, so I am not talking about putting tiny headlines on unimportant stories. No. I refer to fairly good stories that may be unimportant to some readers. The object is to let readers pass up a story without worrying that they have missed something of importance. Headlines share the burden here, obviously, but layout has a role. For instance, let's say something big is going on in China, and we have a lead story and a couple of sidebars on it. If you arrange these three stories so that readers can see their relationship—one is the lead news story and two are subsidiary—readers may readily realize they can skip the two sidebars and miss only some background information. Similarly, a reader deeply interested in the subject can find the news without stomping around through the underbrush on other pages; it's all together, and the stories are ranked in value.

When grading the news, your task is to make sure heavyweight stories are not like desert flowers, left to bloom unseen. Top stories must be presented so that readers cannot overlook them. Readers must pause at the story, if only to decline your invitation to linger.

Layout process

Our discussion of layout now shifts from the historical and philosophical to the practical. And we start with the basics, the building blocks. In an abstract way, we need to consider each newspaper layout element as having some kind of weight. We can say photographs are heavier than headlines; headlines heavier than body type; boxed stories heavier than unboxed. Thus you understand the meaning of a requirement that we have strong element in every quarter of the page.

Most of the following discussion is based on thoughts about page 1 makeup. Although these principles hold true for inside pages, noticeable differences abound. For example, you need to worry about the bottom of the page on outside makeup, but inside pages are normally anchored by ads. Also, inside pages do not have a nameplate. And inside pages with ads call for considerably different treatment of photos, which should not be placed next to ads if other space is available.

Layout editors slight inside pages far too often. Page 1 is the showcase, and editors instinctively focus their attention there. Moreover, page 1 layout wins contests and prizes and plaudits, while inside pages bring you little or nothing. Shame on us all. We may have 20 to 50 chances to impress a reader with good inside layout, and only one page 1. We sin grievously by ignoring the inside.

We turn now to some general rules of page 1 makeup. I sometimes refer to these as the 13 ironclad rules. Some are worthwhile. Maybe all are.

1. Nameplate goes at or near the top.
2. Top right is the key spot.
3. Top left is second best spot on page.
4. Stories descend in value as they move down the page (this rule has a thousand exceptions).
5. Headlines descend in size as they descend on page.
6. Always watch the bottom of your page.
7. Juxtaposed elements must contrast (don't bump two boxes or two unrelated photos).
8. Don't bump headlines accidentally.
9. Vary headline arrangements to an extent.
10. Avoid dutch turns.
11. Use no smashingly big headlines in one- and two-column widths.
12. Do not let the space between columns run the full length of the page.
13. Never hesitate to break any rule for good purpose.

What does all this mean? Well, these are the basics, the conventional wisdom. These rules are in use throughout the world. They make sense most of the time. We will flip back through them and see why.

We put the nameplate—some call it the flag—at or near the top so that the reader will see and identify it quickly and so that we do not break up our page with a horizontal strip across its middle. A nameplate more than seven inches deep on the page disrupts the eye's movement to the bottom of the page. Probably 90 percent of the nation's newspapers leave the nameplate at the top of the page most of the time. Some drop it regularly, of course, and some drop it occasionally for a special story or an over-the-flag headline (sometimes called, picturesquely, a skyline streamer). I prefer a nameplate that runs less than full width of the page and that you can move around as a makeup element.

The tradition of putting the lead news story at the top right has hung on too long. As noted earlier, we used to start in the upper left, the same place you start reading a letter from your sweetheart. The change came when newspapers started using banner headlines. A person reading a page-wide headline would, obviously, finish the headline in the right-hand column, so editors began dropping the stories down the right-hand columns. And that is why, even today, long after the passions of yellow journalism have cooled and banners have generally faded away, most U.S. newspapers lead from the upper right. A few—the *Louisville Courier-Journal* and *Dallas Morning News,* for example—are going back to the more natural spot, upper left, but the trend is not strong. (If you get a job doing layout, you will want to make sure you establish yourself before you make the switch to upper left. Newspaper people are not as eager for change as you may have been led to believe. If you show that you have talent, you have a lot better chance of getting your big changes accepted. Of course, you may not agree with me that the upper left is the natural spot and is much more pleasing to the sensitive eye.)

If we accept the top right as the key spot, that leaves the top left for number two. Fine; it can take either a good news story or a strong feature. Remember that this is a major place on the page, so don't kiss it off. Indeed, the upper left spot is where the reader's eye normally enters the page. Edmund Arnold, perhaps the nation's best newspaper typographer, calls it the "primary optical area." He suggests, sagely, that you offer a major stopper here—a big headline or strong art.

We said our fourth rule, that stories descend in value as they descend on the page, has a thousand exceptions. If you followed the rule (and its corollary, 5, that head sizes descend, too), you would go right out the window and have nothing of importance at the bottom. Don't allow that. But remember that more important stories and bigger headlines are likely to be on stories higher on the page. This rule has its most common application in midpage (see Fig. 11.1). There, all other things being equal, you give a good story a 3-48-2 headline and a lesser story a 2-36-2. However, you have to come back to larger sizes for the bottom of the page so it doesn't turn gray on you.

It is not at all uncommon for a layout editor to begin work on a page by penciling in a story at the bottom as our sixth rule suggests. You

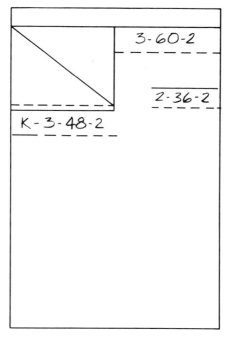

Fig. 11.1

will often have a strong feature or good news story that deserves special treatment but not the top of the page. Such stories are likely to get to the desk early, and you can devise fancier treatment for them while waiting for the lead stories. You anchor the page with such a story and then let the other news flow around your anchor. This practice is much better than working totally from top to bottom and then finding yourself with a special story but no special place to put it. Look ahead. And watch your bottom.

Our next rule (7) says that you do not want to provide some special treatment for that anchor and then take away the effect by surrounding it with similar elements. The basic principle in our restriction on juxtaposition is best illustrated by placing a boxed story next to a photograph. A boxed story surrounded by body type will stand out sharply. So will a photo. But you detract from both if you put them together; neither stands out as much as it would on a background of body type. Furthermore, you do not want to bump unrelated photos. Juxtaposed elements have an affinity for each other, and readers will think they go together. I am all in favor of putting two or three related pictures together as a package, but you need to keep out the interlopers. The nonjux rule does not keep you from putting headlines next to photos, even though you take away a little of the strength of each. Photos are universally used to separate headlines. So are boxes. But boxes do not go next to boxes or to pictures.

Nor do headlines go next to headlines, in most cases (rule 8). You will encounter two kinds of headline bumps: accidental and intended.

Editors generally frown on the first, but they are of mixed thoughts on the second. Accidental bumps are those that occur when headlines in adjacent columns touch or almost touch. These bumps occur more often in the composing room than on the page layout as the layout may look good, but a story may miss its estimated length or be pushed up by a late insert or by another mismeasured story, causing headlines to bump when the pasteup is done.

Most newspapers have loose rules about intentional headline bumps. Some forbid the practice. Others, perhaps a majority, will permit bumps under conditions something like these:

a. The headlines should not be the same size (at least 12 points difference, I would say; more on big headlines).
b. One headline should be in italic and one in roman, or they should be in different families.
c. The headlines should not be the same depth.
d. One of the headlines should be only one column wide; the other should be more.
e. The headline on the left should not be full length.

Actually, headline bumps are not as bad now as they once were. Ten years ago, newspapers commonly used thin vertical lines call column rules to separate columns. These were 1 or 1½ points thick, set on a 3-point base. This left ½₄ inch between columns. Today's newspapers usually separate columns with ¼ inch of white space. This gap is slightly larger than the space between words in most headlines; and it helps take the sting out of bumping, although it does not cure bumping's ills.

Note the final words on rule 9, "to an extent." Admittedly, a page full of multicolumn, two-line headlines has a stale look, with all headlines the same. But a page full of souped-up screamers—every one with a kicker, underline, overline, hood or other special treatment—is perhaps worse. A page with half its headlines in italic is similarly troublesome; you don't need that much italic to lighten a page. Alas, we have no national consensus on what is proper, on what you should use in a given situation. My instincts tell me that a straight news story gets a straight headline, probably two or three lines of type with no subsidiary elements. However, some well-known newspapers, good newspapers, do not boggle at topping the lead headline with a kicker or even using a centered underline on it.

My assessment of what is normal is open to challenge, of course, but I will offer it and await the arrows. A normal page with seven headlines might have them arranged this way:

a. One plain headline with three lines
b. Three plain headlines of two lines each
c. A one-liner with an underline
d. A one-liner with no accessories, just a line of type
e. A one- or two-liner with a kicker

In other words, your unadorned headlines are expected to carry most of the load. If you have more than one single-column headline, you may want some variety there. One-column headlines are more likely to have three lines than two when used on the front page. Those above the fold (page midpoint) commonly have three lines. And if perchance you use one at the top of the page, up with the flag, three lines or more will be almost mandatory. Many newspapers would add a smaller deck, a readout, to such a page-topper.

Since the use of italic type comes under this rule, we might look at it briefly. A couple of italic headlines per page will do nicely, tradition says, though one noted typographer would scrap all italic. I wouldn't. I believe an italic typeface can add a little nonverbal communication to your layout. If you reserve your italic for features, for poignant stories, for something other than rock-hard news, you improve your readers' ability to grasp meanings quickly. The only problem is that we are assuming you have a poignant story every day, which may be asking too much. You may have to say only that you will not use italic on a murder story or something of that nature. Or you may want to use your italic strictly on the basis of geography—wherever it looks good on the page. Fine. The *St. Louis Post-Dispatch* sometimes uses italic for the lead story.

Our next rule (10) has nothing to do with who pays for what on a date. No, a *dutch turn,* or dutch wrap, occurs when you move a paragraph or so of type at the end of a story into the next column, out from under the headline. (A *raw wrap,* a more heinous crime, occurs when part of the body type is moved out from under the headline and placed at the top of a column, with no headline over it at all.) The general rule is that body type should remain under the headline. Violations of this rule mean that a piece of our story is in an adjoining column, separated from some other story only by a thin cutoff line or, more common now, by a dab of white space. It will confuse readers.

Two exceptions come to mind. First, a headline format called the *side head* has caught on in the past five years and is fairly common—and understandable. A side head is simply set at the left side of the story. The headline has no body type under it. It uses white space to fill the gaps between it and stories above and below it. Side heads work fine in many ways, for they can help you eliminate a head bump or, particularly on an inside page, let you use a fairly small headline on a thin, page-wide space above an ad. (Some newspapers have strips as thin as two inches deep, and the layout editor has to put an eight-column headline over a layer of type 1½ inches high.) If you use a side headline on page 1, you may want to use special rules (borders) above and below the story. Otherwise, a reader may go from another story right into a leg of your body type, skipping over the white space you intended to be a barrier.

The second exception to a prohibition against running type out from under the headline occurs in packaging. If you have a story and related art, you can make a nice little package by running the story down one or more columns to the left of the art and then tucking some body type under the art. However, be sure that your readers understand you are offering them a package. Keep the bottom line of your type level across all columns, even under the photo. If one leg of type goes deeper than the others, you lose the effect. You should wind up with a rectangle.

Our restriction on smashingly big headlines in one and two columns (rule 11) is based on pragmatic considerations as well as aesthetics. That is, if you (as copy chief) assign a 2-72-3 headline to a story, you are apt to get a punch in the nose from a disgruntled headline writer. You probably deserve it. Such a headline would count seven or eight, maybe more in extra wide columns. No copy editor can sparkle in three lines of eight count; be reasonable. Besides, from a layout standpoint, such headlines appear unbalanced, regardless of fit.

Finally, we require that all column rules or spaces be crossed (rule 12). This requirement keeps your page from breaking into two parts. The page appears knitted together if you have something across all columns. Moreover, the reader's eye never gets caught on that long slide from top to bottom of the page.

That brings us to the last and perhaps the most important rule of all: Never hesitate to break any rule for good purpose. The catch here is that you have to know what you are doing before you can do something for good purpose. To illustrate this rule, we might look at the previous one. Let's say we are arranging some kind of vertical package, two or three pieces of art with a story. If the package runs the full length of the page, we would be foolish to shorten it and try to slip something horizontal under it just to break the column rules. Or how about the *Chicago Sun-Times* head, a 1-60-7, saying

City's
First
Snow
May
Get
This
Deep

Artificial rules can be bent in good conscience when they stand in the way of good layout and thus good communication. But you are hereby reminded that you have to understand the rules first.

You probably cannot recite the 13 ironclad rules from memory. Do not worry. The point is that some guidelines make your layout better. Follow these guidelines.

Handling a layout

Let's go to the copydesk and see how layout is handled. You have seen (Chapter 2) that inside layout is done first and that the copydesk chief tries to move a large number of pages quickly, keeping copy flow-ing throughout the cycle. Even while doing this basic work, the desk chief keeps an eye out for page 1 news.

Page 1 is usually the last page completed in the day's cycle, sometimes followed by the jump page (the inside page that contains parts of stories too long to be used entirely on page 1). Some layout editors will start their front page a couple of hours ahead of time, but they will not normally get down to serious work on it until 30 minutes or so before the copy deadline. If things are hectic, a layout editor may be sidetracked and wind up with only 5 minutes or so to do a page. A good editor can handle the job in that time, but not if copy editors have to write or rewrite a great number of headlines or if precision copyfitting is required.

Normally, copydesk chiefs like to have half an hour to draw the dummy and get the headlines in from copy editors. They do not have time to dawdle, but they are able to weigh the copy and make sure they are presenting the day's news in the best fashion.

Actual pencil work on page 1 layout is preceded by an assessment of the available news. Newspapers make their assessments in a variety of ways. Some—the larger papers, usually—start with a formal meeting of department heads. Those men and women push their best stories for page 1 and generally try to make sure that their departments come out with plenty of space on page 1 and inside. A typical conference would see the national editor suggesting the use of a story on a California forest fire as the lead, only to have the city editor weigh in with a major budget story.

The meeting on a smaller paper may consist of the city editor yelling across the room to urge the news editor to lead with the big local story and the news editor replying that he prefers to go with a piece on the state legislature adjourning. Bickering may follow.

And on a still smaller paper, the assessment process may consist of a copydesk chief, thinking, "Hmmmm. I wonder if I ought to lead with this fire story or that budget thing."

News editors are helped in their measurement of the news by wire service budgets (see Chapter 8). These brief summaries of the major stories expected each day are sent by wire services near the beginning of the cycle. They include length and a note on whether the story will stand up or will require a change to cover developments. Do not put a changing story on a page with a color ad or on a small page by itself. If a story requires a change for a later edition, extra work must be done in the pressroom in getting the color realigned. Similarly, the pressroom has just as much work to do on a page with one story as on a page with many—a page is a page. Thus you save time and a little money if you have two or three changing stories on the same page; then you can change them all with one make-over.

The budgets do not allow for fresh-breaking news, of course, since wire service people are no better than others at looking into the future. News editors tend to gamble that at least one page 1 story will come in near the deadline, rounding off a perfect page. It doesn't always work that way (as you learned in the Colorado grasshopper vignette). Nevertheless, no newspaper has ever run a blank spot on page 1 because the world neglected to produce a meaty story that day.

News editors normally let their copy editors work with page 1 stories fairly early in the day rather than hold back until all decisions have been made. In the days of hot type, editors would sometimes send material to the composing room with an HTK (Head To Come) designation. (I have no idea why it wasn't *HTC*.) Such copy could be set early, expediting copy flow. Headlines would be applied after the layout began shaping up.

Electronic typesetting does away with the need for early setting, but smart news editors let their copy editors get a look at the stories before the squeeze. They can even edit them, within limits, thinning out the verbiage and awaiting only a final decision on making the trim for length.

Let's look at what happens when the desk chief, or layout editor, or news editor (we have called this person by many names) takes a fresh piece of layout paper and starts to work. The layout page, often called a dummy, is a miniature of the completed page. It is the editor's shorthand message to tell the composing room how the page should look; it is a map (see Fig. 11.2).

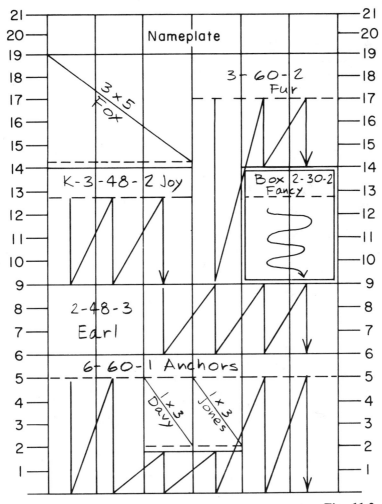

Fig. 11.2

NEWSPAPER LAYOUT SHEETS

Newspaper layout sheets are drawn to scale vertically but not horizontally in most shops. The discrepancy (which you will quickly learn to ignore) exists because newspapers use regular 8½ by 11 sheets for layouts, and full-size papers are not in that proportion. The vertical dimension is the one that makes a difference.

Let's look at the layout in Fig. 11.2 and see what all those funny marks represent. Markings vary from place to place. The ones you learn here will get you through, but you will want to change if other marks are common at your newspaper. The main goal is to use marks your pasteup worker can understand.

We start at the top in Fig. 11.2. The vertical lines divide the page into columns. The numbers stand for one inch apiece; they are a scale to tell you how much material you have placed on the page. Most newspaper layout sheets have numbers on both sides.

The first horizontal line shows how deep our name-plate runs, 2 inches. Some nameplates run deeper; most run about 1½ inches. You do not have any control over nameplate depth.

Next we have an indication that we have a 3-60-2 headline. I require a dotted line at the bottom of the space the headline takes up, simply as a reminder to beginners that they must allow room for headlines. Later, when allowing for the headline comes automatically, you can drop the dotted line.

On the left, we have the marking for a photograph. We indicate the depth in case the makeup person wants to start on the page before the art is ready. (Type often reaches the pasteup area before photographs.) Now, we also need the guideline on our picture, "Fox," in this case. You may draw your diagonal line from either side, in case you are wondering. Many people who do layout draw an **X**, and one person I know draws partial diagonals from all four corners. Do whatever pasteup recognizes.

Under the photo we have a dotted line. I require this for the same reason I require it on headlines—to remind you that you must allow room for cutlines. Again, you can drop this with no harm in your full-time job as long as you allow for lines when drawing in your photo. The makeup person is going to leave the amount of space you indicate in numbers—3 columns by 5 inches here.

The vertical lines showing where body type goes are commonly started in the middle of the first column of type and run down the middle of all columns, ending in an arrow, as shown here. People doing this work for a living usually take shortcuts: They start in the same place and end in the same place, but they round off the corners severely on the way. Just make sure you know where the type goes.

We move now to the right side of the page, where we

encounter a box. The system shown, lines inside the normal lines, is common for indicating that a story should have a line around it. The word "box" in the headline helps. If you have a standard kind of box on your publication, this is all you need. If you want something special (boxes come in a great number of widths and designs, from dot patterns to solid blacks of several thicknesses to Christmas holly), you simply make a marginal note for the printer.

Note also that we have a wiggly type line in this box, which indicates you are using wide-set type. The printer will look for some double-column indented type, rather than the regular stuff.

Moving down the page, we get to a side headline (see p. 220). You put it at the side as shown and assume a printer can figure out your wishes.

The rest has been covered.

Some layout editors automatically pop the flag (nameplate) onto the top of the page as a starter. That's fine, especially if your newspaper wants the flag at the top. Also, early placement there guarantees that you will never forget to dummy the flag. It is not uncommon to find a make-up editor who will admit to having laid out one page 1 without a flag, or getting almost through the layout before discovering this embarrassing omission. You need not worry about going to press undressed, however, for the flag is normally kept with the page 1 form (or in the pasteup area), and the printer will inquire, probably louder than is truly necessary, about any novel plans you may have for the flag today.

Your next step will depend on what you already have in hand. If you are running some kind of special story, a fancy investigative piece with maps and photos, you may want to place that next. Ideally, you spot your special packages early and work the other material in around them.

We'll say for this discussion that you put the package across the bottom of the page. Looks nice. Some editors would prefer to start with the top, placing the lead story and some art and maybe the second and third stories before moving to the bottom. Whatever you like, you do. But we are continuing with the package at the bottom (see Fig. 11.3).

You will probably find it convenient at this point to make a decision on art. If you have a strong photo for the top of the page, you may decide to play it right under the flag, with the lead headline beside it (Fig. 11.4). If you have mediocre art and a strong story, you may want to put a wide headline on the story and run the art lower on the page (Fig. 11.5).

Your placement of the art automatically creates natural positions for other stories. Traditional layout almost always calls for a headline and story under art. The layout shown in Fig. 11.6 also produces a natural spot on the right side of the page. Note that the headline on the right natural spot runs only two columns, permitting a leg of type from the lead story to separate the two headlines. If you incline toward modular

226

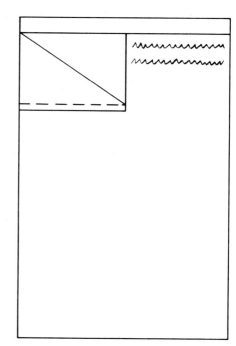

Fig. 11.3

Fig. 11.4

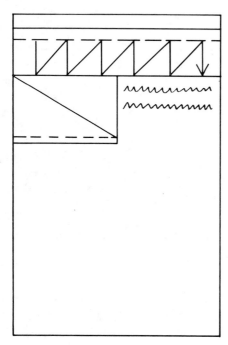

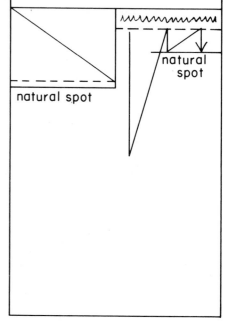

Fig. 11.5

Fig. 11.6

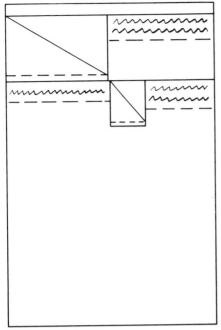

Fig. 11.7

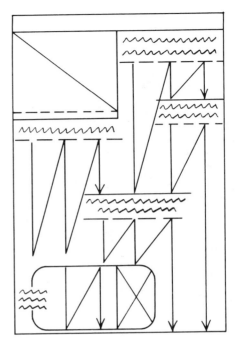

Fig. 11.8

layout, with flat-bottomed stories, you will have some kind of bump under the art unless you either run the story there all the way across the page or use some device to break up the bump (Fig. 11.7).

Your move from here depends, as always, on the stories you are trying to display. Indeed, if your number two story is a whopper, long and strong, you may want to run that headline under the art all the way across instead of breaking it with a one-column picture or box, as done in Fig. 11.7. But if the stories are of only normal value, you will probably make some kind of move in the middle of your page, as in Fig. 11.8.

This leaves you a long gray leg on the right and two moderately long gray legs on the left. You can break them with one-column headlines, again depending on value and length of stories available. If your number two story is good and solid and if your newspaper frowns on jumps, you may have to keep two gray legs at left. If the story is not so long or if you can jump it, you put in a one-column headline. This head and one for the right side are shown in Fig. 11.9. If the number two story is short, instead of long, you can jack it up a little with a short article under the second leg, in column 2. Keep the article short, or you will clutter the page.

If your midpage story deserves more emphasis than we have given it, you may have to drop the one-column story in column six and run a four-column headline. As far as that goes, you can run a five—or even a six. But be sure you have a story strong enough to carry it.

Incidentally, you will note that this layout puts the lead story in the

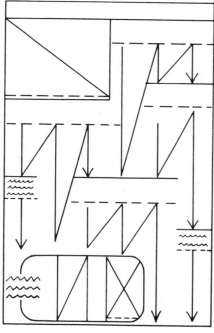

Fig. 11.9

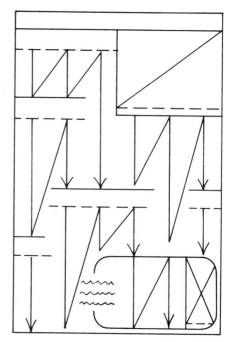

Fig. 11.10

upper right, the traditional spot. If you want to use the upper left, with the advantages cited earlier, all you have to do is flop the page, as in Fig. 11.10. That gives you a mirror layout, putting everything on the side opposite its present position. You have only one exception here: You cannot flop the side head. That package has to stay as is. Our only problem is that the art is loaded up on the right. This traditional layout will do the job, no matter how we flip-flop.

But what happens if we want to go modular? The easiest way to rearrange what we have started is to run across the page with a line under the art—not a physical line of ink on the newspaper page but a straight line of white space. My preference would be to offer a piece of art, two columns wide, to go with a four-column headline (Fig. 11.11). If we did not have any more art, we could box a story that deserved boxing or we might put a hood on a headline over a worthy story. And if we had no such worthy story, we would go with the six-column headline mentioned earlier. Let's use a two-column picture. (A three would be too neat, a formal offsetting of the top three-column art.)

Now, depending on our stories, we fill in the page. If one of our stories is really a biggie, we may want to run all the way across the page with it, as in Fig. 11.12. If it is somewhat less exciting, we might drop to a two-column headline under the art, as in Fig. 11.13. In that case, we would need to use something just to the left of this headline to keep from bumping the headline we know will be on the left side. Figure 11.14

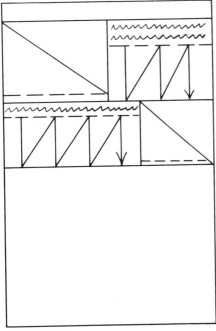

Fig. 11.11

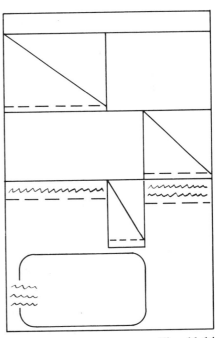

Fig. 11.12

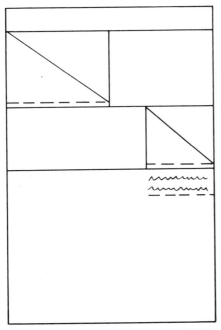

Fig. 11.13

Fig. 11.14

shows the art separating those headlines. A one-column photo would handle this chore best, but a box would do. The drawback of a box is that it sits atop the box we placed on this page earlier. Two boxes do not go well together. The photo is less harmful than a box because it has cutlines under it. Neither device is perfect, but with their help, the layout is nevertheless complete.

We have walked through a layout full of abstractions; you did not have any way to judge the stories as they were dummied. All you could see was form, not substance. And good layout, to repeat, is a showcase, not the merchandise itself. Also, layouts involve aesthetic judgments. Although you will find thousands of wise news editors who will applaud the layout information in this chapter, surely the world of newspaperdom contains one or two no-class guys who think these layout ideas stink. I will neither defend nor condemn, but I will note that newspaper layout comes in a multitude of shapes, that different editors and different cities prefer different kinds, and that the only good layout is the kind that helps readers understand and enjoy their newspapers.

We need to touch now on headline sizes and picture placement. The first of these makes great trouble for newcomers; the other, for everybody.

One of the first questions asked by students newly exposed to layout work is, "How do you know what size headlines to use?" You don't. Nowhere will you find engraved in stone a perfect answer to that question. The closest (watch out for flying stone chips) is that headlines should be of appropriate size.

If you are presenting a sedate, home-delivered newspaper to readers who examine it in comfortable, relatively relaxed surroundings, you may want to use modest type sizes throughout, perhaps no larger than 48 point, sometimes even 36, although the latter is small for my tastes. On the other hand, if you are competing with other newspapers and radio for a hully-gully audience dashing for the subway or bus stop, or racing across the sidewalk in front of the office on the way to work, the appropriate headline may be a 288-point (four-inch) streamer. You can defend either size, and some in between. You will find newspapers that use large headlines throughout. Some have a 60-pointer on almost every page. Even that is defensible, on one condition: The newspaper should be consistent in its headline sizes. That is, if you lead with a three-line 72, you ought not drop to a 36 as your second head and fill up the page with 24-pointers. Hardly. If the lead is 72, the second head will commonly be 48, perhaps 60 if the second story is quite strong. Many newspapers find 36 point about the smallest common size for page 1 headlines in six-column layout.

You cannot put this book under your pillow and let all this information and knowledge soak into your head by osmosis. No, you will have to work at it if you want to improve your ability to choose headline sizes. You need to do two things:

1. Learn type sizes. You will find a chart in Fig. 11.15. It is not

TYPE SIZE

6 pt. Type

7 pt. Type

8 pt. Type

9 pt. Type

10 pt. Type

11 pt. Type

12 pt. Type

14 pt. Type

18 pt. Type

24 pt. Type

30 pt. Type

36 pt. Type

42 pt. Type

48 pt. Type

60 pt. Type

72 pt. Type

Fig. 11.15

precisely accurate for every typeface, since some types of a given size have slightly smaller letters than others; they have more built-in white space between lines. But you can compare most types with the chart and learn approximate sizes fairly quickly.

2. Examine newspaper pages. *Examine* them. Look at a *New York Times.* The lead headline may be a 3-36-2. Do you like it? Is it too large? Too small? Either way, it is probably consistent with other headlines on the page, but *you* must make a decision on the basic size. Look at a *Detroit Free Press.* Most of the headlines are large, 48 point being common. Are those too large or just right? Picture the page with smaller heads. Like it? What would *you* use?

This business of picturing a paper with different headlines is hard to master. A simpler way to accomplish the same thing is to find a newspaper with headline sizes you like, determine what they are, and use it as a general basis for future judgments. If you know what you like and you know what you can do, life becomes much cheerier.

Placement of photos

We cheerily turn our attention to photography, particularly the placement of photos on a newspaper page. A basic thought should come to mind every time you lay out a page with a piece of art on it: Photos should show some relationship to any stories they are related to.

Formerly, the problem was less severe than now. Newspapers used to have column rules on all sides of everything and cutoff rules above and below. To tie art to type, editors would take out the rule or cutoff where the picture touched the accompanying story or headline. Printers accomplished this deletion by trimming off the top part of the rule with a pair of tin snips. The rule was thus too low to make a mark. White space took its place. You will still find column rules on some inside pages and on page 1 in a few newspapers, but most rules have gone the way of nickel coffee. The resulting white space is attractive, but it gives makeup people a new problem in showing a relationship between art and story.

The situation is not one of unrelieved gloom. Thoughtful layout editors are forced into doing what they should have been doing all along—and what many no doubt did—put the art in a normal position in regard to the story. Although research has been slim, we do know that readers have certain perceptions of relationships. When a photo is surrounded by stories, the story immediately under the photo is the one most often considered to be the one that goes with the art. The choice is a toss-up after that—top or side.

Sometimes you cannot put an accompanying story under the art. Where then? I believe a photo will be perceived to have an affinity for a story with which it has a common border along the full length of one side. Test the theory with this layout (see Fig. 11.16.). Since the logo cuts story number two off from the art, we see quickly that the art does not

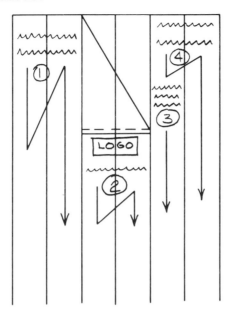

Fig. 11.16

go with what is under it. Story number one shares a border with the art along one full side of the art. Stories three and four do not.

The following layouts have art and type sharing a border. They go along with the basic principle that art should lead naturally into a story or flow naturally out of it. These are thus acceptable placements in which the reader will have no trouble in discerning the relationship (see Figs. 11.17 and 11.18). Note that all these arrangements work in mirror layout; they can be flopped.

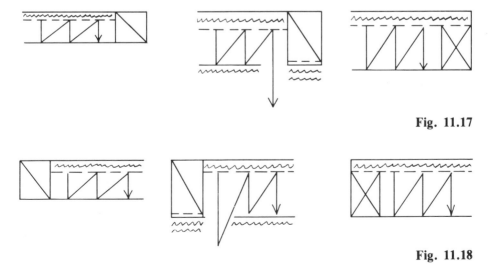

Fig. 11.17

Fig. 11.18

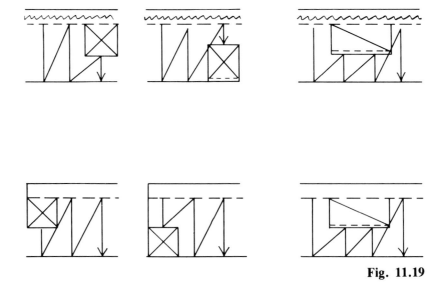

Fig. 11.19

So can those of Fig. 11.19 except for the first layout. Why can't the first one be flopped? Because the research available clearly indicates that readers go from headline to the nearest touching body type; thus they will try to start reading this story just to the right of the picture rather than under it.

We have a related situation when we float a mug shot (the head and shoulders art of one person) in a column, as in Fig. 11.20. The reader's eye does not readily go through the picture, even to the cutline. The eye turns to the next column of type and looks for some continuation of the story there. Type under the picture thus gets lost.

Finally, we come to the transgressions. Here are some things to avoid in putting art next to a story (see Fig. 11.21). A proper rule of thumb holds that you can run under the art with your story only if the body type has a flat bottom. The flat bottom makes the art and story a package deal, purely rectangular. If your story has two different lengths of legs on the part not under the photo, as shown in Fig. 11.21, forget it.

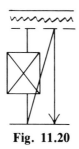

Fig. 11.20

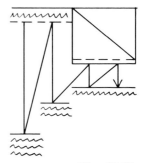

Fig. 11.21

In Fig. 11.22, the art could conceivably go with the top story. You may get caught in a bind someday and have to lay out a page that way. However, the second story will not do for a combination of art and story. The story is trying to sneak in the back door and cannot get in.

Carelessness sometimes produces something like Fig. 11.23. A photo only partly covered by its story is much worse than a photo not covered at all.

The layout in Fig. 11.24 shows that the layout artist was once told that a picture and its story should be side by side. Unfortunately, simple proximity will not suffice. This is the bustle approach; something is sticking out behind. The art does not show its affinity for the story.

On occasion, you might get away with having a one-column story and a multi-column headline under the picture, with either related to the art (see Fig. 11.25). But if the multicolumn headline runs out from under the art, its kinship to that art is in question.

Some people will accept the layout in Fig. 11.26; some forbid it. It is borderline. You will see it in newspapers now and then, and you may even fall back on this arrangement yourself in a bind. But be aware of its imperfections.

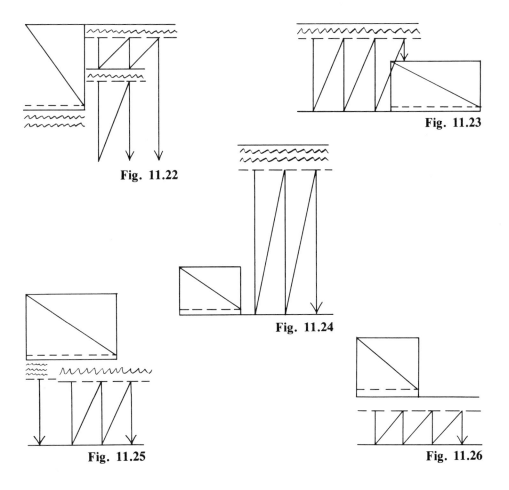

Fig. 11.22

Fig. 11.23

Fig. 11.24

Fig. 11.25

Fig. 11.26

Keeping tabs

Predictions that tabloid newspapers will replace broadsheets are voiced with some regularity. Evidence of a change is rarer. However, the format is common enough on college campuses to cause us to take a longer look at tabloids than we took earlier in the chapter.

Tabloid format has a number of advantages (and some disadvantages) over full-size newspapers. (1) Of particular importance to schools is the flexibility in number of pages and the illusion of bulk. That is, an eight-page tabloid, though small, appears to be a regular newspaper, while a four-page broadsheet offers only a single thickness when unfolded, although it is of substantially the same overall size as the tab. As for flexibility, note that you can have a six-page tabloid but not a three-page broadsheet.

(2) Tabloid format also allows you more ad-free pages than a broadsheet can. An eight-page tab can devote one page to editorials and move ads to the next page, whereas a broadsheet would have to have ads on the editorial page under the same setup. This division of pages provides greater ease of departmentalization elsewhere in the paper. You can give each department its own page or pages and encounter fewer problems of running out of pages than with a broadsheet.

The disadvantages are not ruinous, but they are strong enough to cause professional papers to shy away from tabs for the most part. For one thing, you lose a bit of space to page margins. If you visualize two tab pages as being the same size as one full-size page, you see that the margins between the two tab pages would be like a belt of white space across the middle of the full-size page. That space is simply lost. Also, tabloid newspapers are difficult to break down into sections. You have trouble giving the sports section to Dad, the life-style section to Sis, the news section to Mom, and so on, since tabs come in a single folded section. *Newsday,* one of the country's biggest tabs, tackled the sectionalizing problem by cutting semicircles into the margin, sort of like a dictionary's letter markers. Others have printed alternating sections upside down, so they could easily be distinguished. No one has solved the problem, but it does not seem to be a major hurdle to journalistic success. And it is of no consequence in college newspapers.

Of more importance, no doubt, is the charge that a tabloid is a little paper, sort of a toy, not a real newspaper. This is particularly troublesome on very thin newspapers, which are often found on college campuses. I would say that if a college cannot support a daily tab of at least eight pages, its publication frequency ought to be reduced. Anything under eight begins to look like a newsletter, with resulting credibility problems. Thicker newspapers are less susceptible to this charge.

A discussion of tabloids that fails to go beyond the *New York Daily News* is woefully incomplete. The *News* sells 2 million copies a day, almost always with a poster layout that includes the nameplate, a whopper of a picture, and a giant headline. However, other tabloids shout less, and some even offer the appearance of a scaled-down broadsheet. The

New York Post, for instance, has large headlines, but it also carries several stories on page 1. College tabloids almost universally use page 1 for news, not only for art and headlines.

This kind of tabloid layout is to an extent governed by the same principles that effect broadsheet layout. However, we deal with much more than just a geometric shrinking of the paper. One might think that a 36-point headline in a tab would have the same effect as a 72-pointer in a broadsheet, since one is half the size of the other, but not so. Bear in mind that the tabloid is on a different axis, sort of running crossways to a broadsheet. The tab is thus likely to be 14–15 inches deep, which is approximately two-thirds the depth of a broadsheet. A size reduction of about a third instead of a half strikes my eye as proper for most headlines. Thus a lead head of 72 points in a full-size paper becomes a 48 in the tab; a midpage 36 becomes a 24 (instead of an 18). Beyond that, your work is basically unchanged. You will quickly discover that a tab does not have as much room for long stories, but you remedy that by reducing the number of stories. The lack of space can be a positive factor if you adopt sprightly packaging. A story that might not merit a full page by itself in a broadsheet can get major impact with that treatment in a tabloid. The format lends itself to big-story packaging. The layout editor's job is to take advantage of what is available.

Inside pages

Page 1 is of course an open page, a canvas you can paint with few hindrances other than a nameplate and perhaps an index. Inside pages, on the other hand, offer great variety—meaning problems and opportunities. In some shops, you will find that the people spotting ads on pages will make an effort to accommodate you, to help you with your problems. In others, it sometimes seems that those people are the problem. I find it easy to hate people who leave a two-inch hole all the way across a page top, along with those who think a page with no more than a half-page ad on it is wasteful.

Although we do not want to disparage people who bring us money, you, or the managing editor, or even the editor, must make sure the tail does not wag the dog here. It is incumbent on the news side to make sure that the ad layout people offer you enough space to present the news attractively. We will leave that problem to you to solve, reminding you only that grumbling to yourself does not do nearly as much good as grumbling—or speaking right up—to someone who can change things; the first step is to make sure someone knows you need more space. The advertising people simply may not realize they are raining on your parade. Tell them.

Advertising is laid out in two, maybe three, basic patterns. *Pyramid right* works best for the news department. In this style, ads are stacked as shown in Fig. 11.27. Pyramids to the left, are less common than to the right. Some newspapers occasionally put a pyramid left on the left-hand

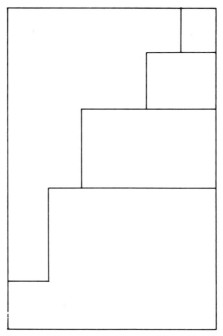

Fig. 11.27

page and a pyramid right on the right-hand page, creating an open space in the middle of the two pages. This would be magnificent, or at least good, if people read the newspaper two pages at a time. William Randolph Hearst used to spread the paper on the floor and turn the pages with his toes, and he may have found the double pyramid proper. Less talented people get along fine without it, as they usually handle only one page at a time.

The page should pyramid to the right so as to open up the primary optical area on the left. You need some room at the upper left, so you can offer the reader something interesting and your art won't be cramped. We call that the primary optical area, to repeat, because Edmund Arnold likes that term and because the upper left is where people start reading most things written in English.

You will occasionally run into *well* layout, in which ads are run up both sides of the page, creating a tapered hole in the middle. Makeup people do not like wells; the only spot for big display is in the middle, and after that you quickly find yourself writing one-column headlines. A well dummy is shown in Fig. 11.28.

Magazine layout is similar except that the taper is eliminated in favor of straight sides (see Fig. 11.29). It's hard to do much with that kind of ad layout.

In inside layout, all the principles that govern page 1 hold good ex-

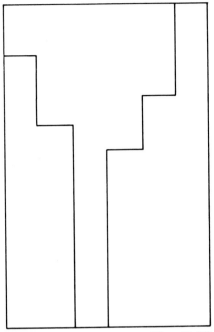

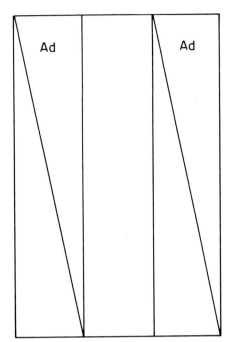

Fig. 11.28   **Fig. 11.29**

cept our ironclad rule that calls the upper right the lead spot. It has been repealed now, and we start with the upper left. Some basic thoughts:

1. You should have art on every page.
2. Every page needs a dominant headline.
3. Keep an eye on the ads.
4. Wrapping is still a sin.

Art. Do not be afraid to lead the page with art. Run it with confidence. Run it big, as big as it deserves. Many pages do not lend themselves to the use of art; then let common sense win out over a rule. Don't force art onto the page. But use it when you can.

Dominant headlines. Your job as a layout expert is to help readers understand the news. Tell them, with headline sizes, which stories are likely to be of most importance and interest to them. Make sure one headline has more muscle than the others; it will tell the reader to look at it first. A rule of thumb would hold that the dominant headline should be at least 12 points bigger and a column wider than the number two headline. You need not break out a calculator here, but you should be aware that a 2-36-3 (two columns, 36 points, three lines) has more bulk than a 3-48-1, even though the latter is a column longer and 12 points taller. Multiplication tells you that $2 \times 36 = 72$ and $72 \times 3 = 216$, whereas

$3 \times 48 = 144$ and $144 \times 1 = 144$; the 2-36-3 takes up more point space. Do not set that multiplication trick in concrete as a guideline, because a 2-48-2, though slightly smaller, is as strong as the 2-36-3. However, a page with those two as the biggest headlines would not have a dominant headline, a headline that the reader would instantly recognize as the page leader. Try for a dominant headline.

Ad watching. You are in control on page 1, and people do not slip up and interfere with your layout. The situation changes slightly on inside pages, for you have to consider the ads there before you start exercising your creativity. You run the risk of putting a headline or photo next to something similar in an ad. The ad layout indicates only that the message from a given advertiser occupies a certain space on the page; it does not tell you what the ad is like. If the ad contains a big, dark halftone (photograph), your news photo is in peril, for it may be overwhelmed by the ad's photo. Similarly, you can lose a headline if it runs low on the page and right next to a bit of large type in the ad. Since you have no control over the ad, you must make the adjustments. You adjust with least trouble by putting body type next to ads whenever you can, rather than art or headlines.

Ideally, you will not ever have to place a picture atop an ad. Cutlines separate your photo from whatever might appear in the ad, but they are a thin buffer if the ad has a dark halftone at its top.

Occasionally, you will have a one-column hole running beside an ad, and you have no choice but to put one or two stories and headlines next to the ad. All you can do is hope that the advertisement uses white space on the outside to concentrate the reader's attention on the central part of the ad.

Wrapping. Possibly the best advice you could have regarding inside layout is this: Do not break rules here that you would not break on page 1. Do not think no one will see or mind if you wrap a story out from under its headline; do not think people will suffer silently as you assault them with naked type at the top of a page. You may have to put type at the top of a page and use a side headline if you get a sneaky page with a thin strip of news space at the top. The side head (which has no type under it) makes the use of raw type at the top appear to be intentional, and we can live with that. But the normal rule is to keep the story under the headline.

(The *Los Angeles Times,* which has achieved a measure of success, has a standard layout for many of its inside pages, a layout directly contradictory to my rule. The *Times* uses a two-line, two-column headline in the top left corner, with the type wrapped buck naked across the rest of the top of the page. The *Times* is happy with this functional approach. It is easy to lay out. I think it's ugly, but readers accept it.)

The trick is to do things deliberately and with some degree of consistency. If readers become accustomed to your way of doing things and if you have no competition to offer them something more attractive, you can get away with just about any kind of layout you want. But you may wake up in the middle of the night sometime and say to yourself, "Gee, but I'm really slopping that sheet together.'' I hope you have a hard time going back to sleep. The rest of us are going to do it right—and sleep the sleep of the blest.

Things to know

You learned in Chapter 2 what the copy editor does. Now I want to mention a few things you ought to learn if you are going to choose what goes into a newspaper or a news broadcast.

Two requirements: know your city and know yourself. We will examine these in reverse order.

You have already been exposed to more education than the average American. You may not be better educated, and I am not even hinting that you are more intelligent. But you have simply been to school longer than many people. In college, you pick up certain interests, certain traits, certain habits and ways of doing things. Other people do not necessarily have these characteristics, but college students generally share them. All of you are roughly the same age. On the outside, things are different. Suddenly you are surrounded by people who have interests totally new to you. What's more, there are more of them than there are of you. While the college news editor can assume that a story he or she finds interesting will interest most readers, the outside news editor has to have other criteria.

Here is an illustration of what can go wrong if you do not realize you must change your perceptions. Earlier this century I got a job as news editor of the *Galveston Tribune.* The newspaper prospered despite that handicap and despite the work of my boss, the grasshopper lover we encountered earlier. One day the wires carried a story on a change in Social Security payments. I had been on the planet less than 25 years at the time, which meant that I had more than four decades to go before Social Security became a burning question. Social Security was for old folks. Accordingly, I gave the story a 1-24 headline and stuck it back in the paper somewhere behind the want ads.

The managing editor discovered it there. He frowned, loudly. Although he was not discourteous, he pointed out firmly that Galveston, a town of balmy climate and gentle breezes, was a retirement haven for many people—many, many people. Furthermore, it had a large number of citizens who were still working but planning for retirement. In short, he explained, every Social Security story was of vital interest to a large segment of our readership. I inferred that he was also suggesting I hold off a couple of weeks on asking for a raise.

The *Tribune* survived that tempest, although it was sunk by later storms. The people got a better version of the Social Security story the next day. I learned a lesson. And now you have learned the same lesson with less pain.

The lesson, in case you are thick, is that you need to know what kind of people live in your city because your job is to cater to their news needs and desires, and you do that best if you know what they want and need. Your knowledge of the people does not stop with their ages. You need to know about their jobs, education, activities, spendable income, ethnicity and anything else you can find out. All these will influence your selection and display of the news.

For instance, most newspapers will not get overly excited at a story on new regulations for shipping iron ore. But readers of the *News Tribune* in Duluth, Minnesota, have an abiding interest in the subject; it affects their pocketbooks because the vast Mesabi range is nearby. If you get a job at the *News Tribune,* be sure you give all your iron ore stories heavy play. Similarly, the people in Watkins Glen, New York, pay close attention to anything involving car racing and wine drinking (not together, of course). They are in wine country and some of the world's finest road racing has been done around there. If your people are big on boating, or Little League baseball, or politics, or finger painting, or whatever, make sure you know about it and give them the information they need to make their lives a little more pleasant.

You learn all these things by asking questions—after you have been to the library. The U.S. Census will tell you most of what you want to know, and the rest will yield to the gentle prying of a helpful librarian or a tenacious reporter or editor.

After you learn about your city, you will be in a proper position to assess news stories as a news editor or copydesk chief. Weigh your stories on a scale that covers the items we mentioned as elements of news in Chapter 4: consequence, proximity, prominence, immediacy and oddity (and others as you see fit). These criteria tell you that you must consider how much impact a story will have on your part of the world as you make decisions on placement and headline size. These criteria tell you that a story about something happening to a famous person or in a well-known place will have more readership than the same thing happening to an unknown person or in an unknown place. They also remind you that a story with immediacy may outweigh one of more consequence—a story about tonight's expected snowfall will have more appeal than a forecast of the cooling of the planet over the next century. And the criteria will remind you that some stories of little consequence should be offered for their own sake, for the rarity of their occurrence or for their entertainment value, if nothing else.

Some publications get along with a diet leaning strongly to the consequential—the *Wall Street Journal* and *New York Times* are as serious as you can get. Some feast on oddity and prominence, souped-up with conflict; you can find an example at nearly every supermarket checkout station. Most newspapers offer something of a mixture, giving readers a great amount of information required for the orderly operation of their lives but adding material for pleasant reading, for entertainment.

Unfortunately for the general theme of this book, which is that you need to know how to edit so you can help people take in more useful information, newspapers that offer titillation universally outsell the serious sheets. I hope you land on or start a publication that offers enough human interest stories to let you feel you are making some contribution to the improvement of humankind. Just a little contribution will do.

A final thought: Be conscious of the news judgment process. Start now to develop your ability to evaluate news. Your news judgment grows sharper almost automatically as you ripen with age and experience. You can speed the improvement if you start looking at newspapers (today would be a good time) as if you were the news editor or copydesk chief or both—and the same goes for the examination of broadcasts. Start reading newspapers with a grease pencil in hand. Mark the stories you think should be played better or less prominently. Challenge every page 1 story: Does it earn its keep; is it honestly worth such outstanding treatment? Ask the same questions about stories on inside pages—you may find one that belongs on page 1 or in the wastebasket.

Learn to read a newspaper with a critical eye, to measure every story against your own standards and with the criteria we have already considered. Absentminded editors can let a good story slip by, giving it an improper burial. Read and think—and do your thinking in the light of what you know about your audience. You will find that the process of putting out a newspaper, including all the headaches of headlines, deadlines and layout, is a fairly interesting way to pass time. Some people enjoy it a great deal.

[12] *Photographs and cutlines*

TO TELL YOU that you live in a generation in which visual images are important would be like telling Noah about the flood—you've heard. Although this book is made up almost exclusively of words, perhaps we can defend the lack of pictures because of the subject matter; it is hard to get a photograph that satisfactorily shows a dangling participle. Noah thought about water the way you need to think about photographs—almost constantly.

Two principles to include in your thinking are: (1) Photographs can tell some kinds of stories far better than words. (2) Photographs can be used as strong lures to attract readers to text matter.

Previous generations of newspeople have grown up with the idea that photographs are primarily something to keep headlines apart or perhaps to illustrate a reporter's brilliant words. But as television has shown us so clearly, the visual image has immediate, heavy impact. It tells a story that draws on your emotions. Photography can show poignancy—a child's tear, an athlete's elation, a sparrows's fall—far quicker than words can tell about it and in far more memorable fashion.

Even on stories that words handle better, photos can be used to attract readership and enhance understanding. Stories of municipal budgets, for example, deal mainly with figures. How much does something cost and how much do taxes have to go up to pay for it? Readers can be drawn to this basically dull material with photographs of what that tax money ultimately produces—parks full of children, highway construction, courtroom action and such things as police and fire protection.

This chapter's primary concern is the work the copydesk must do with photographs: cropping and sizing and writing cutlines. I would leave you with three other thoughts on being a photo editor:

1. If you are in doubt about what size the picture should be, make it bigger. Far more pictures are used too small than too large.

2. Crop it tight. The job of cropping a picture (picking the part you

use) should be handled ruthlessly. Cut out all extraneous matter. Get to the meat of the picture.

3. Look for the unusual. As a photo editor, you will handle hundreds of pictures daily. Look at each one thoroughly. You may find the unusual lurking somewhere inside a traditional shot. Too, you may be able to turn a normal shot into something special by cropping, particularly if your cropping produces an exceedingly deep picture, or one wide and thin. Beware of habitually using all art the same shape, especially square.

Cropping and sizing photographs

The average journalism student's brain tends to clog up on initial exposure to the problem of sizing photographs. The work looks suspiciously like algebra and is thus widely avoided. That is unfortunate, for two reasons: (1) Sizing does not require unusual mathematical skill; really. (2) Difficult or not, sizing is important in many, many jobs in all kinds of journalism.

You can get a fairly good grasp of the intricacies of sizing photographs in this chapter. Take your time with the questions. You will realize that you do not need to be a mathematical genius to handle this stuff.

Your chances of having to size pictures are almost directly inversely proportional to the size of the publication you choose as your employer, or perhaps choose to publish yourself if you prefer to be the boss. That is, almost everyone on a weekly newspaper will frequently size art. On a small magazine, a house organ, most people will do some sizing. The same goes for small public relations companies and the people there who put out brochures. On a large newspaper, however, some reporters (but not copy editors) make it all the way through to Social Security without handling art. On a paper the size of the *New York Daily News,* people can spend a career on the copydesk without doing any photo work beyond checking cutlines.

Electronics people are making welcome inroads in the photo field, too. New equipment on the market (past the lab stage) lets you reproduce art on a VDT screen and manipulate it as you wish—within certain limits. One goal of this chapter is to teach you an appreciation of those limits. The computer equipment will not let you perform magic; its main value is that you can see the picture cropped and sized about as it will appear in print and can change it if you do not like what you see.

We need to distinguish between sizing and cropping. *Cropping* refers to the selection of a part of a picture for publication. A football picture taken from a press box in most stadiums will show about 80 yards of empty Astroturf. Normally, the photo editor (or the photographer) will eliminate much of the empty space, focusing, let us say, on the line of scrimmage. This process is called cropping. If the photo editor narrows the scene further to a runner and a tackler, for example, he is cropping still tighter. If the picture is good enough (it wouldn't be, if the lens could take in all the field from the press box, but that is another subject), the editor could crop down to one player's facial expression.

This sword cuts two ways: Cropping is also the process of eliminating the parts of a picture you do not want to print. You will probably find that this elimination of unwanted material is more important than selection of the good parts. Same result, though.

Sizing (many people prefer the term *scaling*) refers to the decision on how large a photograph will be when printed—the size, not the contents. If you have a cropped photo that is 8 by 10 in the original (called the *copy*) it will appear as a 4 by 5 or a 16 by 20 or a 6 by 7½ in print, depending on how you size it.

Let's look at a photograph. Figure 12.1 is a full-frame shot—everything on the photographer's negative. It is a picture of a family outing. It tells a story in a neat, tight package, for the photographer cropped it with his lens. He positioned himself and focused so that he did not take a picture of 50 yards of creek bank or 20 feet of weeds; he shot the family. News photographers do not always have the time, and perhaps not the skill, to crop with the lens. They focus on the central object, their main quarry, and get the news picture. And then they or the photo editor can crop out the excess baggage, the parts of a photo that do not contribute to communication of the message. (Photo editors universally prefer to work with the full-frame photo. That gives them more leeway in sizing.)

J. B. Colson Photos

Fig. 12.1

We are not forced to accept the picture as it comes from the darkroom, even if it is a good shot like the one above. We can manipulate our photos by cropping. Let's say we want to use our family outing shot in a photo layout depicting a small boy's afternoon at the creek. We can crop it as shown in Fig. 12.2. We thus not only confine the art to the subject we have chosen; we let people see something about our strong-armed young friend that they probably missed before. (Did you see the flying rock on the first pass? I overlooked it. The cropping makes you look for the lad's missile.)

Fig. 12.2

Two more croppings of our photo appear in Figs. 12.3 and 12.4. (1) We have Mom and the two boys, romping on the creek bank, full of life and action (Fig. 12.3). (2) We have the father-and-toddler shot, in which Dad passes down the wisdom of the ages or acquaints the kid with dangers of running water, or whatever it is that we are trying to tell in our picture (Fig. 12.4). We simply crop to concentrate on parts of the photo that help us tell our story best.

You will recall a mention of cropping to eliminate things, as well as to highlight parts of a picture. Check Fig. 12.5. This full-frame photo shows much more than the pianist who is our subject. It shows a recording engineer at right, a great expanse of wall at left, and somewhat more ceiling than we need. In addition, the pianist's face is small and thus hard to recognize. So we crop to Fig. 12.6. Now you know what we can do. We cut out the bad parts and we emphasize the good parts.

Fig. 12.3

Fig. 12.4

In addition, we need to have the photo in whatever shape we want; that's the tricky part. You can handle it, but you will have to pay attention. You have no cause for panic, even though we are going to arrange our sizing work into something that has a vague resemblance to algebra (maybe it's not so vague). But you can do it.

J. B. Colson Photos   **Fig. 12.5**

Fig. 12.6

This is the process we go through in sizing a picture. We set up an equation (although you do not need to call it by that name if you dislike math). Starting with the copy (the original art, the glossy photo, etc.), we write down our first number. We will use the bottom part of the equation here. We always write the width first—*always*. Then we give the depth (call it *height,* if you prefer). We will use 3 inches by 2 inches for a piece of copy. (Rarely will you have such small copy. I am using it only for illustration, to make the math easier.) The figures go into an equation this way:

$$\frac{}{3} = \frac{}{2}$$

Remember, those are the copy dimensions. Let us say that we want to enlarge this picture. We arbitrarily choose to expand it to 6 inches wide. That could represent two columns in the magazine you edit, let's say. Now we have three figures: 3 by 2 in the copy and 6 by something in the reproduction. Our job is to find the fourth dimension: How deep will the reproduction be if it is 6 inches wide? We are almost home. We ride in on the wings of a formula, the like-on-like formula. Say that out loud: *like on like.* It means width on width. And if you have width on width, you also have depth on depth—*like on like.*

So let's try *like on like* in our equation. Here's one side of it, using the figures we have worked with so far:

$\frac{6}{3}$ (reproduction width we chose for our magazine)
(copy width, measured on photo)

We know our copy depth is 2 inches. So we finally get a full equation:

$$\frac{6}{3} = \frac{d}{2}$$

(If you have fond remembrances of your algebra class, you may use *x* instead of *d* for the missing part. I use *d* to stand for *depth.*) You know enough math to cross multiply and see that 6 times 2 is 12 and 3 times *d* is 3*d*. If $3d = 12, 1d = 4$.

Look at it another way: If reproduction width (6) is twice as big as copy width (3), then reproduction depth (*d*) must be twice as big as copy depth (2). It is: 4 inches.

Q. *Copy width is 3, copy depth 2, repro width 4½, and repro depth d. Write the formula, with like on like.*

$$\frac{4½}{3} = \frac{d}{2}$$

Q. *With that formula, what repro depth do you get?*

You get 3. Cross multiply: 2 times 4½ for 9 and 3 times *d* for 3*d*. Divide 3 into 9 for the answer, 3. As before, it's a matter of proportion. You see that your 3-inch copy width is ⅔ of repro width, 4½. Thus you know that copy depth, 2, will be ⅔ the size of *d*.

Q. *Of course, few pictures will come to you in the size we have used,*

3 by 2. Most are more like 8 by 10. Let's do an 8 by 10 and run it 9 inches wide in our magazine. What is the formula?

The formula is

$$\frac{9}{8} = \frac{d}{10}$$

If you cross multiply, you will find that $8d$ is 90. Thus d, for repro depth, is 11¼. Note that 9 is a little more than 8; thus d will be a little more than 10. Makes sense.

Q. *Say you have that same 8 by 10 picture but you want to run it only 6 inches wide. What is your formula?*

The formula is

$$\frac{6}{8} = \frac{d}{10}$$

Q. *And what is the figure for d?*

Simple: $8d$ is 60. Division gets you 7½. Note that 6 is ¾ of 8; d must therefore be ¾ of 10.

Not all our sizing problems come in such simple formats. We need to look at one of the basic premises, namely: To size, you must somehow arrive at three of the four dimensions. Then, when you apply proportional math, you get the fourth dimension. What that means is that *you* have to come up with three dimensions yourself—any three—by hook or crook. Then, finding the fourth is automatic.

An illustration: Ignoring cutlines, let us say we have a 5 by 5 hole on a magazine page. No matter what dimensions our copy has, the reproduction must be square, 5 inches by 5 inches. Consequently, in sizing our photo for this square hole, we can use any dimension we wish—as long as all sides of the picture are equal. We could crop the copy to 5 by 5 or 6³⁄₃₂ by 6³⁄₃₂ or 8 by 8—anything square.

Q. *Which of these would fit the space just described?*

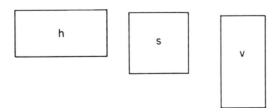

Too easy, but important: *s*.

Q. *Which of these is a wide shape? Which is deep? Which is square?*

In order, *h, v, s.*

Get them all? You may be a mathematical genius and not realize it. You may have discovered that you cannot put a wide photo in a deep hole, assuming you do not run it sideways.

> **Q.** *If the hole in our magazine is 6 by 3, which of the above shapes will come nearest fitting, without cropping?*

The answer is *h.* The hole, and thus the art, is twice as wide as deep.

> **Q.** *If the hole in our magazine is 6 by 3, which of the croppings below would come nearest fitting? (The shaded parts are those we cropped out.)*

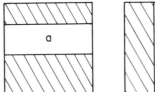

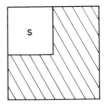

The one closest to our dimensions is *a.* Our cropping had to produce copy twice as wide as deep. Remember that we always write down width first.

> **Q.** *What would happen if the hole we just filled were not 6 by 3 but 3 by 6? Which of these shapes would likely fit without cropping?*

The vertical, *v;* we have a picture twice as deep as wide.

> **Q.** *Which cropping would be best for that same hole, 3 by 6, in the figures below?*

It still has to be vertical: *v.*

Q. *If we want a reproduction to be 6 by 3, which of the three incomplete formulas below would be the starting place for the proper formula in the system we have been using?*

a. $\dfrac{6}{} = \dfrac{3}{}$ b. $\dfrac{}{6} = \dfrac{}{3}$ c. $\dfrac{6}{3} = \dfrac{}{}$

In our format, the proper answer is *a*. A clever person could work it out in any format, but that would mean abandoning the like-on-like rule, and I do not want to give that up just yet.

As indicated, dimensions for your formulas do not just drop in on you out of the blue; we have to make some kind of decision on what we want. In this case, we chose 6 by 3, the size of the hole we found in our magazine, as the size of our reproduction. If the next hole is a different size, we will choose different figures.

Q. *We have a piece of copy that runs 8 by 10. We want to put it into the 6 by 3 hole we just discussed. But it won't go, since 8 by 10 is not the same proportion as 6 by 3. Consequently, some dimension must yield. We must choose three dimensions and then accept as the fourth whatever the math forces on us. Let us say we decide to run the picture 6 by 3 in the magazine, our repro size. Say further that we want to use maximum width; that would be 8 inches. How deep would our copy be? (Hint: Write down the three known parts of the formula, including the 6 by 3 and the 8, putting like on like.)*

The answer is 4 inches. We find our answer the regular way: $6/8 = 3/d$. Cross multiplication gives you $6d = 24$, and $d = 4$. Examine it sideways: 6 is 2 times 3 and 8 is 2 times d. This art is twice as wide as it is deep.

Layout people sometimes get a perverse streak and decide they will just run the picture however they want to run it; they will force it into the hole. Their efforts sometimes bring them to grief. See what would happen if you turned stubborn and insisted that you would crop your 8 by 10 to be 5 inches deep and then stick it in that 6 by 3 inch hole. Set up your formula.

Q. *Which of the following does the job?*

a. $\dfrac{8}{6} = \dfrac{5}{3}$ b. $\dfrac{6}{8} = \dfrac{d}{5}$ c. $\dfrac{6}{w} = \dfrac{3}{5}$

c. $6/w = 3/5$. Remember, we said you insisted the hole would be 6 by 3. And you insisted the copy would be 5 inches deep. That means you have to accept the width you get. This sort of compromise is not at all uncommon. It happens dozens of times daily (or weekly, depending on how much cropping you do).

Q. *Now we have a problem. If we do the math on the problem above, we get 6 times 5 for 30, 3 times w for 3w, then 3w = 30, and our width is 10. What is wrong with that?*

Our copy is only 8 inches wide. Ten goes past the margins.

Take heart. This sort of problem also comes up dozens of times weekly. If you must run 5 inches of your copy, you have one more move. You can set up your formula so that you choose *some other* dimension and the dimension you want is included. Put the 8 by 5 on the bottom for your copy dimensions—the 5 you want and the 8 you must accept as a maximum. (Remember that this means you must change the size of the hole. If the spot you have in mind for the picture cannot change, you need to scout around for another picture.)

> **Q.** *Let's do a problem under the conditions just outlined. We want our copy to be 5 inches deep. It can run no more than 8 inches wide, we know, since 8 is the full width of the photo. Thus we have an 8 by 5 copy. We will choose a hole 6 inches wide. That gives us three dimensions. Write out our formula.*

We know our copy is 8 by 5, so those numbers go on the bottom. We chose 6 inches for our repro width, so that goes on top. We use our like-on-like rule to tell us the 6 goes atop the 8.

$$\frac{6}{8} = \frac{d}{5}$$

If you do the math, you will get 6 times 5 for 30, 8 times d for $8d$; $8d = 30$, d is $3\frac{3}{4}$.

I may be guilty of overkill here, with multiple examples of how to adjust copy sizes to fit whatever hole you want. In truth, probably two-thirds of the sizing done on newspapers is done by choosing copy size (both dimensions) and reproduction width and then figuring out the repro depth. The normal procedure is to make your basic cropping decisions, measure the art as cropped, choose how many columns wide it should run, and then size it for depth. If the picture is the wrong depth, you go back and recrop. More often, you accept the depth and adjust the length of the story that goes under it.

Newspapers are also likely to measure width by columns. That is, a picture marked "2 × 7" will be two columns by seven inches. But I know of places that provide all their measurements in picas and others whose main interest is percentage. The latter is achieved by cropping the picture and telling the engraver to shoot it 110 percent, for example, or reduce it to 78 percent, or whatever. Rest easy: You do not have to know how to calculate all those percentages. Sizing is customarily done on a proportion wheel.

If all our figuring were confined to even numbers, we could handle sizing as we have done in this chapter. with a little cross multiplying. Unfortunately, proper cropping of a photo is just as likely to give you a picture 8¼ by 9½ as one 8 by 10. And columns do not come in even inches. Newspapers that use 13 picas, for instance, have a column 2⅙ inches wide. Moreover, the use of 18 points between columns leaves such a newspaper with a two-column width of 4⁷⁄₁₂ inches. Work with that fraction would put half the nation's copy editors in the hospital with brain strain.

The simplest way to handle numbers is to go with picas all the way, and then convert the final figure into inches (by dividing by 6). The beauty of the whole situation is that the proportion wheel does not care what kind of measurement you use—miles, rods, leagues, picas or inches. The proportion wheel will tell you that *a* is to *b* as *c* is to *d*, and you can convert those to any measurement you like. Inches and picas are most common. The proportion wheel in Fig. 12.7 mentions inches in reproduction.

The wheel has three charts. The wheel shown here has an outer ring of numbers on a fixed background, a piece of opaque plastic. The next ring is on a separate piece of plastic, clear where it covers the outer ring but opaque for its own numbers. Still another ring is printed on the fixed piece of plastic, but you can see only part of it through a window. This window has above it the words "per cent of original size."

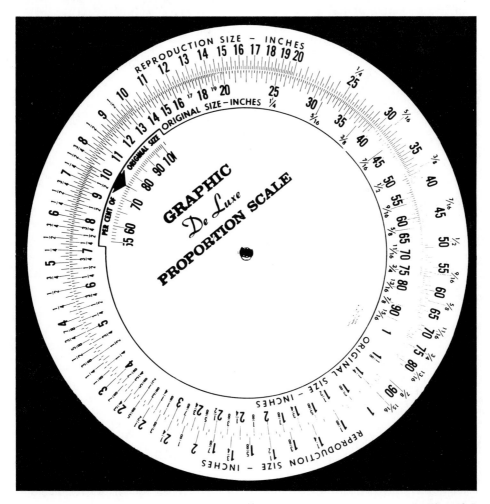

Fig. 12.7

You operate the wheel by putting like on like and then looking above or below the third dimension you have selected. Note that the wheel here is set up for the numbers we dealt with in the problem with a photo 8 inches by 5 and a hole 6 inches wide. Our formula, run the mathematical way, was:

$$\frac{6}{8} = \frac{d}{5}$$

Instead of cross multiplying, we now let the wheel do the work. All we have to do is line up our numbers, 6 on the top (or reproduction) ring and 8 on the inner (copy) ring, called the "original size" ring here. Then we find 5 on the inner ring. If we look above that, we have our repro depth. (See Fig. 12.7.)

The figure is 3¾, as it was when we did the problem with a pencil. Note also that we have a percentage now, 75. As mentioned earlier, the percent-

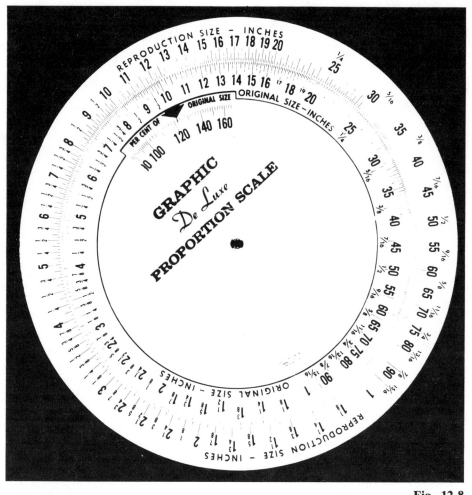

Fig. 12.8

age is the best for many engravers; they use it to adjust their copying cameras without having to do much math themselves.

Let's show another problem, one with tougher math; this may make you appreciate the wheel more. Say our photo is 6 by 10 and we want to put it into a hole 7⅜ wide. How deep will it run, and what will our percentage of enlargement be? (See Fig. 12.8.) The wheel tells us this will run 12¼ inches deep. You find that by looking above the 10. Remember, like on like. Repro width is over copy width; so repro depth can be found over copy depth, which we know to be 10 inches. The percentage, as we see from the scale, is 121.

If you want to work in picas, you simply multiply by 6, because you have 6 picas in an inch. In the work at hand, we would have 44¼ (6 times 7⅜) over 36 (6 times 6) for our first measurement. Then we would look above 60 (10 inches at 6 picas per) and find 74 picas. The percentage would remain the same.

You cannot become proficient in the operation of a wheel by reading about it in this book. You get the basic ideas here, but familiarity comes only with regular experience. We have covered the groundwork in cropping and sizing, however, and you should not suffer unduly as you learn to do the work in real life.

To recap the major points:

1. You must choose three dimensions; the fourth then comes automatically.

2. If the dimensions you choose will not work out, start over and use dimensions that are available to you. That is, your original size (copy) dimensions cannot be larger than the copy, and the reproduction cannot be larger than the hole you have in mind.

3. You handle the math or get the wheel to handle it for you by putting like on like.

4. You cannot put a vertical picture in a horizontal hole.

Most art does not come with a built-in ruler like the one in Fig. 12.9, although the film and paper people are welcome to the idea. The ruler makes it easy to get numbers for your sizing. Let's say we want to crop out the man on the right, but use the full depth of the photo. Then answer some questions.

    Q. *If we reduce this picture to* 4 *inches for repro width, how deep will it be in our publication?*

The answer is 5 inches. (It works just as well with a wheel as with the pencil.) Your formula is

$$\frac{4}{6} = \frac{d}{7\frac{1}{2}}$$

Let's go at this another way. We have just decided we want to run a vertical shot. We want it to come out 10 inches deep. To simplify the math, we will say we want it to be 6 inches wide in print.

Fig. 12.9

Q. *Are those reproduction dimensions or copy dimensions you just received?*

Repro, obviously. Our photo is not that big.

Q. *If we want this picture to run as deep as possible what will be our copy depth?*

Our copy depth will be 7½ inches; we run as much copy depth as we can get.

Q. *What numbers go on the outer ring of our proportion wheel? (Hint: What numbers go on the top line of the formula?)*

As you see from the wheel in Fig. 12.10, we lined up our 10 for repro depth on top of the 7½ maximum copy depth. We then find 6 on the top ring, our third number.

Q. *So how wide is our copy and where could we crop to get a fair 4½ inch width on our copy, eliminating the man at right?*

It's 4½ inches; we could try just to the side of the heads of our two remaining subjects.

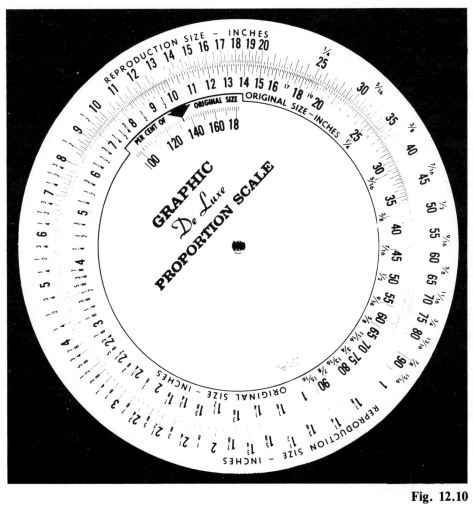

Fig. 12.10

Writing cutlines

Cutlines are one of the stepchildren of the newspaper business. Few newspapers give them the attention they deserve—and need. The *New York Daily News* has a platoon of people who do nothing but write cutlines, but most publications throw the job of writing cutlines to a desk newcomer or an overworked copyreader who doubles as photo editor an hour or two a day. A pity. The quality of cutlines directly reflects the interest and money devoted to them. And cutlines thus often fail to fulfill the important role they should have. What is that role?

Cutlines are the text matter accompanying a photograph. They supplement the photo four ways, sometimes five. Cutlines (1) explain the action portrayed; (2) identify people in the picture; (3) indicate why the picture was taken and is being used; (4) point out for the reader any interesting detail that might otherwise be overlooked; and (5) sometimes, but not always, they give credit to the photographer or his or her organization.

Cutlines greatly enhance the value of pictures. Rarely will you see a photo that can get by without cutlines.

Cutlines come in several categories. We will discuss three: normal (full) cutlines, skeleton lines, and namelines.

ANOTHER KIND OF CUTLINE

Narrative captions help photographs tell a story. Not all photos need cutlines, or at least full cutlines. A photograph of a wounded soldier lying against a tree would normally call for some identification, to be sure. But if the photo is part of a photo essay on, let's say, "war in the jungle," then our wounded soldier might very well represent all wounded soldiers and not need a name.

In a photo story on Tanzania, a shot of Mount Kilimanjaro rising from the plain would usually require identification. But if our work were less a travelogue and more an essay on solitude, or grandeur, or timelessness, we would not need to point out to readers that Kilimanjaro rises majestically from the plain. (Solitary mountains always rise majestically.)

One serious photographer of my acquaintance refers to the *additive caption*. In this, the caption writer is trying to get an idea from one mind into another, building on ideas already filed in that second mind. Picture, if you can, a photo of Kilimanjaro (rising, etc.). With this photograph we use a single word, *forever.* The word immediately calls up abstract ideas for the person seeing the picture. Fine. The photographer is telling the reader something. You have probably had a thought yourself, just now as you read the additive word.

What if we change words? What if we use, instead, *guardian*? Ah! We get a different thought. This book was not meant to promote anthropomorphism, but the word *guardian* certainly gives the mountain a life. The mountain now stands there as a sentinel, making sure that nature's rules are carried out.

Try one more: *young.* That changes the picture, too, so to speak. With half a dozen more words, we could make a philosophy course out of this.

The point is that you must not go through this chapter thinking that pictures are used mainly to dress up newspapers or separate headlines and that cutlines must read like a five Ws lead. Most of the time, news photographers do their work as a witness to news. Sometimes they will go beyond that and become a creator with the camera. Cutlines should help in the transmission of information and in the process of creation.

Normal cutlines are sometimes referred to as *wild* lines, not because they are bizarre but because they go with pictures that are not tied to accompanying stories. Such pictures are wild pictures, free to roam around and end up in any spot in the paper. Some publications use full lines with all pictures. Some use skeleton lines with all or almost all pictures. Normal cutlines explain a picture and identify the people in it. Indeed, they perform all the functions mentioned earlier.

Skeleton lines are customarily used with pictures that have accompanying stories. Inasmuch as some of the information usually contained in cutlines is also in the story, skeleton lines eliminate details, saving space and reading time. Some publications use one line in skeleton cutlines; some, two. Here is an example:

PRESIDENT CARTER TOURS LOW INCOME AREA
Workers told him they want factories reopened

Namelines are those used on mug shots. They usually give the person's name on one line and add a bit of elaboration on a second line, sometimes called an *expository* line. Some publications use only the nameline. On occasion, a mug shot will be used with fairly full cutlines and without an accompanying story. If the story is not burdened with detail, newspapers convert it into full lines on a one-column mug shot and use it as a layout breaker. A mug shot can separate two headlines quite nicely, but that is another subject.

NORMAL CUTLINES
Although the basic principles are the same, we will deal with the three kinds of cutlines separately: Normal, full cutlines often have headlines (called *catchlines* or captions).

A spot news photo freezes an instant of reality. It figuratively carries the reader to that spot for a single long look. Therefore, generally, the first sentence in the cutline will be in present tense and will describe the action of the picture. We call such a sentence the *main descriptive sentence*—the action sentence. All sentences that refer to this action, this frozen instant of reality, will be in present tense.

Sentences referring to action that occurs outside the instant the picture was taken may be in past or future or some other tense. Example:

> Trailing thick black smoke, George Snider's skidding race car smashes into the retaining wall in the first lap of the Indianapolis 500. Snider was unhurt in the crash Sunday but was forced out of the race.

Our photograph shows the car smashing into the wall. We have frozen that moment. If we look at the picture tomorrow, it will show the same thing. So our action sentence, our main descriptive sentence, uses the present tense. However, we cannot say "Snider walks away unhurt," because the picture does not show Snider walking away, hurt or un. We must use past tense in that piece of information; it is outside the instant the photo was snapped.

Note also that we used the active voice: "car smashes." Active voice is normally better than passive.

The time element in cutlines is handled differently from that of regular sentences. It is best placed in one of the secondary sentences. If you say, "George Snider's skidding race car *smashes* into the wall *yesterday*," you create an awkward shift of tense there at the end. Ruinous? No, but it trips a few readers. (The *Milwaukee Journal,* one of the nation's more prominent newspapers, uses past tense and a time element in the bulk of its cutlines, without any noticeable effect on circulation. But I argue that you get slightly livelier lines with present tense.)

Sometimes we encounter a measure of inconvenience in working the time element into a past tense or future tense sentence. If that happens, we can slip it into the action sentence with a little thought. The easiest way is to make it a modifier. Look at our race car lines. We could change them to say that Snider's car smashes into the wall "in Sunday's Indianapolis 500." That is sufficiently unobtrusive. Or, for another example: "Four victims of the Monday riot at the state prison receive medical attention in a makeshift hospital on the prison grounds." (The problem here is that it may sound as if we were distinguishing this from the Tuesday and Wednesday riots. However, that is probably not a major danger.)

> **Q.** *How would you edit this action sentence to make it conform to the major cutline function of telling what is happening in the photo?*

```
Lee Trevino joked with the gallery while his caddy
took a sip of water during the second round of the
British Open Thursday.  Trevino's choking gesture
indicated his great thirst.
```

```
Lee Trevino joked with the gallery while his caddy
took a sip of water during the second round of the
British Open Thursday.  Trevino's choking gesture
indicated his great thirst.
```
(edits shown: "joked" → "jokes"; "took" → "takes"; "British Open Thursday." → "British Open"; added "in Thursday's play" after "choking gesture")

You might have done the following, but it would be rewriting instead of editing:

```
Lee Trevino joked with the gallery while his caddy grabs
took a sip of water during the second round of the
British Open Thursday.  Trevino's choking gesture
indicated his great thirst in Thursday's second round.
```
(edits shown: "joked" → "jokes"; added "at the British Open"; "took" → "grabs"; "during the second round of the British Open Thursday." deleted; "Trevino's" → "Trevino made his"; "indicated his" → "indicating a"; added "in Thursday's second round")

(Free tip: If you are given lines like that to edit, check the story and see if there is some reason for the fellow's thirst. Hot day? Water fountains out of order? Beer too cold? Cutlines are much like news stories in that they look better without holes.)

So far, we have dealt with cutlines without seeing any pictures. This practice works out all right for what we have done, but we cannot carry it a great deal farther; it's sort of like a mail-order pamphlet that tells you how to kiss someone. You can practice by yourself only so long. We will find some photographs and go on with our work.

Fig. 12.11

Q. *Write an action sentence for Fig. 12.11, using some or all of this information:*

The men, from left, are Billy Clayton, speaker of the Texas House, Lt. Gov. Bill Hobby, and Gov. Dolph Briscoe. They are enjoying a laugh because someone unknown clipped a chili recipe to the title page of a speech Clayton made this morning at the University of Houston. The speech was entitled, "Where are the Texans with fire in their bellies?"

We are starting with a toughie. You might try something like this: "Texas House Speaker Billy Clayton registers his approval of the addition someone made to a speech he prepared."

The odds are moderately good that you came up with something better as an action sentence, a main descriptive sentence. But here's what the one above has going for it: It adds to what the reader can see, rather than pounding the reader on the head with a restatement of the obvious. The trite approach is to say the three "enjoy a laugh," and then get around to telling what happened. Although my "registers his approval"

Fig. 12.12

is not a great deal better than the cliché, at least we do not say people are laughing; the reader can see that. Much of the success of this cutline would depend on how subsequent parts were handled.

Q. *Here's another photo (see Fig. 12.12). Write an action sentence, using some or all of this information:*

From left, these people are Mrs. Luci Johnson Nugent, former President Gerald Ford, and Mrs. Lyndon Johnson (Lady Bird). They are visiting the LBJ Library at the University of Texas in Austin. Ford, who was in town for a speech, is waving to well-wishers. The people nearest the subjects are Secret Service agents.

Former President Gerald Ford acknowledges greetings from a crowd as he begins a tour of the LBJ Library in Austin, Texas.

Is that all? Yes, that's all for the action sentence. You will have to come back and identify Mrs. Johnson and her daughter, and you will want to mention the cast (badly twisted ankle; Luci stepped in a hole at a parking lot). The main point is that we refrained from saying, "Ford waves." Readers can see he is waving; your job is to tell them why. Again: Do not state the totally obvious. Although "acknowledges greetings" will win no prizes, it at least explains that Ford wasn't signaling for a fair catch.

Dallas Times Herald photo by Mike Smith   **Fig. 12.13**

Q. *Let's try one with plenty of action (Fig. 12.13). Write an action sentence for this photo, using some or all of the following information:*

From left are Umpire Greg Kose, Texas Ranger catcher Jim Sundberg and Detroit Tiger runner Ron Leflore. Leflore is out at the plate in 2–1 Ranger victory in Arlington Monday.

Umpire Greg Kose rises above the dust to tell Detroit runner Ron Leflore he has just been buried at the plate by Ranger catcher Jim Sundberg.

If you prefer something more sedate, you can say simply that our ump called the guy out. The connection between "above the dust" and "buried" is on the tenuous side, anyway, although I like it.

Identification. We had an easy time with identification in the sports photo, since the three subjects wore different uniforms. Sometimes, identification gives us a harder test. Usually, you make an effort to name anyone whose face is clearly identifiable and who appears to be part of the main action. In a crowd gathered around a political candidate, for example, you would identify only the candidate and the people directly involved. However, if the candidate's husband were standing nearby, even doing nothing, you would probably identify him. (Remember the functions of cutlines?) Photographers should not be encouraged to pose masses of humanity for group pictures.

In the Ford–Lady Bird picture, the Secret Service people's faces were hidden. But it would not have been a problem if that fellow behind Luci Nugent had been visible; unless he had her by the arm, he would not be considered a main part of the action, and thus we could leave him out without causing readers any extraordinary grief.

Turn back to our photo of the laughing officials. The cutlines read like this:

> Texas House Speaker Billy Clayton registers his approval of the addition someone made to a speech he prepared. Clayton, on a program with Gov. Dolph Briscoe, right, and Lt. Gov. Billy Hobby, spoke Monday on "Where are the Texans with fire in their bellies?" An unknown practical joker clipped a recipe to the title page—a recipe for chili.

Although the picture has little action, it offers examples of identification by action, by position, and by elimination. Clayton is identified by *action*—he obviously is holding the speech and laughing. Briscoe is identified by the most common method, *position* (Gov. Dolph Briscoe, right, . . ."). And Hobby is identified by *elimination;* he is the only one remaining. A more common case of identification by elimination would occur in a picture showing a husband and wife, particularly if the husband had short hair and the wife wore a dress.

Another aspect of identification could be called *obviousness.* If you have a picture of a governor standing behind the desk and shaking hands with a new appointee, you need not tell which is which unless the appointee has for some reason managed to move the governor over and get behind the nameplate. Most pictures of governors are used only within those governors' states, where, presumably, most voters already know what they look like and do not have to be told. Similarly,if you run a picture of the U.S. president and a visitor, you need not specify which is which.

Credit lines. Photo credit lines are handled in two major ways: (1) in small type above the cutlines; and (2) in type the same size as the lines, at the end of the cutlines. The first way is probably more common. It provides a neat little touch, and it adds pleasant white space. The other way is more functional, because the credit line can be set without changing type fonts. The credit line is for identification, of course. Newspapers customarily give credit lines to all wire service photos. Credit for staff-produced pictures is usually handled about the same as bylines on news stories—credit the good ones.

Here are some ways that credit lines can be set. These are abbreviated, on the assumption that you have had your fill of chili:

> State of Texas Photo
>
> Texas House Speaker Billy Clayton registers his approval of the addition someone made to a speech he prepared.
>
> Texas House Speaker Billy Clayton registers his approval of the addition someone made to a speech he prepared. (State of Texas Photo.)

Texas House Speaker Billy Clayton registers his approval of the addition someone made to a speech he prepared.
(State of Texas Photo)

The last two would work just as well with dashes (one each) instead of
parentheses:

. . . a speech he prepared.—State of Texas Photo.

SKELETON LINES

Skeleton lines are short because they omit details covered in a story accompanying the photo. Readers waste time if cutlines contain the same information that is in a story. Worse, there is a chance that the reader will
abandon a story if the first few paragraphs have little information not in the
cutlines. (Generally, a reader will look at a picture and lines before getting
into the story.)

We showed one kind of skeleton lines on p. 261: an all-cap line followed
by one in lowercase. The top line, all caps, is like the main descriptive
sentence used in full cutlines. The bottom line, using headline style capitalization, adds explanatory matter. The second line may be in any tense
and may further describe the photo's action, or it may tell of some event
that occurred outside the time frame of the picture.

Some publications prefer a single line, often italic. These lines are
usually in a type size larger than normal body type. Fourteen and 18 work
well for a single line, though you might go up 6 points more for a very wide
picture.

Skeleton lines usually emulate headlines in dropping articles *a, an, the.*

Q. *Flip back to the picture of President Ford. Write skeleton lines for it.
(We will have a story with the picture.) Make the first line of your
skeleton lines all caps. On the second line, cap the first word and all
other words except articles and prepositions. Use 6-8 words on the
first line, 8-12 on the second. You do not need to write in caps. The
printer will set the line according to your instructions.*

Perhaps something like this:

GERALD FORD ACKNOWLEDGES CROWD AT LBJ LIBRARY
Mrs. Johnson, daughter Luci Nugent accompany former president

Note that we did not refer to Luci's sore ankle. Something had to
go. However, if you believe the ankle deserves attention, you could try:

Luci Nugent, with twisted ankle, and Mrs. Johnson on tour

The best choice is to put the information in the story.

You need to be aware that cutlines are not written in a vacuum. You are
influenced by circumstances. Take the Ford picture, for instance. I would

bet that few newspapers used it with full cutlines, mainly because few newspapers used it. The picture was certainly of interest in the city concerned, and it got skeleton lines and a full story there. Elsewhere, it was of scant interest and received no play at all.

That moves us to the last kind of cutlines, those that go on mug shots. Publications use mug shots for a variety of reasons: to dress up a page layout, to separate bumping headlines, and to show what a person looks like. Occasionally a mug shot will capture a facial expression unusual enough to justify use of the photo for that reason alone.

Most mug shots are run with stories, and they consequently use a form of skeleton lines. Styles vary, but the trend is toward the use of a single line, containing nothing but the name. (I report this trend on the basis of an examination of 50 newspapers presumed to be representative.) Names are run in caps or caps and lowercase in regular body type, or they may be boldface or even italic—your choice (or the boss's).

Some newspapers and magazines add a second line to the nameline. This line offers further identification of the subject, often summarizing the accompanying story in two or three words. For instance:

Bruce Crampton
wins third title

I like the second line on namelines, and I hope you will stand fast against those who would eliminate it. A mug shot with only a name, especially on an unknown person, forces readers to dig for information if they want it. And readers do not want extra work. Remember that readers look at pictures first; thus the mug shot is your first chance to hook a reader. If the face and naked nameline are unfamiliar, you have less chance of landing anything. You need better bait.

Typographically, you have a number of choices—not as a copy editor but as a newspaper. Style is usually set by the boss, and you follow that. But you may get to be the boss; and before that you may be able to talk him or her into changing styles. Here are some of your options:

Bruce Crampton **. . . wins third title**	*Bruce Crampton* *wins third title*
BRUCE CRAMPTON **Wins Third Title**	**BRUCE CRAMPTON** **wins third title**

What is best? That is up to the publication. The easiest method (and ease must at least be considered) is to set both lines in the same face as your body type. Such lines do not stand out, however, so the next easiest thing is usually to set the lines boldface. In hot metal, particularly, boldface is the common departure in type faces. But in cold type, which is now dominant on newspapers, the switch of typeface makes little difference. You can achieve the greatest change by using a different type race, as in the sans serif of our last example. Sans serif stands out starkly from the roman body type.

The explanatory or expository line after a nameline on a mug shot should describe the person, tell what he or she has done, or complete a thought, using the name as the subject of a partial sentence.

Let us illustrate by looking back at the Crampton lines. We completed a thought there: . . . wins third title. We would have accomplished the same thing with these:

Bruce Crampton	**Bruce Crampton**	**Bruce Crampton**
winner of 3rd title	**again a winner**	**$34,000 richer**

All those are thought-completers, though they omit the verb "is". Each second line might be said to be prefaced by an understood "is": Crampton is winner, Crampton is richer.

Watch your step at this point or you will be in a pit that traps many cutline writers. I refer to lines like these:

Bruce Crampton	**Bruce Crampton**
New car for hole-in-one	**one shot wins car**

Eschew that approach. Mr. Crampton is not a new car, and cutlines saying he is are inferior, below your standards. He is not a shot, despite our second explanatory line. Under the philosophy set forth a minute ago, our explanatory line should say something like one of these:

wins car with one shot

he rolls one in   (a Rolls Royce)

quite a driver

has new wheels

Q. *Using our criteria, decide which of the lines below would be acceptable as second lines for a nameline reading:* **Nancy Westmoreland.**

a. **Miss America candidate**	*n.* **wins in Columbus**
b. **job secure**	*o.* **victory expected**
c. **in new role**	*p.* **expected to win**
d. **scholarship recipient**	*q.* **expects victory**
e. **$3,000 scholarship**	*r.* **stolen property found**
f. **too much a tomboy?**	*s.* **robbery victim**
g. **vacation in Bahamas**	*t.* **reports robbery**
h. **vacationing in Bahamas**	*u.* **finds stolen property**
i. **vacations in Utica**	*v.* **hired by NASA**
j. **prize-winning Iowan**	*w.* **called NASA genius**
k. **top racer at rodeo**	*x.* **NASA hires genius**
l. **top prize at rodeo**	*y.* **new NASA scientist**
m. **winner in Columbus**	*z.* **quits NASA**

All are fine except *b, e, g, l, o, r, x*.

    How did you do? Some publications would accept most—perhaps all—of those we rejected. Here is why the rejects do not meet our criteria: *b*. Miss Westmoreland is not a job secure. You could say "has secure job" and be all right. *e*. Our young lady is not a scholarship. A scholar, maybe; a scholarship, never. *g*. You could say "has vacation in Bahamas" or "on vacation in Bahamas." But plain old "vacation in Bahamas" lacks the smoothness of other approaches, as in *h* and *i*. In *l*, we call her a rodeo prize, which is unlikely. *o*. This is not far off but we are asking the reader to supply a "her" as well as the understood "is," which would give us a line saying "her victory is expected." That is asking quite a bit of a reader. If we used "expected victory," we would be all right, since the name would be the subject of the sentence formed by our namelines, and the sentence would be in past tense. *r*. We have here a repetition of the problem just examined. Our *r* is to *u* what *o* is to *p* and *q*. (Look at them again; *r* is wrong and *u* is right; *o* is wrong and *p* and *q* are right.) Finally, in *x* we have the wrong subject. This one would not confuse most readers, but it is wrong by the criteria we set up.

    These namelines show the high-class way to identify your photos. I am not saying newspapers that take another approach are wrong; they are just less right and they may not care as much about details as you do.

CATCHLINES

    Research sponsored by the American Newspaper Publishers Association clearly indicates that a good headline over cutlines enhances a reader's understanding of a picture. Some people call these headlines captions; I prefer the term *catchlines*. Catchlines come in a variety of styles. Magazines usually forgo them. Newspapers commonly use them in 18–24 or 30-point type, all caps, clc, italic—you name it. They are most often centered, but it is not at all unusual to find one flush left or flush right. Here is an example of a centered catchline atop full cutlines:

They Follow Polluted Air

Government scientists Cheryl McIntire and Tom Swinnea check chemical readings as their helium balloon drifts with a mass of polluted air across Missouri. They said their preliminary evidence from the flight indicates that pollution from cities can foul the air of rural areas hundreds of miles downwind.

    Catchline writing is an art. Cleverness draws a premium, although you do not want to be funny on a totally serious picture, such as our balloon art. The good catchline writer will extract all the humor that a picture has to offer, if any, employing puns, word plays, literary references and other things. But the writer must always stop short of forcing the humor. The writer must remember not to be cute on a serious subject; your goal is communication, not entertainment.

    In the catchline above, our key elements are pollution and movement—tracking the stuff. Our catchline, though bland, hits both elements. A reader would know what the picture was about just by reading the catchline. Although "Up in the air, down in the mouth" would be catchier, it would not convey to the reader as much information as the one we have. Use lines that inform. If the wording is clever, that's a bonus.

Q. *Think about the criteria we have discussed. What is wrong with the following catchlines for the pollution picture?*

a. Scientists take to air
b. Pollution testers wing it
c. Balloonists check pollution
d. Pollution checkup-up-up
e. Pollution trackers go aloft

Our first one, *a*, does not tell us what kind of scientists we have. They could be looking for bugs, testing balloons, or photographing sunspots. Do not mystify readers. Our *b* is catchy but inaccurate; balloons do not have wings. Answer *c* is fair, but it does not mention movement; it offers no hint that our guys are following a cloud. Answer *d* opts for a gimmick at the expense of clarity. I could live with answer *e* if the word "trackers" indicates movement, and I think it does. It does not tell us what kind of pollution we are dealing with; readers may think our scientists go up to spot pollution from above. Nevertheless, we could use this, although the original is better.

Are you hot for a pun? We will say our picture shows a large group of bicycle riders milling around at Valley Forge, waiting to start a two-day ride to the state capitol in Harrisburg, Pennsylvania. They plan to give the governor a petition calling for more bikeways. A hundred bikers started the trip at dawn today, just after we got the picture.

Q. *Write a catchline of at least 15 and not more than 40 counts (as in headline counts). Cleverness is encouraged, but don't get hokey.*

Here are some possibilities, in no particular order:

> They wheel for a better deal
> They spoke for bicycle paths
> Petition gets rolling
> Bikers pedal their views
> Out to start a new cycle

I would defend any of these. The pun in the second one may be too subtle; perhaps we should have said "Spokesmen for bicycle paths," or you could use "spokespersons" if you are inclined that way. The one on bikers pedaling their views gets my vote. It's a pun, of course, but it carries the same meaning either way you read it. They do "peddle" their views, too, in the sense that they are asking someone to support them.

If you wrote a better catchline, congratulations. I suspect many catchlines with more zip than the ones above are lurking out there somewhere. Your job is to write one.

We will do a catchline for Fig. 12.14. The pictures show Russell Erxleben of the University of Texas kicking an NCAA-record field goal of 67 yards. The holder is Ricky Churchman and the opponent was Rice University. One of the things to consider is your own location. If you are writing cutlines for an Austin newspaper, for example, you can call the lad "Erxleben," perhaps even "Russell." A newspaper in California would probably refer to him as "Texas kicker." Determine what you want to call him at your place and see if you can boot this catchline problem right through the uprights.

Q. *Since this is a wide strip, the catchline should be five to eight words long. Write three or four catchlines. Pick your best.*

Don't beat around the bush on this. Forget those clichés about getting a boot out of the record. Go at it head-on, perhaps with this one, which tells the story.

Texas kicker hits record 67-yarder

Let me repeat a point: If we are dealing with a local product or person whose name is nationally recognized, we can use the name. In that sense, "Erxleben" (pronounced IRKS lay ben) is a far better name than "Johnson," the subject of a previous catchline.

Q. *Now we are going to consider a series of rejects for the panel of photos. What is wrong with each of them?*

a. **Kicker also a jumper and a hugger**
b. **Happiness follows record field goal**

Daily Texan photos by Mike Smith

Fig. 12.14

c. Getting a kick out of a record field goal
d. Record field goal is a real kick
e. Kicker goes for high jump record, too

They all have the same basic problem: They do not give as much information as they might to the reader. They add the element of happiness, and we can applaud that, but they add it at the expense of other details. Net: No cheers. Our *b*, *c*, and *d* get the record but do not hint at identification.

Let's look at them individually: *a*. This asks the reader to do too much and offers little in return. The reader is not told that the fellow was happy because he had set a record. *b*. This one could be used, although it focuses more on player reaction than on the accomplishment. It does not give the length of the kick or tell the perpetrator's name. Usable, but flawed. *c*. Cliché; shun clichés. *d*. Again, the trouble with *d* is that it does not give any details. You could use it in a pinch. It does contain a play on words—a pun on a slang saying. *e*. Not bad, but it focuses on the reaction at the expense of information.

Q. *It is time for us to put all this stuff together. Go back to our baseball picture. Write full cutlines for a Colorado newspaper; include a catchline; put the catchline first.*

I would mention the dust, since it is so conspicuous in this picture. You could have a catchline saying "Tigers' hopes bite the dust," unless, of course, you want to argue that I am trying to sneak a cliché past you only a minute after getting a kick out of the football picture. Maybe, "Tiger out in a close, dusty call," or, "Down and dirty . . . and out." I like the first one, because it mentions fading hopes.

Next we take up the cutlines. Perhaps this: "Umpire Greg Kose rises above the dust to tell Detroit runner Ron Leflore he has just been buried at the plate by Texas Ranger catcher Jim Sundberg. Leflore was tagged out trying to tie up Monday's game in Arlington, which the Rangers won, 2–1."

We can try one more to close. Figure 12.15 above shows a lad named James Wickett, who lives near the West Texas town of Monahans. He is surfing on sand at Sandhills State Park, not far from his home. Hundreds of youngsters and a few oldsters do this. The local kids build their own surfboards, usually out of old plastic counter tops. They wax them up and generally have a fine time. No drownings, no worry about Jaws—just fun, a growing sport.

Q. *Write cutlines for the picture, based on the preceding information. Your main descriptive sentence need not be first, but it must be in there somewhere. Write the main lines of your cutlines first; we will wrestle with the catchline after a discussion.*

This rather weak picture has only one action element. You may back into the cutlines with such a picture—set the scene or explain something before telling what is going on. Or, we can go right to the action with something like this:

Fig. 12.15

James Wickett knifes down the face of a big wave as he enjoys a growing new sport in West Texas—sand surfing. James and hundreds of others surf at Sandhills State Park, near Monahans. The surfing is not as stimulating as that at Malibu or Waikiki, but very few sand surfers drown—and there is no chance of being nibbled on by a shark.

Perfect? No; the lines run to corniness, but they will suffice. Note the use of a strong verb, "knifes," in the action sentence. Also, our first sentence explains why we are running this picture—to show the reader a growing new sport the reader probably does not know about. Our second sentence fills in the details, and our last one is meant to leave readers with something light. The joke comes close to being forced. Anything more would have been heavy-handed; even this may be too much for you.

Now the catchline. Do a couple if you like. Good cutline writers will look at this picture and think. They will see that it is not complex; readers will not need a great number of clues to understand what is being presented. Our cutline writer can communicate with this:

Texas sand surfer

That would do. It is bland to a fault, but the reader would understand it.

Perhaps we can come up with something brighter. What are the word plays here? How about the natural contrasts: sand and water, desert and water, surf and dirt? What else can you call sand? Grit, silica, or waves. Anything odd about the surfing? Tracks, harder falls, absence of fishes, hell of a beach.

All these things would go through the mind of a caption writer. This catchline requires fewer details than the field goal catchline, because this picture has somewhat less action. This one calls for cleverness. Maybe:

Surfing, desert style

We would assume that readers would quickly see that our surfer was on sand. Such a catchline would be legitimate. So would these:

Where surfers leave tracks

Desert surfer

Surfing in the sand

A gritty surfer

The last is my favorite candidate. You may like one of the others or your own better, but this one has a little charm. It is a pun and it contains a measure of accuracy. Not much courage, not much true grit, is required to surf, admittedly, but a sand surfer who falls is sure to be gritty all over.

Not all publications use the kind of catchlines offered here. Some use words in capital letters at the beginning of the lines, with no other headline. This policy takes two forms, one in which the capped words are a separate unit and one in which they read right into the lines. You will find different terminology at different publications. I refer to the first as a *read-through* and the second as a *read-in*. Here's an example of a read-through and a read-in, repectively:

> **A GRITTY SURFER**—James Wickett knifes down the face of a big wave as he enjoys a growing new sport in West Texas—sand surfing. . . .

> **RIDING A WAVE OF SAND,** James Wickett enjoys a growing new sport in West Texas, sand surfing. . . .

The difference, to repeat, is that the second example has its bfc material as part of the main descriptive sentence, part of a thought contained in the lines. The bfc material in the other one is a self-contained thought. Careless or lazy writers will start with

> JAMES WICKETT KNIFES DOWN the face of a big wave. . . .

That's a mistake. Rather than start with the unknown boy's name, focus on the thing that makes the picture interesting, the sand surfing.

The art of writing cutlines requires a great deal of concentration. You must impart a sizable amount of information in a limited space, preferably with phrasing and style that will please readers as well as help them understand the picture. You will find the work challenging and enjoyable. Sometimes it is a chore, but it is a job worth doing, and worth doing right.

Index